Francisco Fanucci · Marcelo Ferraz

brasil arquitetura studio

Francisco Fanucci · Marcelo Ferraz

brasil arquitetura studio

Introduction

João da Gama Filgueiras Lima

Max Risselada

Essays and project analysis

Cecilia Rodrigues dos Santos

Vasco Caldeira

Comments and interview

Francisco Fanucci

Marcelo Ferraz

COSACNAIFY

For Madalena de Oliveira Fanucci and Isa Grinspum Ferraz

Introduction 1

João da Gama Filgueiras Lima (Lelé)

I first met the Brasil Arquitetura Studio team when we worked together in 1986 on Lina Bo Bardi's designs. The project consisted of restoring the historic site of Ladeira da Misericórdia and the Benin building, both in the city of Salvador, Bahia, in the Brazilian northeast. At the time, the team was formed by three young architects: Marcelo Ferraz, Marcelo Suzuki and Francisco Fanucci. We found we had a lot in common because we shared an interest in the many possibilities offered by the reinforced concrete block masonry technique used on those two projects, but mainly because of the great admiration we had for the genius of Lina (1915-1992, Italian-Brazilian architect) – a most wonderful character, who ranged with exceptional sensitivity and confidence the many realms of culture. Her conceptual clarity and her strong and impetuous temperament intimidated many, but she revealed an uncommon sweetness and benevolence to her close friends. Despite her Italian upbringing, she had the ability, matched by few Brazilians, to fully understand and interact with the richness and diversity of Brazilian culture. I recall being struck by the admirable potential of those talented young architects and recognizing the importance of their close association with Lina, at a time when Brazilian architecture faced the tortuous alleys of postmodernism.

Today, twenty years on, I am greatly satisfied in examining the team's magnificent body of work. Every design is testimony to the importance of the architect Vilanova Artigas in shaping the whole generation of architects to which they belong. One can also identify the influence of many other masters of modern architecture – such as Le Corbusier, Mies van der Rohe, Alvar Aalto, Luis Barragán – always impregnated with a vivid Brazilian-ness. This is due to a careful study of the work of Lucio Costa, our greatest master, who, in the 1930's, revolutionized the teaching of architecture in the city of Rio de Janeiro, enabling the development of a genius like Oscar Niemeyer and of a whole generation of great architects, such as Affonso Eduardo Reidy, the brothers Marcelo, Milton and Maurício Roberto, Alcides da Costa Miranda, Jorge Moreira, Aldary Toledo, among many others.

The teachings of Lucio Costa, always present in the work of the Brasil Arquitetura Studio, are more obvious in the house projects. They are carefully located and integrated within the landscape, and are built with innovative constructive techniques, denoting the permanent intention to explore to the full the available technical possibilities appropriate to each material to the full. The reading of the construction techniques employed is always clear, indicating they have been carefully selected from the very beginning of the creative process and refined or improved in the course of its development, in perfect harmony with the project's chosen approach.

The healthy intention of participating directly in the entire process of construction is manifest in the team's concern to maintain Marcenaria Baraúna as an extension of the practice, where they devote themselves to the design and production of furniture. In their own words: "At Barauna we design architects' furniture. The reasoning, the concepts, the way of approaching each question are the same as those we adopt in our architectural projects or in urban planning. The logics of structure, balance, behavior and strength of materials, comfort, economy of means and inputs, essentiality, all of this draws us to render the constructive system explicit".

The work of the Brasil Arquitetura Studio conforms to modernism while rejecting the easy models of international architecture, without giving in to nostalgia or being anachronistic. On the contrary, it has very contemporary expression and Brazilian character, and is a lucid interpretation of the country's cultural and social-economic context. It may be taken as regionalist architecture, but not because it is impervious to external influences, but simply because it absorbs, digests and transforms these influences according to a view that respects our memory and traditions as well as the tropical character of our climate.

For all this, in such turbulent times, when one of the cruellest aspects of globalization is the destruction of cultural references, the publication of the body of work of the Brasil Arquitetura Studio offers us, along with the high quality of the work itself, a clear and daring professional stance that is a very important contribution to the shaping of generations of architects to come.

Introduction 2

Max Risselada

My knowledge of the multifarious work that the Brasil Arquitetura Studio team has been producing since 1978, as well as my view of the place they occupy in the complex picture of contemporary Brazilian architecture, is limited and very much impregnated with the many myths disseminated by the media in recent decades. In spite of the current globalization, Brazil remains to me a context in which forces and movements operate which I can barely surmise.

These observations come, therefore, from a foreigner; from an "other" who, in recent years, has had the opportunity to visit Brazil a few times, to talk with Fanucci and Ferraz and to see firsthand some of the projects they have carried out in the vast subcontinent that is this country. I was thus able to apprehend certain aspects of this specific architectural culture. Speaking as a teacher, I consider this process of "apprehension" – in certain cases, even of identification – important to a position of critical balance. It is necessary then, to create a framework to enable this process to happen, with the double purpose of tracing an overall view of the team's work and displaying the perception and the values of the viewer. The positions of the observed and the observer, the object and the subject, are ever changing and depend, on one hand, on the temporal perspective and experience of the subject and, on the other, on the object and its context. This has to do with a mode of perception that is indissolubly linked to my view of how knowledge in architecture develops and is passed on, and how a specific tradition in this field is constituted – which turns out to be particularly necessary in the current practice, multiple as it is – and reflects in the teaching of architecture.

I got to know the Brasil Arquitetura Studio team by way of an exhibition of the work of architect Lina Bo Bardi, in 1994, at the Faculty of Architecture, Technical University of Delft. Marcelo Ferraz, who was then director of the Lina Bo and P. M. Bardi Institute, organized the travelling exhibition. Our meeting meant a lot to me, among other reasons because it revealed a body of work unknown to us then, which drastically changed the idea we had at the time of modern Brazilian architecture. Lina Bo, Italian by birth, seemed to develop an architectural language capable of combining the universal trends and values of modern architecture with the reality of the Brazilian context. It seemed she had solved the dilemma inherent in modernity – the sensation of loss of the existent, frequently highly esteemed, as consequence of necessary and deliberate innovation. Aldo van Eyck, the Dutch architect, pointed out this quality of Lina's better than anyone else at the opening of the show.

Lina Bo and Aldo van Eick reached adulthood during the Second World War. It instilled in their generation what we may call an "everyday life utopia". For them, the experience of war meant not only rupture with the past, but also a new outlook on ordinary life, the banality of day-to-day, from which all that was natural and logical had been lost in the wake of deprivation, the rubble to be cleared away, the rationing and the reconstruction, etc. This generation, to a great extent, built upon ruins, as it was amongst the ruins that they perceived the fragility of daily life – and if this was an opportunity to implement progressive and in some degree even utopian tactics, it was also a reminder of the value of what is ordinary and of endeavoring to secure new forms of stability.

Thanks to her background and experience, Lina not only discovered affinities with the modern architectural establishment in Brazil (where she moved with her husband after the war), but also felt very much at home with the life in this country, apprehending it in its contradictions and its wealth of cultures – an attitude that seems to have been strengthened after the military coup in 1964. More than ever she associated with the opposition and, in a way, went underground. Most certainly because of a lack of commissions at the time, she redirected her activities to the theater and to the production of exhibitions dealing with society and culture in Brazilian everyday life. This way, the "ruins" reappered in the form of abandoned industrial buildings and degraded neighborhoods. It was during this period that the young Brazilian architects began working intensively with her – which brings up back to Brasil Arquitetura Studio.

When I came across the team's work for the first time, completely free of preconceptions, I was immediately impressed by the way they used very basic, commonplace materials and ordered them in relation to form, space and time. In my view, the quality of this work does not reside, mainly, in programmatic innovation, but rather in the way the program is manipulated to suit a given context, so that unexpected aspects may surface and play an active part. While, as is often the case in public or institutional projects, the main action is the transformation or metamorphosis of preexisting buildings – usually anonymous, but of historic and social value – the important thing with private residences is, above all, the way the architects' stance brings out the hidden possibilities and qualities inherent in the context.

The team's working methods are clearly demonstrated thoughout these pages. However, I would like to briefly focus on one particular aspect – the interlacing of the building's interior and exterior – calling attention to three house projects: Casa do Muro Azul (p. 126 – 131), Casa Ubiracica (p. 132 – 139), and Casa Morumbi (p. 152 – 157).

The three are located on small plots of land, naturally different from one another in aspects such as orientation, shape, nature of boundaries, terrain, etc. These ordinary and physical "limitations" are treated as positive information for the design and are explored so that the inconsistencies implicit in the requirements become evident and isolation from the surroundings is diminished, when desired. Thus, the regular distance to be kept from the plot boundaries, usually fixed by building codes, does not result in lost, dull space, but takes on the form of diversified, interlaced space, where the different levels of the terrain are made to interplay in a very creative way.

The key point is that this never means taking possession of the plot with a bold statement – as with many houses designed by the so called *Paulista* (from São Paulo city) school – only to soften the contrast between internal and external spaces later. Isolation, in this manner, is merely established, not properly emphasized, as would be desired. The aim, in the above-mentioned projects, is to ensure that the plot boundaries have an active role in the design, making them part of a changeful space that, in this way, contributes to the spatial quality of the house and at the same time mediates its relation with the surroundings – the city as living space.

This strategy also holds consequences for the organization of the program inside the houses as such, which undergo a careful process of deconstruction and reaccommodation, so as to enable the spatial relationship between interior and exterior and so achieve the desired interaction. By means of certain "adaptations", specific attitudes and especially designated external spaces, connection is established with the outside world, turning the concept of dwelling, literally, inside out.

These descriptions suggest an overall view of the team's work; at the same time, they reveal the perception and values of the observer himself. The dual relation created by the bilateral focus relativizes the difference between the observed object and the observing subject, opening the way for the emergence of unexpected convergences and harmonies. There is a visible link with the European tradition of giving shape to transitions – between interior and exterior, between private and public – making it possible to compare them with the referential and apparently disparate works of modern architecture, such as the Schröder House (1925), by Dutch architect G. Rietveld, and Baensch House (1932), by the German H. Scharoun. This is a tradition strongly echoed by the Italian roots of Lina Bo and which finds new resonance in the work of Brasil Arquitetura.

METRÔ

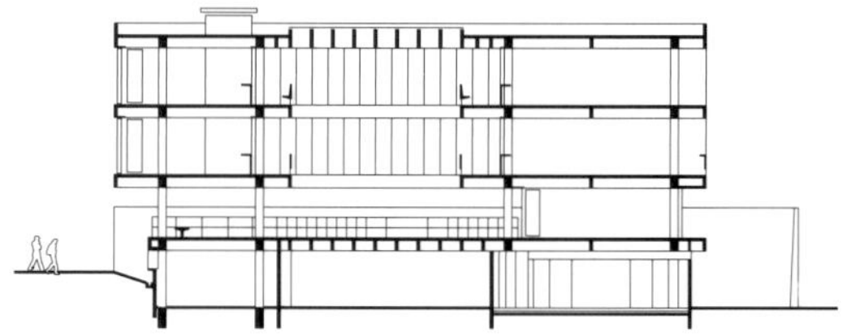

Marcelo Ferraz, Marcelo Suzuki, José Sales Costa Filho and Tâmara Roman, Cambuí City Council Hall.

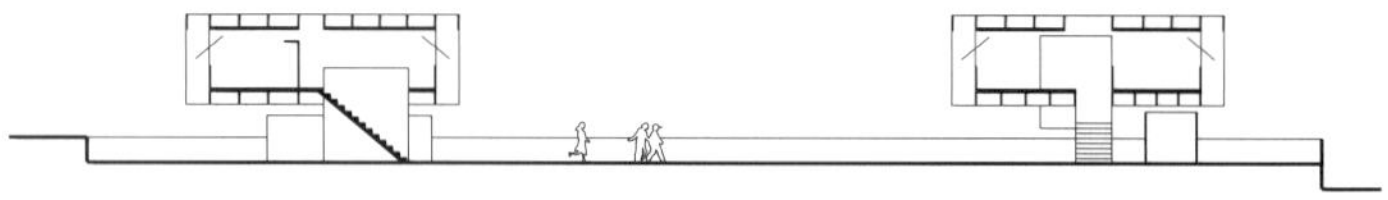

Francisco Fanucci, Antonio Carlos Barossi and José Calazans, Residential Housing Estate, 1977.

Brazilian Architectures: Brasil Arquitetura

Cecilia Rodrigues dos Santos

[...] Many are the Brazilian modernists that are learned in Modernism. However, we may be very learned in a given subject without it representing for us an object of knowledge...
Mário de Andrade

It is a difficult task to tell the story of this country named Brazil. It is not easy to tell the story of contemporary Brazilian architecture either. Nor is it easy to select a period in this broad history, of which many chapters remain to be written, that can furnish an understanding of the particular route taken by a generation of São Paulo architects who sought to treat architecture, above all, as a cultural matter – a generation of which Brasil Arquitetura Studio, the practice led by Francisco Fanucci and Marcelo Ferraz, is part.

This generation entered São Paulo University in the mid-70s and found the school stripped of its most politically active lecturers, architects with the courage to create a discourse and an architecture of confrontation and resistance, and so were silenced and forced into exile by the dictatorial government that had taken power ten years earlier. A school that, above all, offered resistance. In this way, it strove to preserve the memory of its masters by keeping their teachings alive and, at the same time, by fuelling the myth of its founders. It was a question of keeping alive the dogmatic, combative and even "heroic" *Paulista school*, and of learning and putting into practice the precepts of its pioneer, Vilanova Artigas. This involved commitment to a necessarily left wing ideological stance.

Taken to extremes, to be politically engaged meant abandoning the drawing board to devote oneself to the crucial discussion of the cities' great collective problems: a generation of planners, far removed from architectural design and urban planning in the broadest sense. It meant practicing an architecture of resistance, that is, a rationalist architecture, complete and inflexible in its rustic structural truth, exposing its rough concrete, modern despite having been moulded from crude timber boards by unskilled workers. An architecture of huge spans, concrete slabs and exposed concrete walls (ornament was then a crime), an architecture of which the spaces were designed first and foremost to operate the social revolution.

We – this architecture and its architects – were rebellious, earnest, dogmatic, obstinate and rigorous. Perhaps for being *Paulistas* (from the city of São Paulo), historically a very particular people, who chose to build their village and their culture upon the plateau, isolated from the coast. Portuguese and Brazilian Indians alike confounded in the hard struggle for survival, having had to crawl their way up the mountain escarps to find their

Tâmara Roman, Marcelo Ferraz, Marcelo Suzuki, José Sales Costa Filho and Francisco Fanucci, team of Vila Madalena Studio, 1980.

Cambuí City Council Hall.

dwelling place, they would then have to travel every time they yearned for new horizons or for a glimpse of the sea. After overcoming this geographical obstacle and trying to destroy this barrier with rails and smoke, we welcomed, housed and mixed together peoples from all over Brazil and the world, patiently learning from each in order to create a new culture, a combination of so many faces it might appear to have none. Brute, yes; and our modernity could only be brutalist, just like the city of São Paulo with its suicidal development dynamics, which devours and rebuilds itself over its own ruins. An excluding, hard city that forces its own inhabitants to hide in modernish houses, behind high walls and metal railings, with their backs turned towards the street.

The reality of São Paulo city is far removed from the happy synthesis of modernity practiced in the 1940s by Rio de Janeiro's architects, enlightened by the thought and the work of Lucio Costa. Spread along the shore, nestled among the quietude of the mountains and the winding rivers, clustered in lush vegetation, Rio, at that time, offered its architects the chance to create the "anthropophagic" (related to the modernist cultural movement originated in São Paulo in the 1920s) synthesis devised by São Paulo artists, though never put into practice there. One may say it was natural for Rio's architects to observe the Corbusian directives, either designing roof terraces and gardens so as to enjoy the landscape and sea breeze, or raising buildings on *pilotis*, so hammocks could be hung, as is always the case in the midst of palm and coconut trees, to take advantage of the shade for a siesta. The windows were, of course, panoramic, so one could immerse in the magnificent landscape. Informality being the lifestyle in Rio, free plans and façades came naturally. Veiled by traditional trellises, the façades were protected by verandas and jalousies, favouring intimacy, shade and coolness, maintaining a furtive but uninterrupted dialogue with the city.

In São Paulo, a view of the horizon, in architectural terms as well, had to be ripped open, conquered by force. Thus, in 1977, Marcelo Ferraz and André Vainer dared to follow a dissonant and solitary tune emanating from the district of Pompéia, ignored by architects at the time. They sought out architect Lina Bo Bardi and worked, as trainees, on the project for the SESC-Pompéia cultural center, a collaboration that would last until her death in 1992. Other colleagues from the São Paulo University School of Architecture with the same concerns joined the debates and workshops, from which the practice named Brasil Arquitetura Studio would emerge, led by Francisco Fanucci, Marcelo Ferraz and Marcelo Suzuki, who quit the partnership in 1995.

The internship period with Lina, which later led to partnership, can be considered a second graduation. Essential to the direction their the professional work would take, this experience drew their attention to the limitations of the *Paulista* school and to the possibility of scaling the city's wall of mountains to contemplate the world outside (the big, wide, world!), to want the whole of Brazil and pursue it (...longings

Sketches by Lina Bo Bardi for the design of Vale do Anhangabaú, 1981.

Vale do Anhangabaú Project: Francisco Fanucci, André Vainer, Lina Bo Bardi, Marcelo Ferraz, Paulo Fecarotta, Guilherme Paoliello, Bel Paoliello, Marcelo Suzuki and Ucho Carvalho.

for Brazil!): "Internationalism with our own baggage so we won't be swallowed up or dispersed in our own selves", in the words of Marcelo Ferraz. The openings resembling holes in the concrete façades, which Lina Bo designed for the walls of the SESC-Pompéia sports building, are the most significant expression of the struggle for new horizons, a different city, a new *Paulista* architecture. They also express the melancholia ever-present, just like the *paulista* drizzle, in the miserable background, whatever way the windows may face.

Looking at those houses, those churches, a good surprise after another, one can find one's own self, so to speak, feel content, happy, and be reminded of things long forgotten – things one was unaware of, but which were always there.
Lucio Costa

By the time modernism, no longer a leading movement, was reduced to a set of academic principles and was being contested, when ill-famed fragments of history and classical language were just beginning to be recuperated for the sake of image communication, of complexity and contradiction, the din of postmodernism sounded so remote as to be almost inaudible to the students of architecture in São Paulo in the late 1970s.

Far removed from the centers of debate, they obstinately worked on the various tracks of modernity. More than distant, but following the opposite direction, the young Brasil Arquitetura Studio architects militated for a different kind of modernity in São Paulo: one that swayed to the sound of João Gilberto's album *Brasil*, which he recorded with Caetano Veloso and Gilberto Gil, and would inspire the name they adopted for their recent partnership. This modernity was also inspired by the ideas of Brazilian anthropologist Darcy Ribeiro, by the images of the *cinema novo*, pioneered by director Glauber Rocha, by attention to the vernacular and the ordinary, and by the rediscovery of the work of Dr Lucio and Dr Oscar. This approach led them to extend their range of interests and they turned towards Eastern architecture, then to that of European Antiquity; to take a new look, with other eyes, at the immediate post-war period, present in the discussions and in the work of architects such as the American Louis Kahn, the Mexican Luis Barragán, the Finn Alvar Aalto, Sverre Fehn from Norway and Geoffrey Bava from Sri Lanka. Inevitably, they also kept an eye on the universality of Le Corbusier's modernist postulates and on the challenges of Team X when it expounded the human scale and the importance of the particularity of every community.

Meanwhile, curiosity took flight and the soul questioned. They kept to the construction sites of sorceress Lina Bo, who, by then had become very learned and at ease with the local art of cultural "anthropophagy", providing the clues so that the architects could begin to elaborate one of the most instigating syntheses of our contradictory country by the end of the 20th century, the construction of Brasil Arquitetura Studio's body of work.

Rodeio Real Brasil Circus canvas, in *Arquitetura rural na serra da Mantiqueira*, by Marcelo Ferraz, 1992.

Book cover.

The lack of gentleness, the roughness, the reckless taking and transforming, is a source of strength of contemporary Brazilian architecture [...] This process combines technical awareness and the spontaneity and ardour of primitive art.
Lina Bo Bardi

Lina Bo Bardi got her degree from the Rome School of Architecture between wars and moved to work in Milan. Contrasting with the architecture practiced in other European countries, architecture in Italy comprehends many cultural fields, combining technology and functionalism with cultural heritage and the poetics of everyday life. This broader range of the work of Italian architects ensured they provided a rational response to the challenges of the present day, in spite of the solidness of an education intimate with history and ruins. It also made them modern, regarding investigation on form and building technology, while they turned themselves towards the anthropological research of primitive forms, "poor in the more modern sense of the word", as Lina affirmed, because essential in the economy of materials, strict functionality and inventive creation.

From her arrival in Rio in 1946, and during the many years of working with culture in Brazil, the architect Lina Bo Bardi was able to discover, with enchantment, what she describes as "the extremely simple and fresh constructive solutions", "a modesty allied to a festive sense of life", "the intimate poetry of the Brazilian land". She searched for the soul of the people, the way they lived and went about their daily activities, "a way of being that manifests itself in the manner of looking at things, of moving, of resting one's foot on the ground, totally unaffected, artless, close to nature, to the "true" human quality". Her modern architecture, expressive in its structure and materials, took on traces of spontaneity, adapted itself to the place, identified with the simplicity, sought the landscape and made itself Brazilian. When choosing the name for a journal on culture which she began publishing in 1951, in São Paulo, Lina opted for *Habitat*, "a word intimately linked to architecture", which she associated with environment, dignity, the sharing of spaces, and spirituality as forms of cultural expression. And so the essential link was defined, the product of a particular way of looking, of researching, of registering and incorporating the local wisdom and craft, disseminating new viewpoints and approaches to modern architecture. All of which converged with the sensibility and the questioning attitude of those young, *paulista* students.

Hey, winds, winds of the city of Natal, going through me as if I were a veil. I am a veil. I do not clutter the landscape; I am not obliged to see exotica...I'm living the life of my country...
Mário de Andrade

Lina's manner of thinking and acting – European rather than Italian, Brazilian by choice – would have a profound impact

Illustration panels for Gelbes Viertel revitalization project for submitted to international competition, Berlin, 1997.

on the work of the Brasil Arquitetura Studio, putting their upbringing and education in perspective and aiming at an intrinsic Brazilian-ness which transcended their origins. It encourages them to get to know their country better, the people, the cultural archetypes, causing them to travel throughout the country, taking notes, pictures and sketching. These references will be used in their future projects.

The resulting architectural action is plural, tolerant, diverse, adapted to place and promotes the harmony of different historical moments dealt with in the present. At the center of this architecture is the human being, the Brazilian people, their life and culture, because the foremost concern is with the life that unfolds in the designed spaces and gives them meaning. If the result is architecture, something beyond mere building, it is because one works towards the human scale and strives to occupy the shapes made of stone and brick with intention and meaning. Architecture is indeed a question of compositional methodology, of esthetics, of program, of function and technology. But above all, or prior to everything else, architecture is a cultural matter.

Consequently, the Brasil Arquitetura Studio no longer fitted the *Paulista school* from which it developed. Nor did it fit any group or school; not even a certain category thought up by international criticism and labeled "critical regionalism". This variant of modern international architecture would incorporate certain elements of local cultures by making concessions to the climate and environment of countries and places almost always peripheral to the main economic and political centers. If this definition were to be accepted, Lucio Costa would be one of the first "regionalists", with many disciples, especially in the 1980s, who championed the Brazilian reality and its history as they presented themselves, a hybrid of many cultures, even in details such as the manufacture of a brick, or the design of a minute space for a dwelling, profoundly contradictory in its expression, technology and use; and invariably pointed out as impure and imperfect.

We must know how to correctly interpret Lucio Costa when he affirmed that "authentic regional architecture has its roots in the land", as we ought to perceive that neither the work of Lucio Costa nor this typical architectural production of the 1980s, which includes that of the Brasil Arquitetura Studio, may be simply labeled "regionalist". These architects are, in fact, positively Brazilian: "modern and Brazilian". And this generic synthesis, which at a superficial level reads as the incorporation of materials and techniques of traditional architecture to the basic postulates of international modernism, actually involves, at a closer examination, a complex process of cultural deglutition, a lot of mastication (in reference to the so-called Anthropophagy movement, of the early 1920s) and plenty of poetry, with huge doses of alternated daring and restraint. Not to mention considerable learning and no little modesty, as, after all, good architecture can be recognized by the virtue of rendering itself invisible. "Take rather than add, blend rather than emphasize, juxtapose to the existing city, to the terrain,

Antonio Ceppas Residential Building, Rio de Janeiro, Jorge Machado Moreira, 1952.

Sesc Pompéia Cultural Center, São Paulo, Lina Bo Bardi, 1986.

Tamanás House, detail of latticed opening, São Paulo, Brasil Arquitetura Studio, 2001.

to the residues: share", thus ran the motto of Brasil Arquitetura Studio architects.

The frog doesn't jump for prettiness, but because it has to.
Guimarães Rosa (Brazilian writer)

Is it still possible, in times such as these, "to be absolutely modern", as wished Rimbaud? The anthropological gaze at the contemporary world characterizes the current moment as the age of individualism, of similitude, of high technology. The legitimating paradigms of architecture identified by Josep Montaner are no longer universalism and progress, a consequence of the machine age, as had been with the vanguards of modernism; they are no longer a new humanism nor the post-war organic references, which caused European architects to travel in search of the vernacular in primitive or exotic countries; it is not even the new formal abstraction derived from a rereading of those vanguards. Perhaps what distinguishes this supermodern age is the absence of paradigms.

So, to keep in tune with present time, the architects' permanent challenge involves huge complexity at the beginnings of the 21st century. The usual references and the traditional tools are subverted or have simply disappeared. Places have become non-places and old boundaries have vanished. Relations have become virtual and man as individual, man as a cultural being, has ceased to matter. The speed of transformation matches the speed of communication. Values, ethical and esthetic standards are reinvented every day. Memory no longer holds the facts and history goes unregistered. The timeline that teachers drew on the classroom chalkboard has snapped; it is now a beam. Certainly, the crisis of supermodern man is one of identity. As Marc Augé infers, it is in the anonymity of the non-places, of contemporary landscapes emptied of meaning and history, that today, solitarily, one experiences the communion of human destinies.

It is up to contemporary architects, equipped with monitors and cell phones, to adjust to their time and decide whether to clutter it with construction or to transform it. The Brasil Arquitetura Studio team believes, as does Steven Holl, that architecture has the power to transform the way of living, combining intellect and intuition, objective and subjective aspects. However, creation based on cultural reality, accountable in civil and social respects, ethical and plural regarding its references but particular in relation to esthetics and to results; committed to structural logic and to the truth of materials and further committed to the simple comfort of furniture equipment and utensils, buildings and cities – this humanistic architectural reasoning finds itself counter-current in relation to globalized time. Ours is a moment when to act professionally has come to mean to fight against, to transform, to challenge, to practically become a militant activist. A militancy which differs from that of the *Paulista* school of the 1970s, in that composition, form and structure are organized in relation to man as a cultural human being in his habitat, of which the city,

Native Brazilian people's dwelling (*maloca*), Aldeia Camanaus, Upper Rio Negro, Amazon, 1994.

City Showcase, Santo André, Brasil Arquitetura Studio, 1999.

Study for Afro Brasil Museum, Brasil Arquitetura Studio, 2004.

house, furniture and utensils, and his particular way of life, all take part.

So, when the challenge was to design a rail and coach terminal in the city of Santo André, near São Paulo, on a site surrounded by railways, highways and overpasses, when everything indicated the construction of a difficult complex, anonymous and isolated from the surrounding city, a typical non-place to house anonymous multitudes in transit, the architects pursued a bold idea, a concept capable of turning the situation around and affecting change. In this case, it involved the inversion of the municipal administration's proposal for the building by transforming it into a bridge over the various traffic routes, a walkway over the obstacles to urban fluidity, linking the terminal to areas previously fated to isolation. By envisaging the multiplicity of functions and the heavy flow of pedestrians, they transformed the character of the station into that of a high street, providing it with a healthy singularity, allowing it to take on a new functional and symbolic role, that of a new focus for urban centrality. Due to the specificity and clarity of the architecture – achieved with a metallic structure that responded well to the physical contingencies and the construction deadlines – and because of its strategic site location, this building is an element of integration and an important landmark in the geography of a region in need of identity.

Regarding the adaptation and use of historic buildings, the architects express the desire for a 'respectful but not submissive juxtaposition', to build with the present time in mind. According to this principle, decisions vary from case to case. To recover the popular and multiple character of the Polytheama Theater in Jundiaí, state of São Paulo, it was necessary to completely rebuild its interior, stripping the plaster from the structure and remaining walls, and opening up the proscenium.

To deal with the extensive plans for the Japanese Immigration Memorial (proposed by the architects) in conjunction with a managerial training center (the client's initial request), to be installed in the industrial warehouses of KKKK, an industrial plant in the state of São Paulo, or with the plans for the Rodin Museum, to be established in an eclectic style mansion in Salvador, Bahia, both sites protected as architectural heritage, the architects opted for similar procedures. They began by carefully restoring the historic installations; then they designed pure prismatic elements and juxtaposed them to the main buildings, as annexes. The internal plans for the prismatic cubic boxes, with exposed concrete or white rendered masonry walls, were conceived in accordance with the program of necessities, without abdicating geometric simplicity. They respect the scale of the historic constructions, and at the same time affirm the contemporary nature of the solution, a confrontation without conflict. The necessary connection with the preexisting buildings is achieved by concrete walkways and canopies or *marquises* that, besides lending a contemporary aspect to the circulation areas, establish physical elements of continuity and fluidity for both sets.

Monument to the 3rd International Socialist, Vladimir Tatlin, 1925.

"Velvet and Silk Café" exhibition, Mies Van der Rohe, Berlin, 1927.

Passageway in Polytheama Theater, Brasil Arquitetura Studio, 1996.

KKKK Complex marquise, Brasil Arquitetura Studio, 2001.

Since, for the architects, "to design is to relapse", these canopies and walkways are repeated in other projects, under different forms and solutions. They gain autonomy when they embrace a map of Brazil built with petrified remnants of Amerindian culture –, as is the case with the Monument to the Brazilian Indian Nations, created by artist Siron Franco – defining, independently, an architectural plan for the protection and recognition of the set: "Add little, in order to emphasize what already exists".

The relapsing action is not restricted to spatial solutions or solutions related to the set as a whole. It is also present in details that, almost as trademarks, become standard components of the design repertoire. Such is the case with the wood trellises in the manner of *mushrabeyeh*, a Moorish-style trelliswork. In the KKKK industrial complex, they enclose gardens between different blocks. They are also present in the Rodin Museum façade and at the offices of Instituto Socioambiental, under construction in the Amazon. In the office building in Brasília the trellis panels, added to two of the façades, have monumental proportions. Besides operating as sun-breaks, keeping out the weather and veiling direct sunlight, they also work as a quotation of the colonial tradition and its recovery brought about by the work of architect Lucio Costa. In Brasília, the trellis panels are applied to the contemporary façade to act as a counterpoint, that of good, solid, tradition, of the adequate Brazilian way of living, bringing the architects' spirit of modernity to prominence.

All of a sudden an anti-geographic sun tropicalizes the fall of night, and hits the city's metal sheet. S. Salvador contorts herself, enjoying the light that is hers, very gently. Not even Utrillo's palette!... No one will ever accomplish these gilded pinks, these Virgin Mary blues, these scorching sand yellows and the mango tree greens. Color of the years, color of the centuries piled up one over each other...
Mário de Andrade

Perhaps the project that best summarizes and illustrates the architects' way of working is the one in response to a rather unusual program that signaled the possibility of effective resistance to the supermodern assumptions: the revitalization of the Gelbes Viertel (Yellow District) in Berlin, Germany. The trouble in finding a word to define this project – already called revitalization, restoration, upgrading, revamping, remodeling, facelifting and renovation – is directly related to the fact that it is not an architectural or urban planning project in the traditional sense. It has even been described as a merely "skin-deep" intervention in a housing estate, a superficial treatment. As if the skin were not an inseparable part of the body, as if it were not a surface vital to the perception of the environment, the first to react to contact and to communicate sensations.

With the fall of the Berlin Wall and the beginning of Germany's process of reunification, the architecture of East Berlin needed to be revised and thought over in the new context. The main criticism to the endless housing estates –

Selection of Kadiwéu tile designs for Gelbes Viertel.

Tiled panels in Gelbes Viertel.

Architects with the artists invited to visit the Gelbes Viertel project: Miguel dos Santos, Franz Krajcberg, Amilcar de Castro and Siron Franco, Berlin, 1997.

solidly built of pre-cast concrete components, with good infrastructure and located in the midst of common areas – related to their uniformity and monotony. Countless initiatives were undertaken to give them individual character, to renew this urban landscape, which, in our globalized reality, has become the essence of disaggregating contemporary spaces, trenchant examples of non-places. In addition, they also became the symbols of an ideology and of a way of life that needed to be identified and altered.

The decision to create an identity for Gelbes Viertel attracted 56 competition entries from Latin America. It was, above all, an operation that intended to transform non-places into places, or, in the words of Marc Augé, "re-characterize places so that they may come to have an identity, a new relation to the city as a whole and a sense of history". The challenge was, above all, to propose a new significant universe even if that meant drawing on specific cultural references and identities far removed from German culture and geography, so long as those references could communicate by force of their artistic and cultural expression and by the delicate but determined move towards aggregation and humanization, against the cold, supermodern reality of oppressive, characterless spaces.

In their proposal, which won the competition, the Brasil Arquitetura Studio clearly sustained the discourse that informs their work, a discourse based on historic and architectural quotations, on Brazilian culture in its different times and hues, including the ordinary and the vernacular, symbols of renovation and identity. The project was based on four basic ideas: to provide landmarks by way of installing sculptures by contemporary Brazilian artists; to adopt different color schemes for the block façades, using bands of color (with pigments borrowed from popular culture) painted over white coated walls, a reference to the lime-wash once applied to the colonial walls of Spanish and Portuguese America; to design a series of trellised wood panels after *mushrabeyeh* work, and panels of decorated ceramic tiling with designs created by Kadiwéu Indians from Brazil – both elements of the Moorish tradition inherited from the Portuguese; and finally, to give the common areas a landscape treatment that, in its irregularity and variety, would invoke the native American forests. The architects sought to draw, from the timeless vernacular universe of Latin America, especially from Brazil, those qualitative and identity giving elements that are universal because specific of these cultures, elements which the housing estate communities would recognize and relate to, including the modern ones.

To dialogue with the past it is necessary to construct the present.
Sverre Fehn

Project *Árvore Resistente* (Hardy tree), located in Tacaruna, between the cities of Recife and Olinda, in Pernambuco state.

The project proposed was the restoration of an old factory building and the construction of a convention center. Once

Fig tree embedded in wall at the Tacaruna Factory, Recife, 2002.

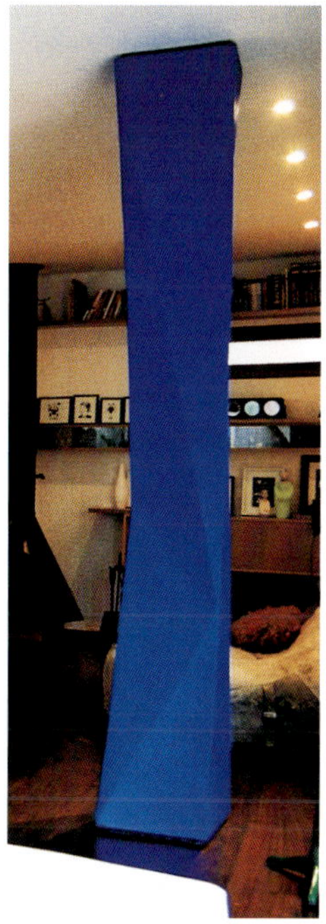

Tamanás House, alteration, São Paulo, Brasil Arquitetura Studio, 2001.

"What is your part?", Marcelo Ferraz,1997.

again it involved preservation and innovation, a plurality of requirements, meeting places, communal areas, celebration areas – in short, living spaces.

The symbol of this unbuilt project embodies the architects' response to the challenge of thinking and practicing architecture. *Árvore Resistente* (Hardy Tree) is merely a huge fig-tree embedded in the wall of a former dilapidated shed, maintained by the architects along with the supporting wall as a sort of sculpture, paying homage to the strong and symbiotic integration of the Brazilian people with their natural and cultural landscape.

The design as the contained gesture that singles out and enriches a consolidated cultural reality, in a perspective of creation in continuity.

BIBLIOGRAPHY

ANDRADE, Mário de. *O turista aprendiz.* São Paulo: Duas Cidades, 1976.

AUGÉ, Marc. *Não-lugares: Introdução a uma antropologia da supermodernidade.* São Paulo: Papirus/Travessia, 2001.

BASTOS, Maria Alice Junqueira. *Pós-Brasília: Rumos da arquitetura brasileira.* São Paulo: Perspectiva, 2003.

COHEN, Jean-Louis. *La coupure entre architectes et intellectuels, ou les enseignements de l'italophilie* Paris: École de Paris-Villemin/In Extenso, 1984.

COSTA, Lucio. *Lucio Costa: Registro de uma vivência.* Rio de Janeiro: Empresa das Artes, 1997.

FANUCCI, Francisco; FERRAZ, Marcelo. *Theatro Polytheama de Jundiaí.* Jundiaí: Prefeitura Municipal de Jundiaí, 1996.

FERRAZ, Marcelo Carvalho. *Arquitetura rural na Serra da Mantiqueira* São Paulo: Instituto Lina Bo e P.M. Bardi, 1992.

—— (Org.). *Lina Bo Bardi.* São Paulo: Instituto Lina Bo e P. M. Bardi, 1993.

MONTANER, Josep Maria. *Después del movimiento moderno.* Barcelona: Gustavo Gili, 1993.

PEREIRA, Margareth Campos S.; PEREIRA, Romão da Silva; SANTOS, Cecilia Rodrigues dos; SILVA, Vasco Caldeira. *Le Corbusier e o Brasil.* São Paulo: Tessela/Projeto, 1987.

PÉREZ, Fernando; ARAVENA, Alejandro; QUINTANILLA CHALA, José. *Los hechos de la arquitectura.* Santiago de Chile: Ediciones Arq, 2002.

ROSA, João Guimarães. *Sagarana.* Rio de Janeiro: José Olympio, 1946.

SEGAWA, Hugo (Org.). *Arquiteturas no Brasil: anos 80* São Paulo: Projeto, 1988.

—— ; FANUCCI, Francisco P.; FERRAZ, Marcelo C. *O Conjunto KKKK.* São Paulo: Takano, 2002.

ZEIN, Ruth Verde. *O lugar da crítica.* São Paulo: Pró-Editores, 2001.

Grisbi Textile Industries

Camaçari, Bahia state 1980

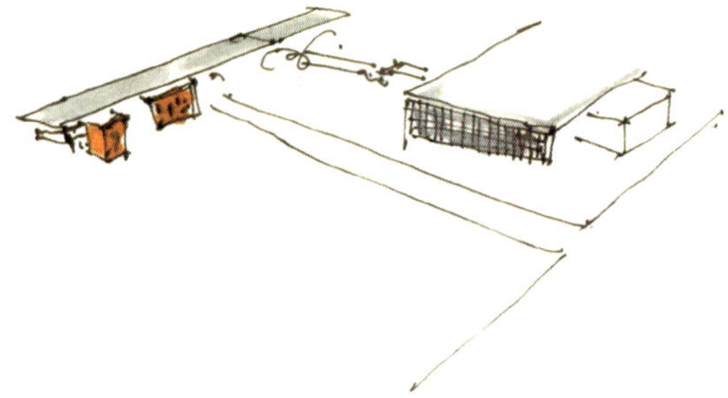

The buildings to house the textile mill in the Camaçari industrial plant, state of Bahia, do not constitute an *opera aperta*, intentionally incomplete and conceived with the participation of the viewer or user in mind. Nor are they an *opera incompiuta*, the product of a design process abandoned before term. It is a complete project, although construction was interrupted by the sale of the estate and by lack of interest on part of the new owner, who abandoned the site soon after, leaving it to a permanent state of premature ruin.

Although incomplete, the building presents itself as evidence of the materialization of the plans. Window and door frames as well as various finishings are missing; so is the red ceramic tiling. Some of the rendered walls lack color. There are no roof gardens. Some elements required for industry are lacking, but none of this detracts from the powerful expression of the sun-bleached skeleton.

In this project, along with attention to the program of functional necessities related to the technological production, which is the starting point for the design of any building devoted to industrial ends, the architects privileged the adaptation of the buildings to the physical/geographical and cultural environment. The result was a highly expressive architectonic design and the potential for significant savings through reduced construction costs from the use of local manpower and materials; energy saving due to an innovative scheme that increased thermal comfort; greater production efficiency resulting from the study and rationalization of the plans and the location of the installations at the site.

In the administration building, the constructive solution adopted to reduce the heat in the working areas was the use of a double protection system, slab/slab or slab/terrace. A sheltering slab, supported by an independent metallic structure, is positioned like a shield 4 ft above the roof slab, which in turn is treated and waterproofed, as an integral component of the building's structural framework. The big sun barrier spreads over an irregular alignment of self-supporting brick masonry cubes topped by gardened terraces. Projecting from the flush-perforated concrete block façades, the cubic elements constitute spaces that are separated from the panoramic central offices by the huge, two storied, and vertical circulation hall. Between the perforated curtain wall and the line of windows behind it, an intermediary garden space was designed to further ensure the coolness of the work environments.

Perforated concrete blocks of various shapes, designed by the architects and moulded on-site, operate either as sunscreens filtering the light, as shades or as ventilation devices. They are present in the lateral enclosure of the administration building, in the ventilation space between the two superposed slabs of the changing room block, as a parapet wall on the terrace in front of the restaurant, and on the second floor of the workshop and of the maintenance building. Borrowed from traditional Brazilian architecture, these blocks mitigate the heat and allow for air conditioning to be used only in the industrial shed, thus meeting the technical requirements of the industrial equipment

The external walls of the buildings also had to withstand the sun. In deciding to use bricks in the masonry self supporting walls and in the ones enclosing the large concrete structures, the architects were not only referring to the architecture of the first factory buildings constructed in Brazil, but were opting for local knowledge, for convenience and economy. Bricks are inexpensive and plentiful in Camaçari, and allow the use of the region's abundant labor force. The extensive structural wall surfaces, which add to a 1,200-sq yard area, as in the production block, are built of irregularly shaped bricks, manufactured locally with varied traditional techniques, using thick layers of mortar. The reddish surfaces, irregularly burned, regular in rhythm and repetition, are the factory building's basic unifying element, underlining the fundamental opposition between the local tradition and reality and the transplanted industrial technology.

Low cost materials, simplicity in construction derived from the project's sophisticated constructive solutions, and a precise functional and technical program, are the combined elements that worked to transcend the banality of industrial facilities and to establish functional efficiency and the desired plasticity. The language is modern, rational and international. The accent, on the other hand, is local, influenced by the language of the people from Bahia and their culture. The result is that this architecture, in its so nearly fulfilled promise, is above all, strong.

CRS

- Three connecting walkways: from the offices; from the entrance to the changing rooms; from the restaurant to the administration area
- Location plan:
  1 administration area
  2 cafeteria
  3 spinning and texturing unit
  4 entrance
  5 changing rooms
  6 workshops
  7 utility room

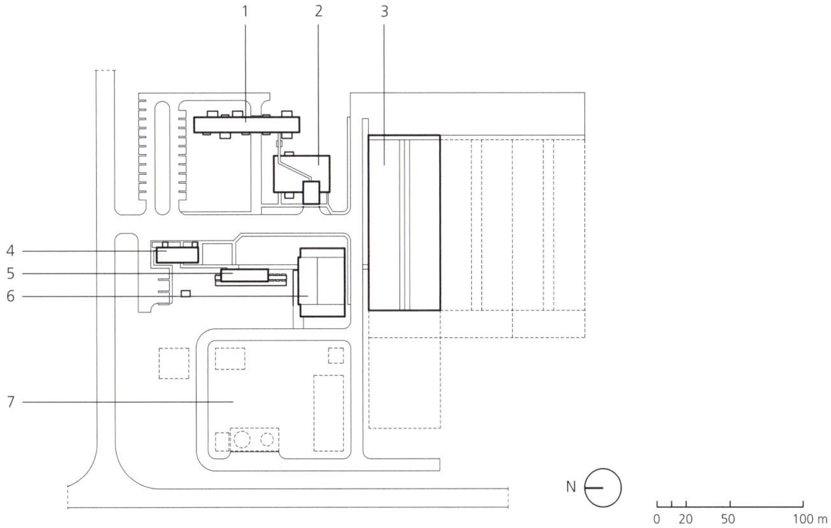

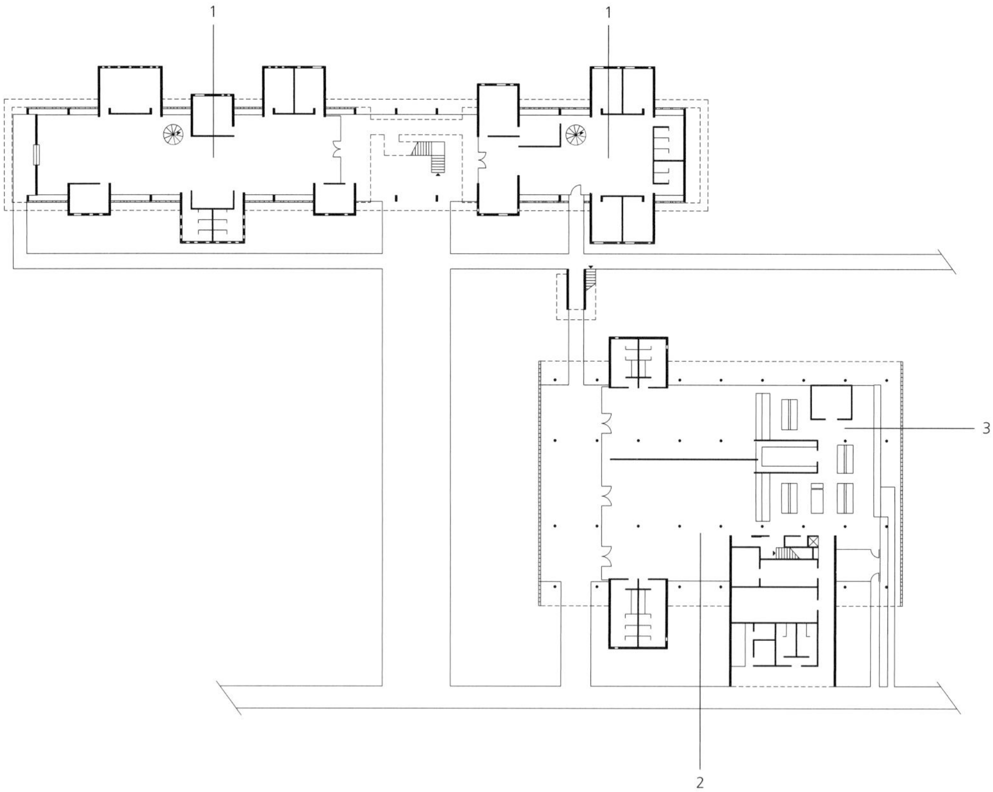

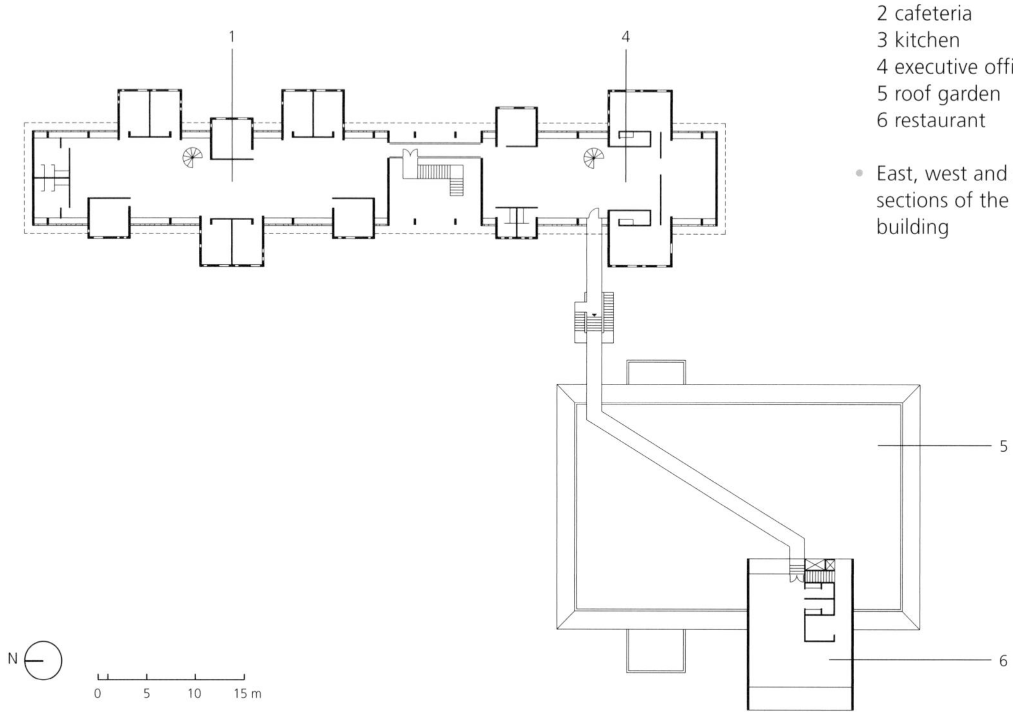

- Ground and first floor plans:
  1 administration area
  2 cafeteria
  3 kitchen
  4 executive offices
  5 roof garden
  6 restaurant

- East, west and south elevations; sections of the administrative building

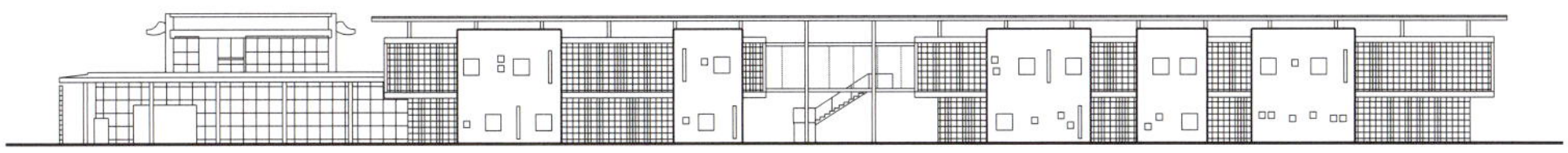

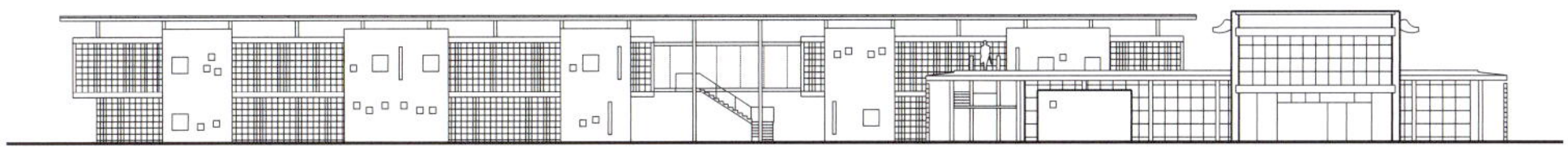

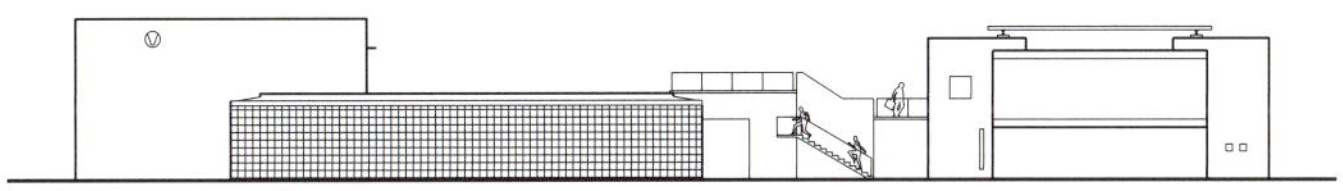

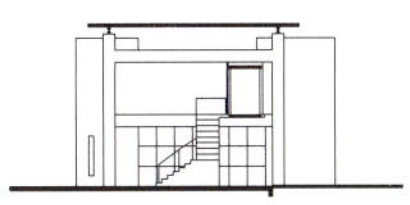

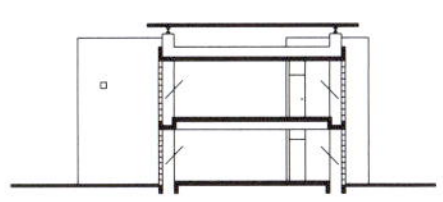

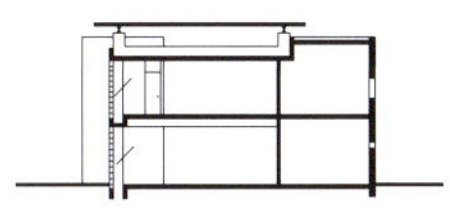

Polytheama Theater

Jundiaí, São Paulo 1995

In 1911, in the town of Jundiaí, near São Paulo, a pavilion was inaugurated to house the Teatro Polytheama, which would become the town's main cultural and leisure center. Removed from the town center, it staged events ranging from theatre and cinema productions to circus and equestrian shows in an improvised circus ring.

Between 1927 and 1928 the building underwent extensive renovation, losing its pavilion-like appearance and gaining an eclectic style two-story façade. It became a proper theatre, equipped with the modern technology of that time, and hosted political meetings and Carnival balls.

The theater stood out in relation to the town's urban profile, but remained confined to the same area, the same narrow street. Aligned with more modest buildings, many of which were residential, it was not accorded an urbanistic or plastic treatment. For the next 40 years it provided the city with cultural service, whereupon it was closed, dilapidated due to lack of maintenance, no longer suitable for use.

The first move to restore the Polytheama dates to 1986 and was coordinated by Lina Bo Bardi, with a team formed by architects André Vainer and Marcelo Ferraz. Lina's objective was to restore its original multifunctional character, giving it technical capacity to house different kinds of shows, both sophisticated and popular. The main façade, with its candid eclecticism, would be restored, and a passageway, in the shape of a nautical tube of light concrete, would be attached to the lateral façade, using the neighboring plot, to give the public access to the tiers and lateral galleries. The interiors would be totally renovated, revealing the original iron roof trusses and the brickwork, increasing seating capacity and enlarging the proscenium and stage, the back wall of which would become an open window to the town.

The project was only resumed in the mid-1990s by the Brasil Arquitetura Studio, without Lina's involvement but following the same guiding principle – to recover the popular and multifunctional character of the building. The architects, however, had to restructure the project, because the adjoining plot was no longer available. The administration of the flow of visitors and artists would have to be dealt with inside the building. In the end, the annex, which was to be located at a lower level at the back of the plot and was planned to provide support to the artistic and administrative activities, was not built either. The alternative was to build a concrete gallery and stairwell by the side of the building, between the boundary wall and the lateral façade with its brick buttresses. The new circulation scheme, now internal, also features elevated concrete walkways in the double height foyer and along the sides of the building, which lead to the seating areas.

On the main façade, white homogeneous coating deliberately attenuate the decorative designs in relief, becoming a subtle eclectic style quotation. Glass panes, used to soften the horizontal segmentation of the façade, replaced the ceramic roof tiles of the canopy. The entire interior of the theatre was redesigned and modernized following Lina Bo Bardi's guidelines: to maintain the horseshoe shape of the seating area, enlarging the stage at the front and deepening it, and to restore the expression and simplicity of the structure and materials of the original pavilion. Only the large opening of the backstage wall was not carried out as proposed.

Materials of superior quality were specified for the interior in order to contrast with the rusticity of the outer case: *pau-marfim* (a fine light yellow Brazilian wood) cladding was used on the floors, box parapet walls and amphitheater; a vivid coating of strong blue on the walls (a pigment named *ultramar* in Portugal); a silver coating on the doors to the boxes; a heavy red velvet stage curtain; and, finally, a chandelier conceived by José Roberto Aguilar, a Brazilian artist, made of 365 crystal canes grouped together and suspended between the air conditioning ducts and the roof's iron structure. The sculpture is a fixture that doesn't generate its own light, but reflects the light projected on it – a precious and mystifying finishing touch.

CRS

The Polytheama Theater in the 1970s and the restored façade with glazed marquise.

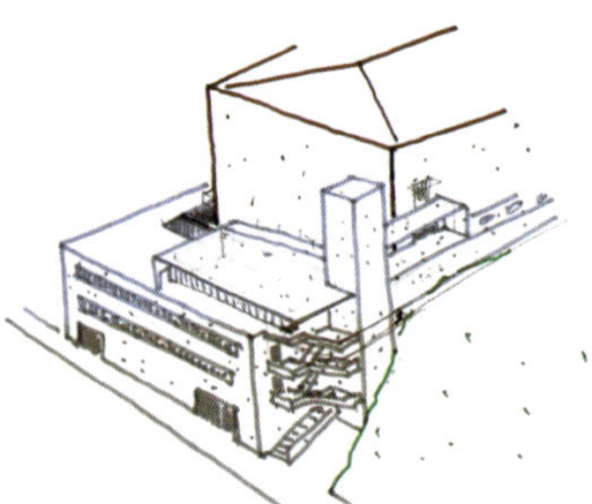

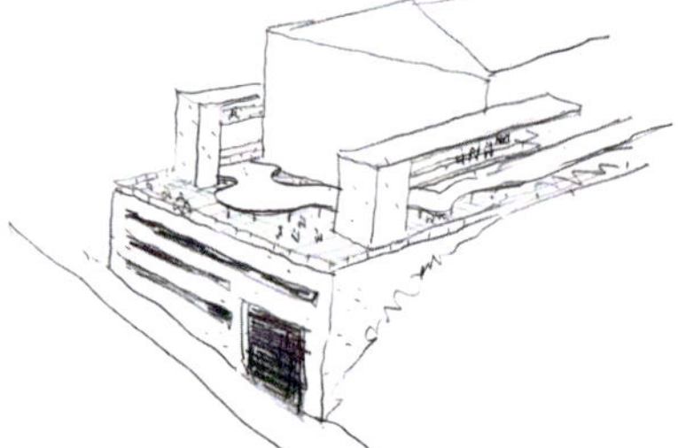

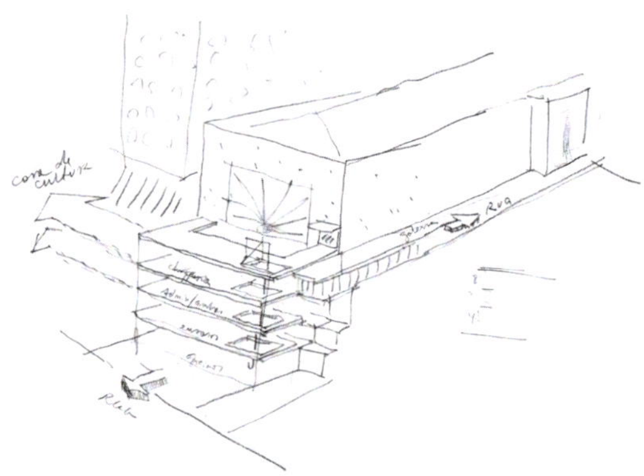

- Study for the support building (unbuilt).
- Location plan:
  1 theater
  2 support building
  3 passageway connecting two streets/gallery
  4 Barão de Jundiaí street
  5 Vigário J. J. Rodrigues street
  6 vertical circulation
  7 restrooms

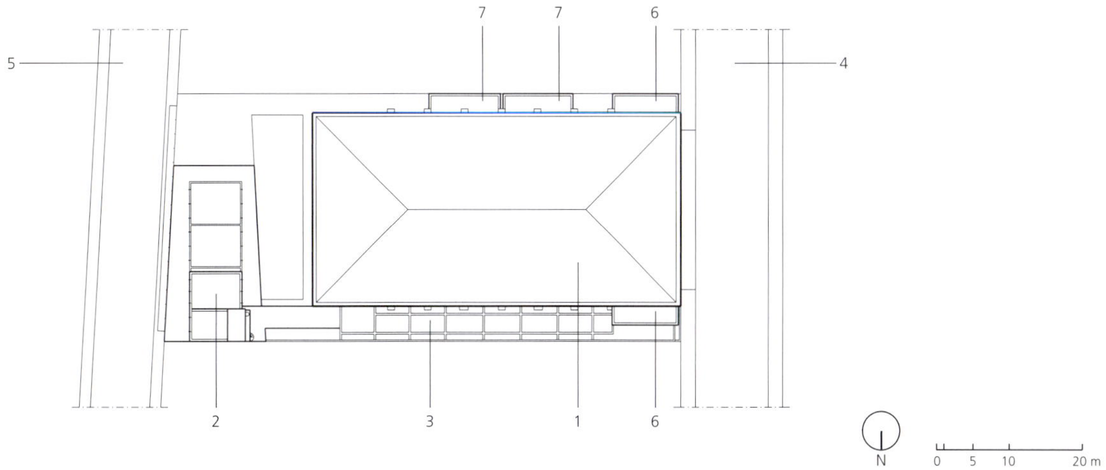

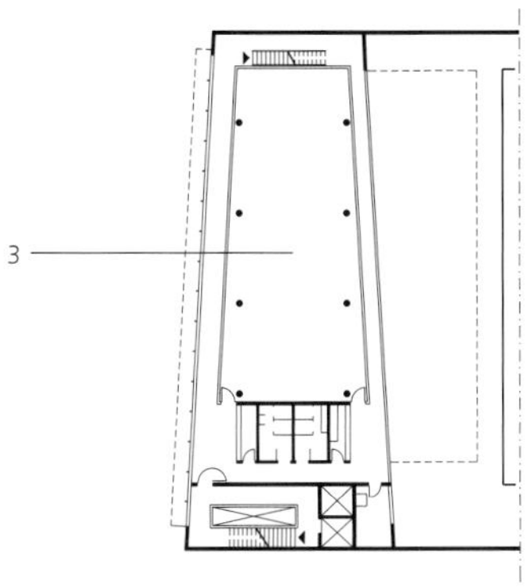

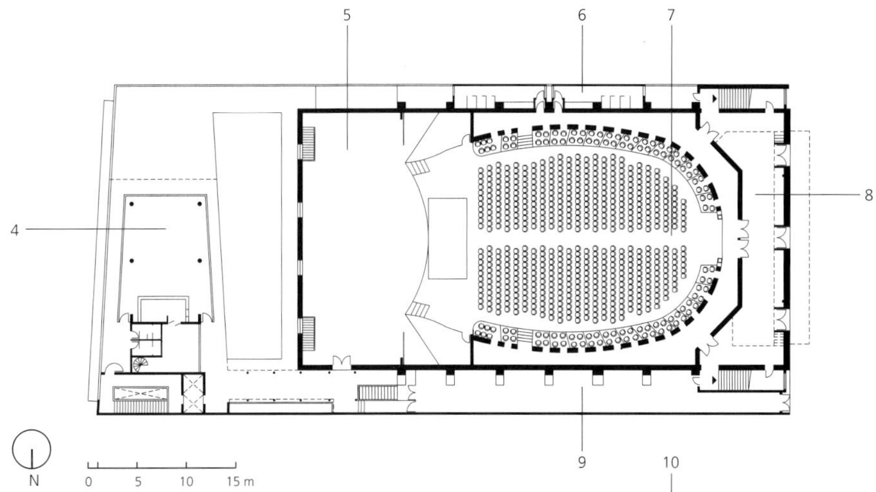

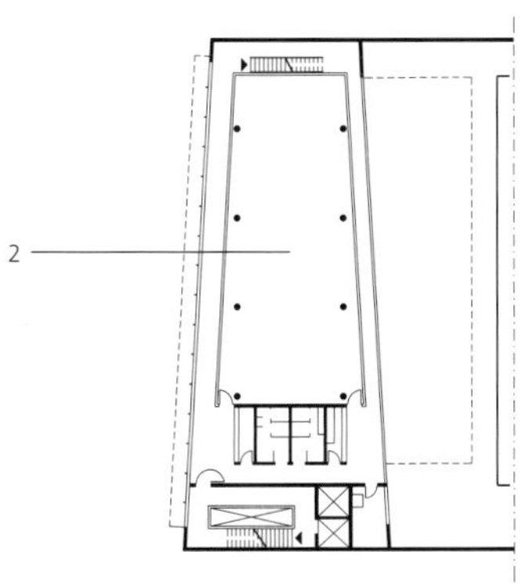

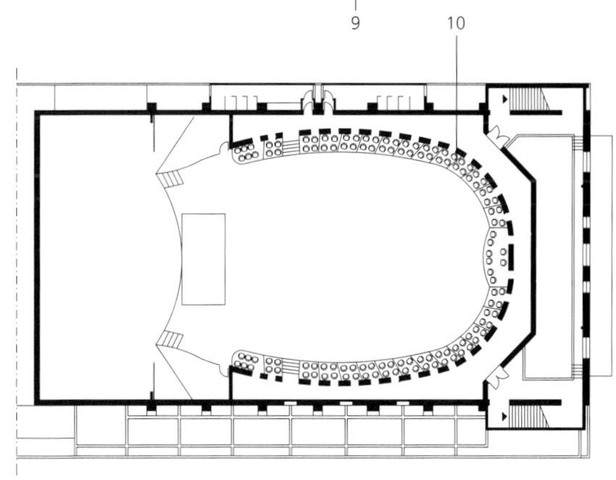

- Level 0.00 plan:
  1 workshop
- level 3.50 plan:
  2 courses and rehearsals
- level 7.00 plan:
  3 administration
- Plan levels10.50 and 13.00:
  4 café/restaurant
  5 stage
  6 restrooms
  7 tiers
  8 foyer
  9 passageway/gallery
- Level 17.80 plan:
  10 boxes
- Level 20.00 plan:
  11 upper passageway; gallery
- Support building elevation
- Longitudinal section

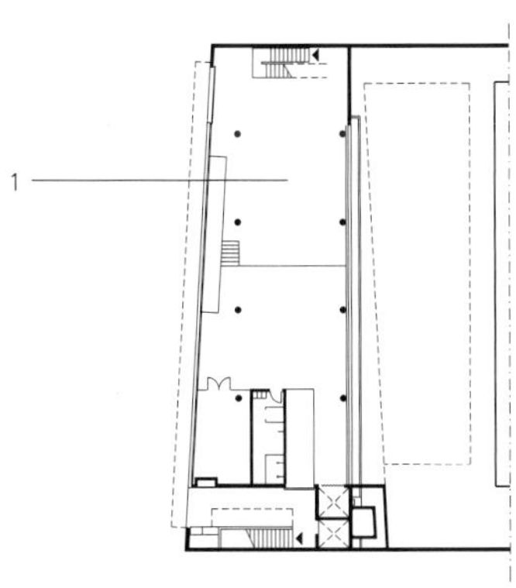

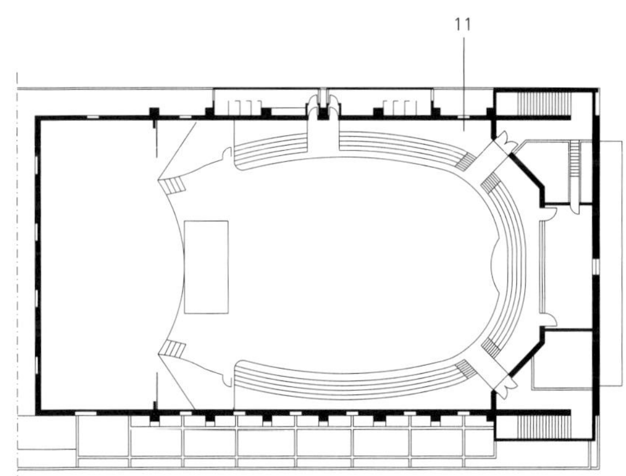

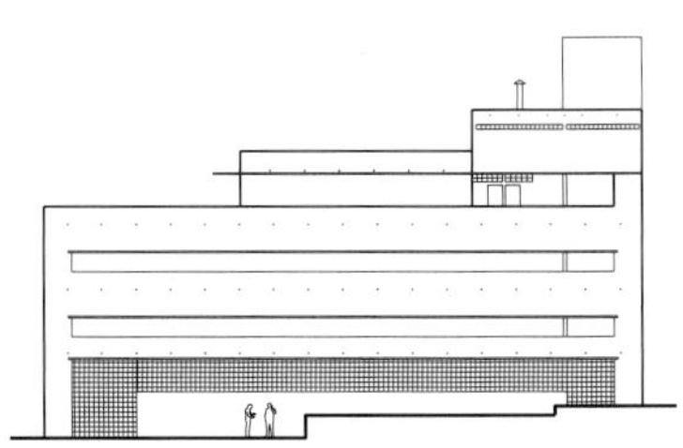

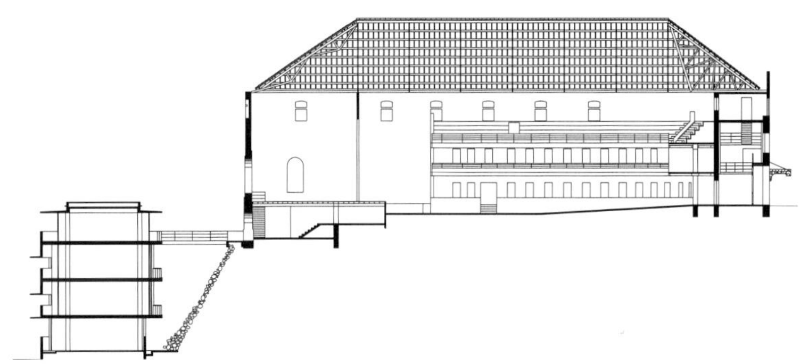

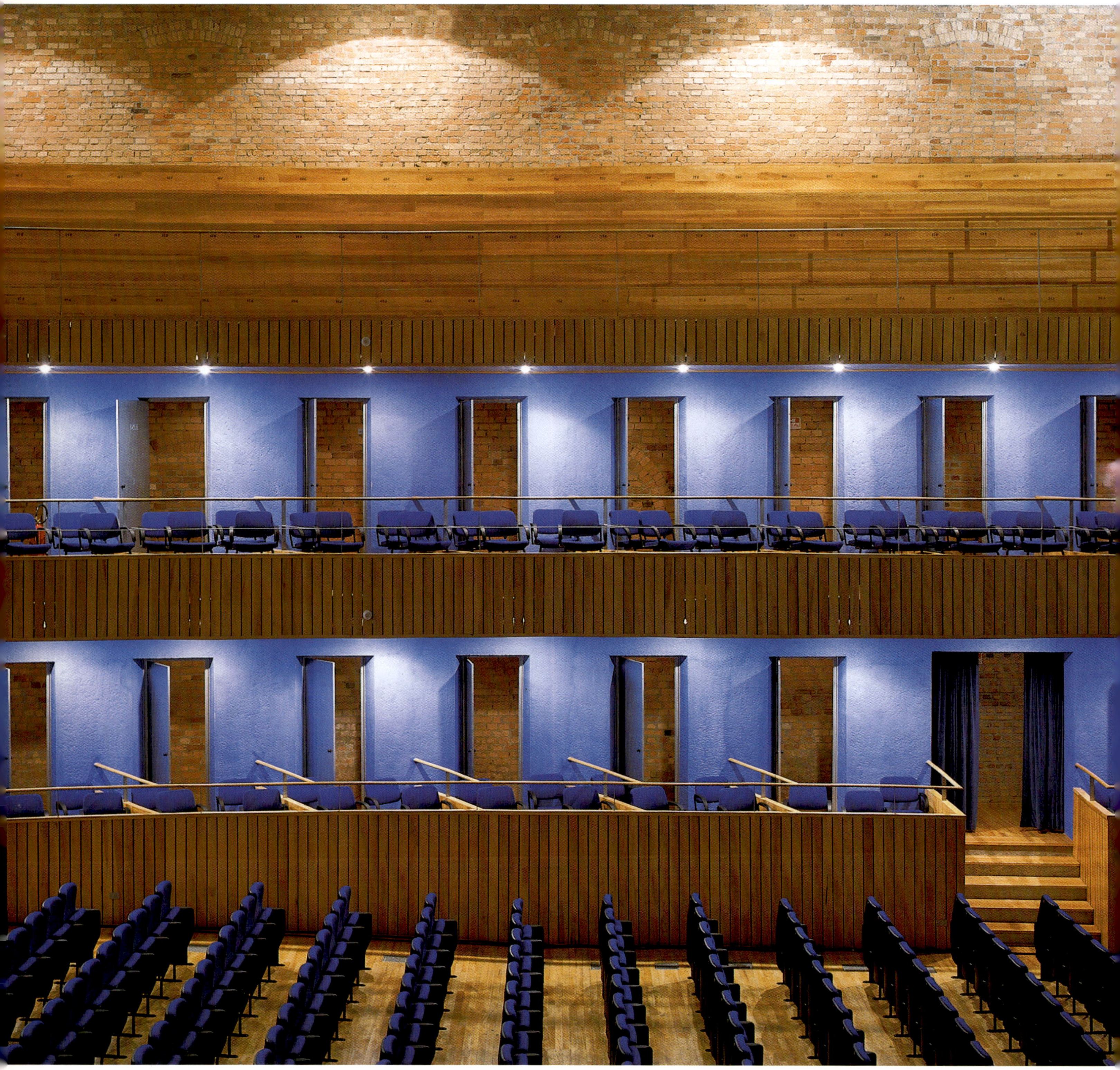

KKKK Complex

Registro, São Paulo state 1996

In 1918, the Companhia Ultramarina de Desenvolvimento KKKK (Kaigai, Kogyo, Kabushiki, Kaisha Company of Ultramarine Development) was authorized to operate in Brazil, in the city of Registro, south São Paulo state. It was a small village, established around a registration post for gold ore extracted from the mines of the Ribeira Valley to be shipped away via the local port. The development of the city and the region was accelerated in 1920, when KKKK brought 450 Japanese families to the colony. The company was responsible for selling land for agriculture – mainly rice fields – and for the distribution of the production, which meant opening roads to silos, to the port and to the Juquiá rail terminal.

To house its commercial, administrative and industrial rice processing operations, as well as to store the grain, KKKK erected an industrial plant on the banks of the Ribeira de Iguape River, on the site of the earlier port. In 1924 four brick storage pavilions were inaugurated, plus a three-story building to house the rice processing machinery. An open sided passageway running along one of the façades interconnected the five buildings. The complex, of industrial character and strictly functional, contrasted with the other buildings the immigrants had built to live in, strongly influenced by traditional Japanese architecture.

The restoration plan for the complex, which was in a much deteriorated condition after years of abandonement, was a Brasil Arquitetura Studio initiative, supported by the municipal administration of Registro and the state government. Priority was given to the restoration of the official historical heritage site, the remains of which carried great significance for the local population because of its direct relation to the town's origins. Along with restoring the buildings, a historical reference institution was established: the Memorial to the Vale do Ribeira Japanese Immigration. This museum has a significant collection, provided by artists of Japanese origin living in Brazil, along with photographs, tools, industrial equipment and other donated items, assembled to illustrate the story of Japanese immigration in the region.

The second important aspect is the integration of these revitalized heritage buildings with their historic and environmental landscape, relating them to the city and to the river in a broader project, the Beira-Rio Park. The objective is to restore the riverbanks and control the floods, integrating the set with the city by designing a market square, establishing communication routes and flux control, all combined strategies to recover the city's historic relation with its river.

The four warehouses constitute, in fact, two large spaces, united and separated at the same time by a garden-corridor enclosed by wood trellises on the façades. This area was destinated as a social center for the local population, and features spaces for exhibitions and for training courses and other educational activities undertaken by the Management Continued Training Center, run by the Government Department of Education. The buildings' load-bearing masonry brick walls, with their expressed relieving arches, were restored. The timber-structured roofs, clay tiled and supported on steel columns, were maintained. The natural light enters through the only original openings – semicircular metal-framed windows above the sliding door transoms – and by rows of glass tiles applied to the roof. The infrastructure necessary to the new administrative and educational functions, particularly in the buildings to be used as a Training Center, was accommodated in independent two-storeyed cubic blocks built inside the warehouses, interconnected by concrete stairs and walkways.

The three-storeyed building that houses the Memorial also had its original brickwork and roof restored. The narrow central timber stairs that join the timber floors were restored as well. And, juxtaposed to the façade, a red prismatic element was added, encasing the service elevator.

RIVERSIDE PARK

The complex in 1995.

Interlinking the blocks, two canopies, one supported by columns and a narrower one attached to the pavilion walls and suspended by steel rods, run alongside the old constructions almost touching them, referring to the original tiled roofs and recovering their function. They work as a contemporary seam between the pavilions, creating sheltered paths, of no little importance in a rainy region.

The design of the canopies, along with the metal sculpture commissioned from the artist Tomie Ohtake – a gigantic tree baptized *Guaracuí*, whose original was a symbolic city landmark while it lived – constitute two contemporary and artistically handled elements of the project, both referring to the history of the city and to the KKKK group. A third, stronger presence, a reference to the architects' body of work, is an immaculate white rendered cube delicately placed on the lawn. With the entrance emphasized by trellis panels and a projecting concrete canopy over an external stage on the opposite façade, the theatre evaded the warehouses where it was originally meant to be, proudly illustrating the architects' attitude: respectful in their interventions in historical buildings while, at the same time, vigorously willing to affirm the contemporary quality of their work. In simple, clear and geometric language, it sets itself apart from the warehouses yet always maintains an alignment and a scale relation with them. The project is neither confusing nor aggressive; at the same time it is not at all submissive: just like a gentle Japanese bow.

CRS

- The guaracuí tree, a symbol of the old town of Registro, *c.* 1920
- KKKK in operation, with boats moored at the port, *c.* 1920
- Approach to the port, with KKKK on the right, *c.* 1920
- The KKKK complex in 2002, with the sculpture *Guaracuí*, by Tomie Ohtake

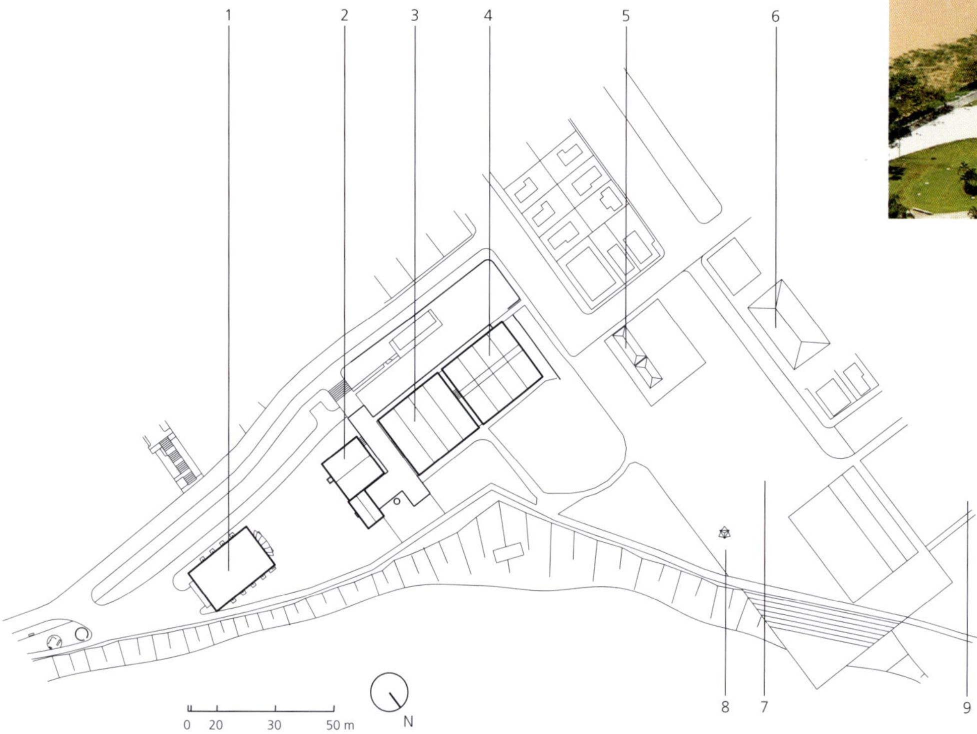

- Location plan:
  1 theatre
  2 Memorial to Japanese Immigration
  3 hall for exhibitions, receptions and other social activities/multiple use hall
  4 classrooms
  5 restaurant/old immigrant's lodge
  6 Town Market Building
  7 Market Square
  8 *Guaracuí* sculpture
  9 Riverside Park

- The new theatre and restored complex

- West, south and east elevations; longitudinal section
- Ground and first floor plans of theater:
  1 stage support
  2 reversible stage
  3 tiers
  4 foyer
  5 cabin
- Space for external use of the reversible stage

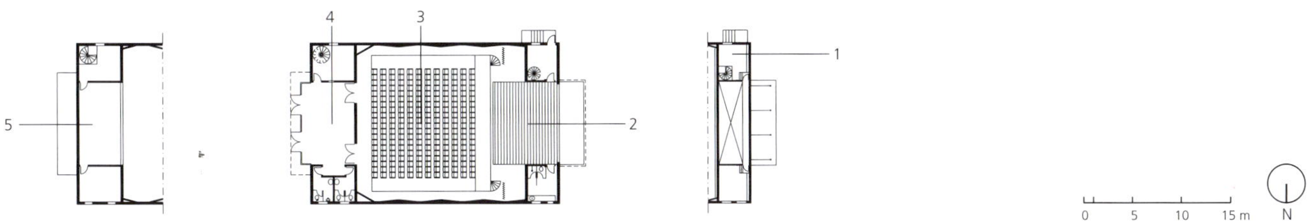

The old passageway and the new, covered by concrete blade/marquise

A few words about a project

In 1995, we prepared a concise architectonic study for the transformation of the old KKKK buildings into a cultural and educational center. For some time we had been aiming at the set of buildings, the abandonment of which caused us heartfelt indignation due to their historical character – also because we avidly yearned for the challenge of a new project. We were impressed not only by the unusual architecture, but also because of its physical and symbolical presence in the formation and development of the city of Registro.

With a privileged geographical and urbanistic location, those impressive – given the local scale – warehouses, were for many years the portals to the city, in a time when one could only get there by boat. Their strategic location on the external side of a pronounced bend of the river allowed a longitudinal view of its course, up and down. From there, when the river was still navigable, one could spot approaching boats from a long distance, coming downstream or from the port, transporting rice, tea and a variety of commodities.

With a small brochure for this hypothetical project, we began a pilgrimage to municipal governments and state departments in search of support. We believed that restoring the complex with the tools of "industrial archeology" would contribute to giving some self-esteem back to the residents of Registro and also serve to revive an entire area of the city that was underdeveloped and held memories only of the floods and other related problems brought by the waters

Many were the trials we had to deal with in carrying out the project, closely followed, and not without suspicion, by the citizens of Registro, especially those from the Japanese community. After all, for forty years the site had remained abandoned, and many promises and attempts at restoration had been made, without success.

As the project neared conclusion, a beautiful and growing movement of adhesion began to take shape. At the blink of an eye, just before inauguration, the three-storeyed building designed to house the Memorial to Japanese Immigration was filled with donations from families of Japanese origin, the descendents of the pioneer immigrants. Personal items, domestic and religious utensils, tools and machinery, written documents and photographs, drawings, maps and books brought from Japan today make up a collection that testifies to this small and little known piece of Brazil's recent history.

Concerned with the need to create a collection of art works, we asked some artists, friends of ours, of Japanese origin, for donations. Astonishingly, the response was immediate: within two weeks of the appeal we were receiving donations and new indications of artists willing to donate – friends of friends. Surprisingly, our precious few first pieces were soon to become a collection of 50 valuable pieces, representative works of Nipo-Brazilian art.

With the completion of this project after six years of twists and turns, we renewed our belief that architecture, or rather, architectonic action, has an enormous power to transform. Even as a single intervention, it can change the reality and affect a whole town.

In the case of the KKKK Complex, a new town/river relationship was established: the heart, or central core, of a riverside park is already a reality; the recovery and re-examination of the town's history from a new "riverside perspective" has already found its document and space; meeting people and sharing have become the key words for this new urban equipment.

FF and MF

Exposição Inaugural
Acervo de Doações

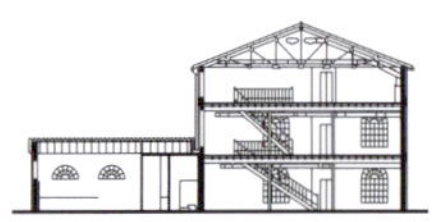

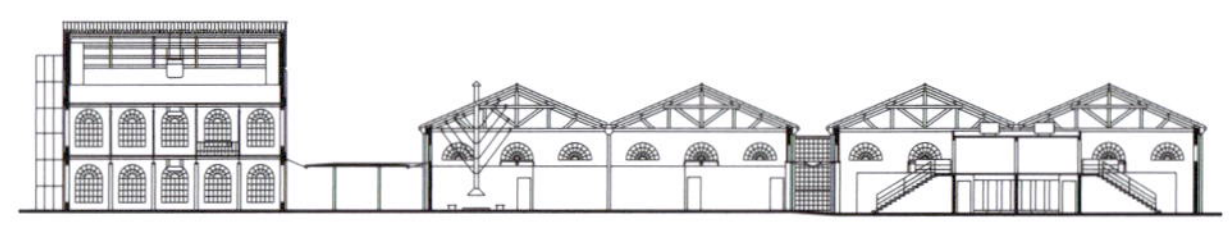

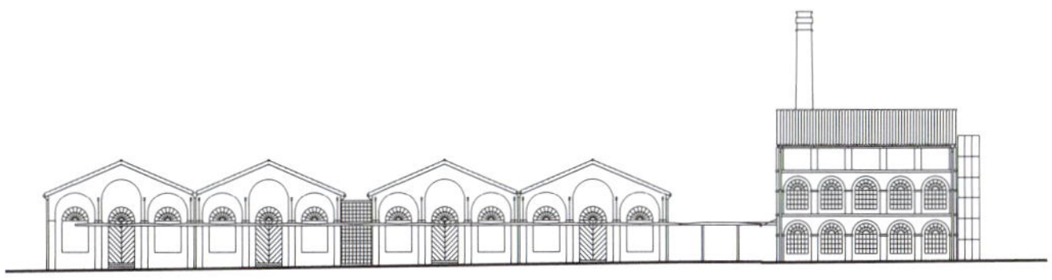

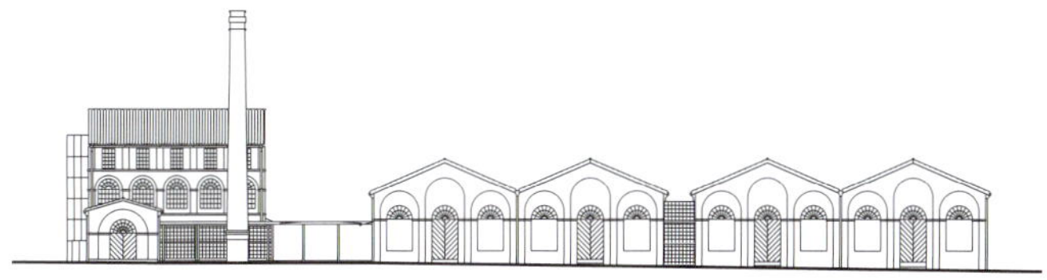

- Area for exhibitions and receptions
- Garden between warehouses K2 and K3
- Classrooms on two levels
- The café, the Memorial to Japanese Immigration, and area for exhibitions and receptions in K1

- Sections and elevations
- Plan, level 7.20:
  1 memorial, library
- Plan, level 3.70:
  2 memorial, art collection
- Plan, level 2.70:
  3 computer and meeting room
- Plan, level 0.00:
  4 memorial/permanent exhibition
  5 café
  6 exhibitions/social activities
  7 classrooms
  8 atelier

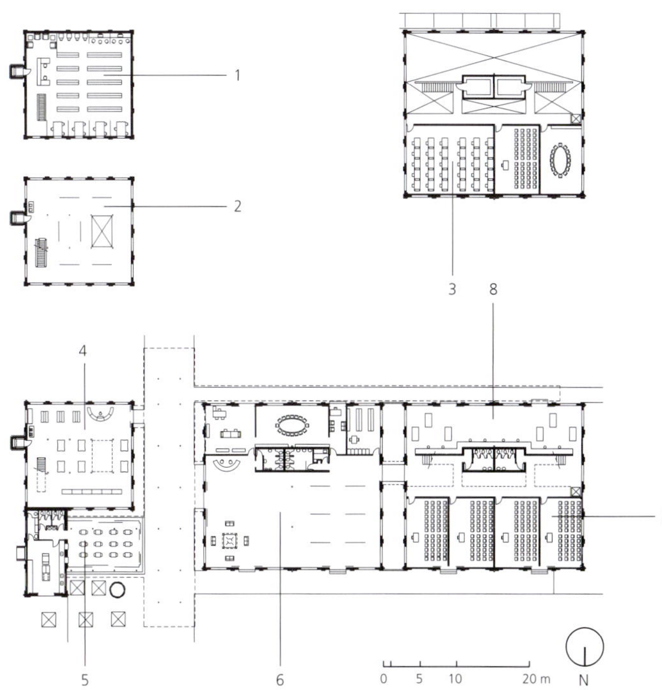

Revitalizing Gelbes Viertel

Berlin, Germany 1997

The trouble in finding a word to define this project – already called revitalization, restoration, upgrading, revamping, remodeling, facelifting and renovation – is directly related to the fact that it is not an architectural or urban planning project in the traditional sense. It has even been described as a merely "skin-deep" intervention in a housing estate, a superficial treatment. As if the skin were not an inseparable part of the body, as if it were not a surface vital to the perception of the environment, the first to react to contact and to communicate sensations.

Before commenting on the concrete results of the intervention, it is essential to think about the nature of the project and the discourse preceding it, and also about the contemporary reality that rendered it inevitable. With the fall of the Berlin Wall and the beginning of Germany's process of reunification, the architecture of East Berlin needed to be revised and thought over in the new context. The principal criticism to the endless housing estates – solidly built of pre-cast concrete components, with good infrastructure and located in the midst of common areas – related to their uniformity and monotony. Countless initiatives were undertaken to give them individual character, to renew this urban landscape, which, in our globalized reality, has become the essence of disaggregating contemporary spaces, trenchant examples of non-places. In addition, they also became the symbols of an ideology and of a way of life that needed to be identified and modified.

The challenge was to construct a new significant universe, even if one had to draw on particular references and identities far removed from German culture and geography, as long as they could communicate by the force of their artistic and cultural expression and by the gentle but determined move aimed at aggregation and humanization against the supermodern reality of oppressive, solitary, spaces, with no references whatsoever.

Gelbes Viertel (or "Yellow District"), located in the center of the former East Berlin suburb of Hellersdorf, is a housing estate that is home to 12,000 people in 3,200 apartments built with pre-cast concrete components and occupied by white-collar and industrial workers. The decision to create an identity for this complex attracted 56 architecture practices from Latin America to a competition aimed at revitalizing the complex.

In their winning proposal, the Brasil Arquitetura Studio clearly sustained the discourse that informed their work, a discourse based on historic and architectural quotations, on Brazilian culture in its different times and hues, including the ordinary and the vernacular, symbols of renovation and identity. The project was structured on four basic ideas. The first involved the highlighting of the four main entrances to the estate. Each of the four entrance squares, measuring 50 by 130 ft, was personalized with the installation of a significant piece of work by the Brazilian sculptors Amilcar de Castro (work in steel, with an accent on geometry), Frans Krajcberg (work in timber, symbolizing the restoration of nature), Miguel Santos (ceramics, expressing social diversity) or Siron Franco (work in concrete, paying homage to the culture of the Brazilian Indians).

The second idea was to give the buildings a chromatic treatment. The drab gray buildings first received a coat of white paint, in reference to the lime-wash applied to the colonial walls of Spanish and Portuguese America. Two bands of vivid color, *ultramar* blue, pink or yellow, one on the ground floor and one along the top of each block, were applied in a rustic, textured manner, to identify and differentiate the buildings with colors borrowed from the vernacular architecture and handicraft of Latin American countries.

The third idea refers to a Moorish tradition rooted in the Iberian Peninsula. It is represented by *mushrabeyeh* work panels, a kind of trellised woodwork used in Brazil since the colonial period, in order to control the light, protect against the weather and preserve privacy. Besides substituting the rails on the balconies and giving character and rhythm to the façades, the panels are present at the block entrances, in the access ways to the stairs, as well as in the passages which cross the blocks, in the form of suspended ceiling panels projected as canopies from the buildings' entrances. The walls of these passages are cladded with ceramic tiling, another element of the Moorish tradition. The ceramic tiles bear designs by the Kadiwéu Indians, in sophisticated graphic patterns.

The forth and final idea that defines the structure of an architectural project focused on the identity of existent, consolidated spaces, is represented by the landscaping of the external areas. The emphasis is on the formal liberty of the composition, on the variety of walkways and on the potential for amusement and leisure activities. The main elements are the treatment of the internal patios and the sinuous paths with stone paving (in a manner known as Portuguese mosaic); the presence of ceramic tiled garden walls; the choice of irregular masses of vegetation, varying in density, evoking the free forms of tropical American vegetation; and the ubiquitous presence of water in the form of discreet waterworks, watercourses and reflecting pools.

CRS

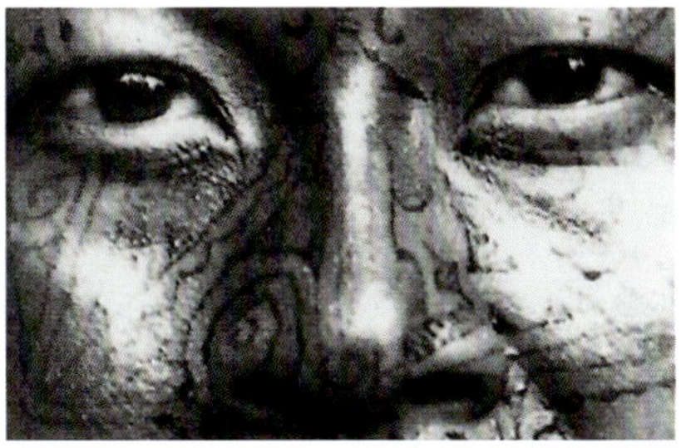

The competition

The fall of the Berlin Wall, along with its well-known consequences for the lives of the German people, opened up a huge, new and unique work front in the architectural field: the revitalization of the prefabricated housing estates, built from the 1960s to 1980s, one of the trademarks of Soviet communism.

This architecture, despite the good quality of the materials and of the construction, especially if compared to public housing in Brazil, has an extremely drab, even ugly aspect, and is endlessly repetitive. It is a huge expanse of gray buildings that starts in Berlin and extends all the way to Moscow, across the central plains, crossing Poland, former Czechoslovakia and Hungary. All these countries adopted the same housing system, which reflected the architectural bureaucracy.

Starting with Berlin, various architects were called in from all over the world, either by invitation or by means of international competitions (as was our case), to tackle this new theme/problem of humanizing and differentiating these neighborhoods, providing them with identity, thus making them more attractive and avoiding exodus.

The selection of our design followed debates with three of the finalists, representatives of the local population, experts and engineers responsible for the construction of the district, along with representatives of the Berlin Senate. Following that, an international panel of judges made the final decision.

We sought to provide that piece of Berlin with its own character and identity by means of a unifying concept, linking it to elements of Latin American architecture and, more specifically, Brazilian architecture.

The great challenge for the architects, in our view, was to introduce new elements, create new contexts and bring forth a cultural and spatial richness without aggressiveness towards what was, nevertheless, a tremendous effort, involving many, to solve one of the greatest problems of humanity: the lack of a proper place to live. To face this matter with resolve and gentleness was our weapon.

FF and MF

- The complex prior to intervention
- The Trabant, economical car in former East Germany
- Model and sketch of proposal

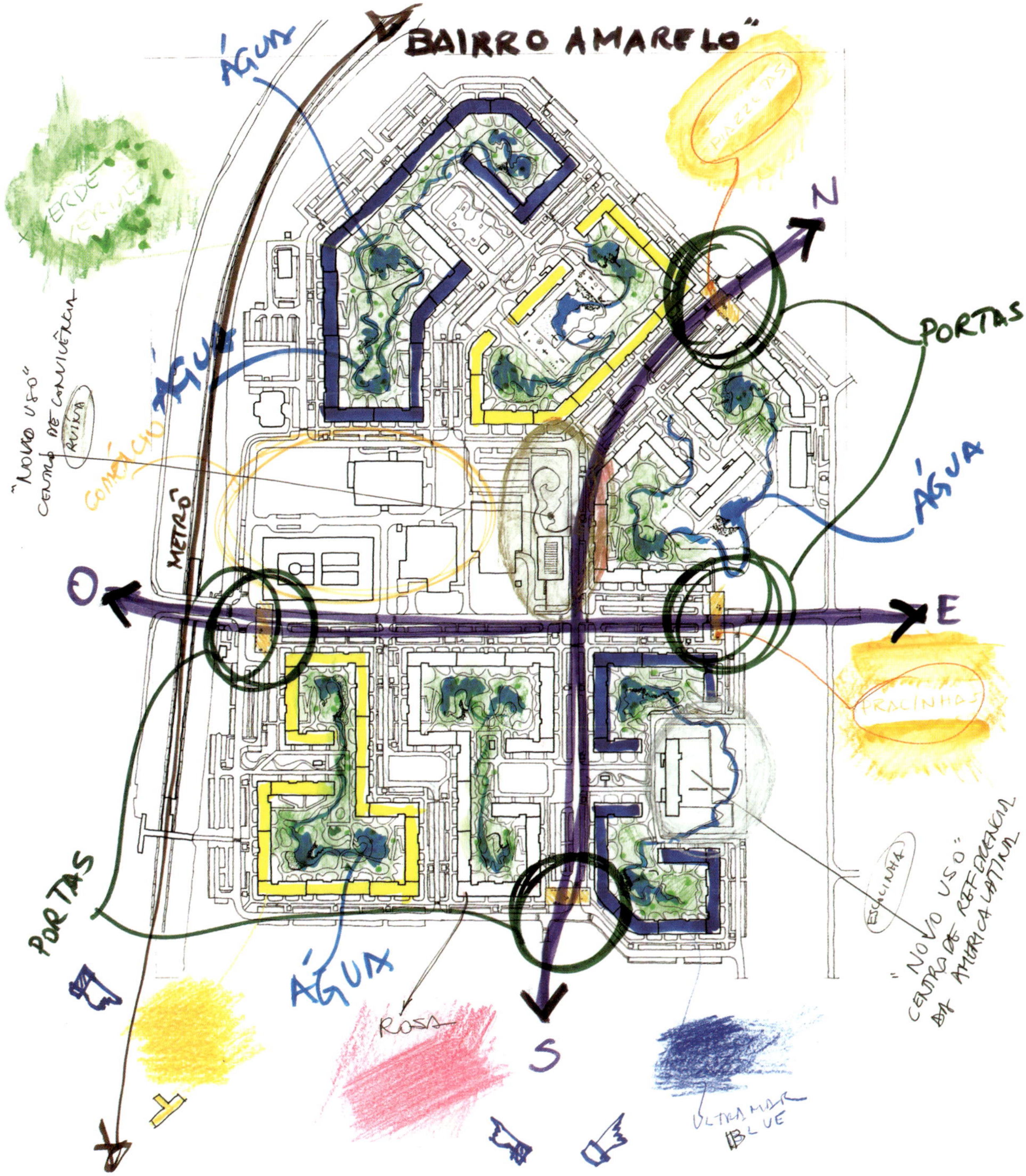
"BAIRRO AMARELO"
ÁGUA
PORTAS
N
S
E
O
METRÔ
ROSA
ULTRAMAR BLUE
PRAINHAS
"NOVO USO" CENTRO DE REFERÊNCIA DA AMÉRICA LATINA

The colors

We draw here on the words of Le Corbusier:

Lime-wash is present everywhere the people have preserved intact the balanced structure of a harmonious culture.

... it has been linked to human shelter since the dawn of humanity; stones are calcinated, ground, diluted with water, and the walls become the purest white; an extraordinarily beautiful white.

... if the house is totally white, the shapes of things stand out without any possible transgression; the volume of color appears clear-cut; the color of things is categorical. Lime-wash white is absolute, everything stands out against it, and one writes absolutely, black on white, frank and truthful.

... lime-wash is the wealth of the rich and the poor, everyone's, like bread, milk and water are the wealth of the slave and of the king.

... the oeuvre of the age, so daring, so adventurous, so bellicose, so conquering, seems to expect that we think against a white background.

(*L'art décoratif d'aujourd'hui*, Paris, 1925)

White symbolically awaits and offers support for the future yet to be written.

To identify each block and in pursuing its identity and proper character, we used other colors also handed down from the Iberian Peninsula to Latin America – *ultramar* blue, pink and yellow. We painted bands of these colors close to the ground and along the top of the buildings.

Blue, farmhouse blue, the blue from the simple dwellings of Brazil or Venezuela, from Caribbean or Mexican houses. The blue of the villages and towns of the Portuguese province of Alentejo, such as Arraiolos. The blue, which is also magical and erudite in the work of Yves Klein, creating the idea of the infinite – the sea – and of the abstract – the sky.

Yellow brings light, heat, and fire. It warms and stimulates. The yellow that recalls Seville and the Plaza de Toros, its *caliente* land. The yellow of the sun, which has no owner; that's there for all.

Pink, the color of the earth, so many different kinds, many pinks. Pink, so often used by the people of Latin America, whether strong or pale, is always the symbol of tenderness and harmony. Flower harmony, that of roses, rose pink.

FF and MF

Kadiwéu art in Berlin

Taking Kadiwéu art to Berlin was one of the driving ideas in the design for Gelbes Viertel. The Kadiwéu people, who live near the border between Mato Grosso do Sul state and Paraguay, are known for the beauty and expressiveness of their designs.

They have achieved a high esthetic standard in body painting and painting on animal hides, as well as in pottery, painted with purely geometric designs, usually by means of green *jenipapo* juice mixed with charcoal.

The idea of placing this rich tradition side by side with the radically modern work of Amilcar de Castro was not gratuitous. We agree with sociologist Darcy Ribeiro that "there is no fundamental distinction between our art and that of non-European, technically less developed peoples", as he wrote in 1980 in his book *Kadiwéu*. "Both can be best understood if viewed as expressions of the different ways of feeling, thinking and doing of their respective societies, and as intrinsically equal, or compatible as results of shared human impulses. [...] They are products of an esthetic concern, of a yearning for beauty, when the result is a work of high technical perfection." Why not show such beauty to the world?

It is in the painting by the women that Kadiwéu art is at its most expressive. The graphic patterns constitute a collective cultural heritage, from which the artists select their favorite themes, combining them in countless variations. At first, we presented the proposal to the Kadiwéu with the idea of using patterns already designed by them, in exchange for proper remuneration. The Assembly of the Association of Indian Communities of the Kadiwéu Reserve concluded, however, that this was not a simple matter of commercial transaction, but rather, of a cultural exchange between two peoples.

To obtain new designs, they organized a competition among the women from the Bodoquena Mountain village and distributed the funds received as payment among all the participants, in an egalitarian manner. Ninety-three women between 15 and 92 years of age presented their works, each of them submitting three designs. Since the Kadiwéu's art would be the link between their people and the Germans, at the end, as a reciprocal gesture, the six chosen artists were invited to visit Germany and to have contact with that culture.

Today the residents of the 3,200 apartments of Gelbes Viertel, in faraway Berlin, live among the beautiful tiles designed by the Indians of the Bodoquena mountain village. And for the first time, in Brazil, the intellectual property of Indian peoples was duly respected. In a legal procedure unprecedented in Brazil, the Kadiwéu have the copyright to their designs protected, registered at the National Fine Arts School, Federal University of Rio de Janeiro.

FF and MF

Kadiwéu women visiting Gelbes Viertel: Sofia de Souza, Saturnina da Silva, Cláudia Pedroso, Acácia de Almeida, Sandra da Silva and Joana Baleia de Almeida.

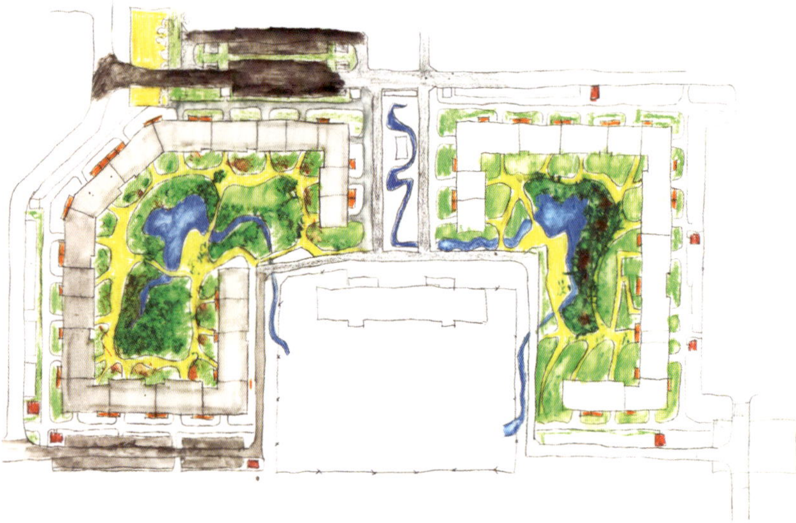

Study for the courts.

- Study for the South entrance
- Sculpture by Amilcar de Castro next to the east entrance
- Before and after the remodelling: Gerbes Viertel in two stages

Rail and Bus Terminal

Santo André, São Paulo state 1998

Along the banks of the Tamanduateí River – which rises high in the Paranapiacaba mountains, the historical barrier between São Paulo and the coast – a trail that has been there since time immemorial has become an important corridor connecting the city of São Paulo to the port of Santos.

A trail for mules and pedestrians, with stretches of navigable river, this first route was replaced definitively by a railway at the end of the 19th century. The railway was located at some distance from the winding riverbed, on higher, drier land. The development of the municipalities along the river in the so-called, "ABC" region, an industrial area to the southeast of São Paulo city, owes much to the existence of this railway.

In the mid 20th century, road transport started to predominate, and along with it came large land recovery projects. The river channel was rectified and the wetlands levelled, avenues were built along the banks, creating new forms of access; and large areas of previously periodically flooded areas were regained for urban development. Furthering a long-standing trend of locating industries alongside the railway, the parallel expressway created a kind of industrial belt along the broad strip between the canalized river and the railway. It is now a primarily industrial zone as well as a circulation zone for people and goods related to the industrial activity, with practically no housing, commerce or services.

Since the 1990s the ABC industrial region has seen the decline of its main economic activity. Many factories have abandoned the region, seeking lower operating costs in emerging industrial zones. Governments have responded to this ongoing transformation by redefining the economic and functional profile of the region. The high point of this new policy came in 1999 with the launching, by the city council of Santo André, of the program *Eixo Tamanduateí*. The overall goal is to redesign the infrastructure and built environment, aiming at the introduction of housing, commerce, private and institutional services, as well as leisure facilities, as part of the central functions of the new tertiary corridor.

The city council anticipated this mega-intervention, but limited the first phase of the project to building a new intercity bus terminal for Santo André, integrated with the existing rail station. The available sites were located in the land between the canalized river and the industrial highway, parallel to the railway and adjacent to a railway bridge which was then the only connection between the two sides of this broad strip, fated to become a wasteland due to the difficulties of access and the industrial evasion. The surrounding area was a mixture of active factories, abandoned warehouses and vacant lots, combining to form a desolate, no man's land.

As a response to this situation, the design went beyond the requirements by rotating the axis initially proposed for the development of the new bus terminal – which ran parallel to the railway – and which was required to refer to the rail station. As an alternative, a huge covered pedestrian walkway was designed, crossing over the rails, joining two new bus stations, one at each end – one for intercity buses, the other for local urban routes. This complex, which bridges two areas of the city largely isolated from each other, was also given the role and character of a high street, offering infrastructure for the installation of commercial activities.

Built with a steel structure combining four types of specially designed standard section components – a half horseshoe, a curved one, a straight one and a curved joint – the raised walkway and both terminals present under their white curved metallic roofs a sequence of ventilated spaces, illuminated and functional, with easy and comfortable circulation thanks to the combination of ramps and escalators. The metallic structure constitutes a technical response to the tight construction schedule, and to the problem presented by the different heights required over the railway, whose traffic could not be blocked at any time.

A section of the complex, just over the railway, was reserved for the construction of a new rail station. Linked to the main halls of the bus terminals, the walkway becomes a mezzanine, with the lower level reserved for activities directly related to the primary functions – platforms, waiting areas, ticket offices, storage lockers, information booths, rest-rooms – and the walkway level provided for parallel activities, such as shops and catering.

Transformed into a composite urban operation, this construction, housing a multiplicity of functions and a heavy flow of pedestrians, came to play the functional and symbolic role of a new urban focus in the city of Santo André. Due to the specificity and clarity of its architecture, and in contrast to the commonplace designs for drab, isolated terminals that often become a focus for the degradation of the surrounding areas, this edifice becomes an element of integration and an important landmark in the landscape of a region in need of identity. Consequently, it is also a source of its humanization.

CRS

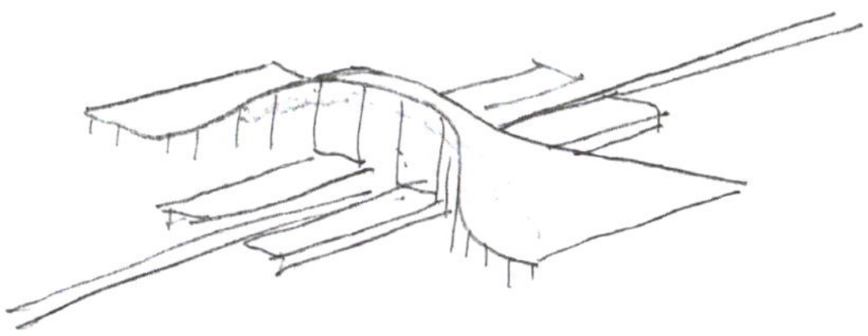

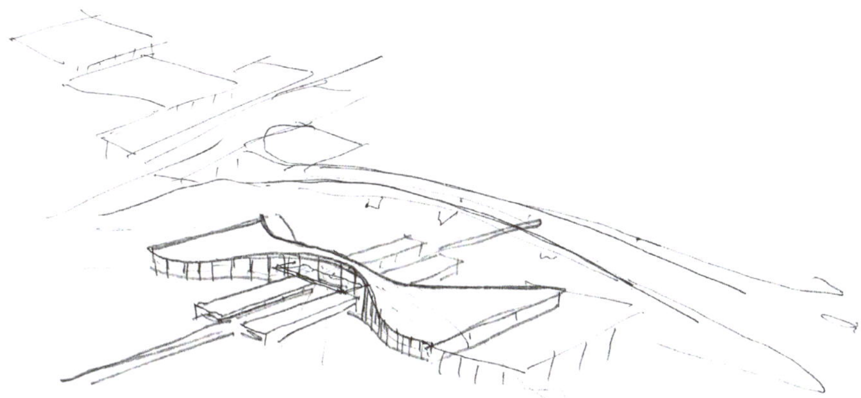

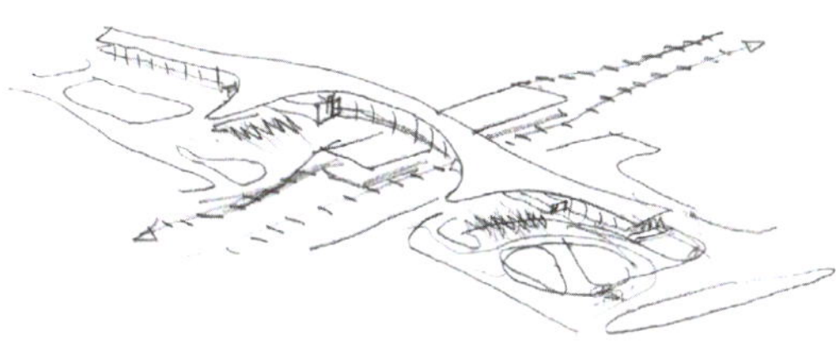

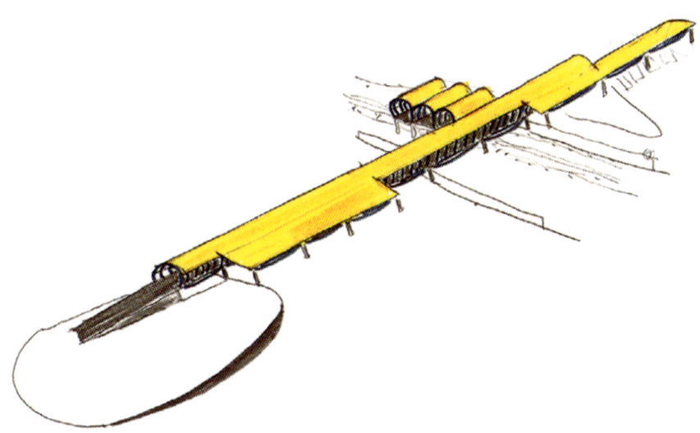

Bridge complex

The idea of a bus terminal often evokes a depressing image of coldness, waiting, discomfort, a place in which one spends as little time as possible, besides evoking all kinds of danger. In Santo André, when we confronted the challenge of overcoming this stigma of urban discomfort, we held to our conviction that our cities can still be dealt with successfully.

A bus terminal does not have to consist merely of platform halls, especially when it is built close to an urban tangle of bridges, railways, expressways and a river.

We projected a complex that would reconstitute the urban fabric, severed and separated over time, due to the uncontrolled growth, or should we say, swelling, of our metropolis.

This structure serves the intercity bus terminal, the rail station for a new fast train system under construction (CPTM), a bus terminal for local routes, and the pedestrians who can now cross the various barriers in sheltered comfort, while contemplating the harsh beauty of the industrial landscape. An urban facility in metropolitan scale, a single intervention that radiates throughout the greater city in contagious waves of improvement and comfort: this is the bus and rail terminal of Santo André city.

FF and MF

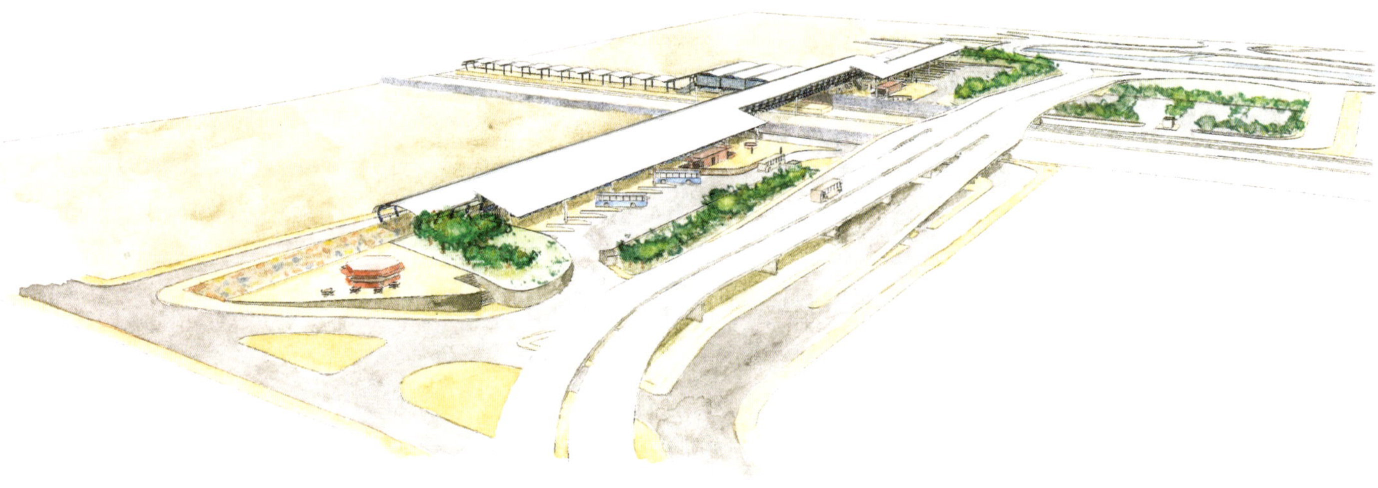

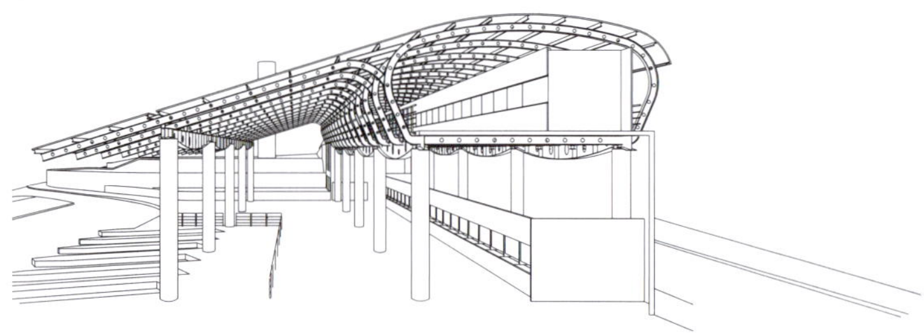

- Platform
- Walkway
- Perspective of bus terminal
- Walkway and stairs leading to platform

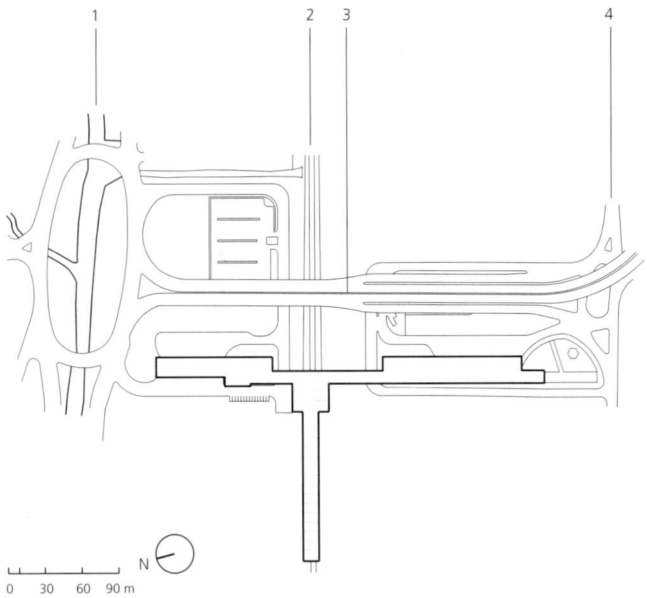

- Location plan
  1 Tamanduateí river
  2 railway
  3 overpass
  4 industrial avenue
- First floor plan:
  5 bus terminal
  6 railway platform
  7 railway station
- Second floor plan:
  8 railway station
  9 walkway overpassing railway

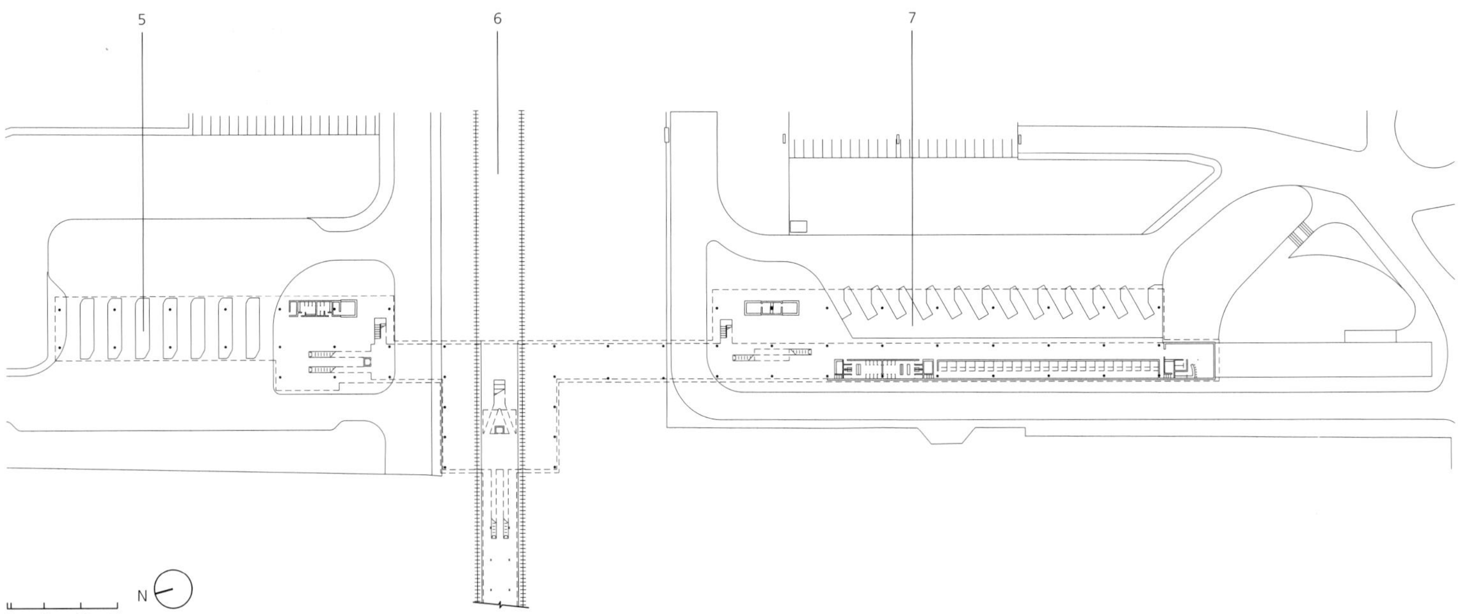

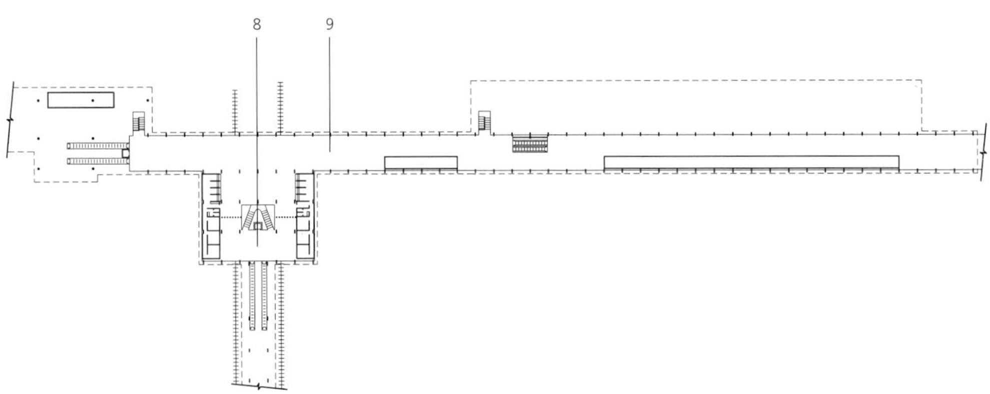

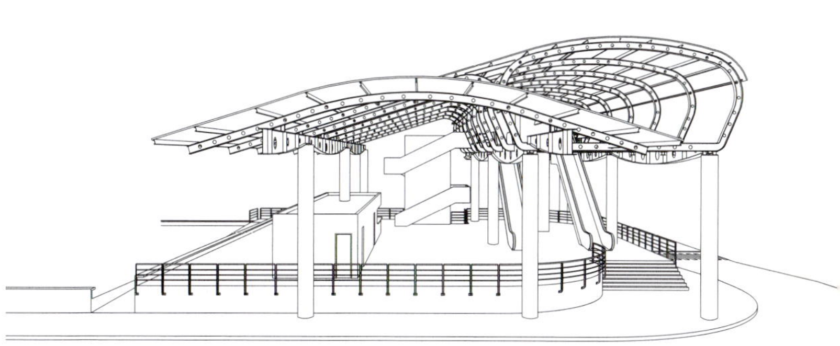

Perspective of bus station.

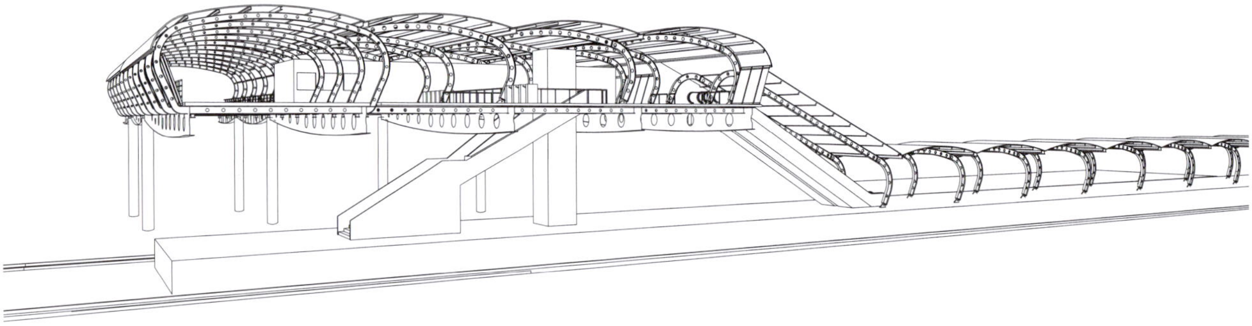

- Perspective of railway station and platform (unbuilt)
- Walkway

- Chicken's nest on a peach tree.
- City Display: information center and forum for debate on projects for Santo André (unbuild); in the background, the road and rail terminal.

Afro-Brazilian Art Exhibition – Brazil 500 Years of Visual Arts

Ibirapuera Park, São Paulo 2000

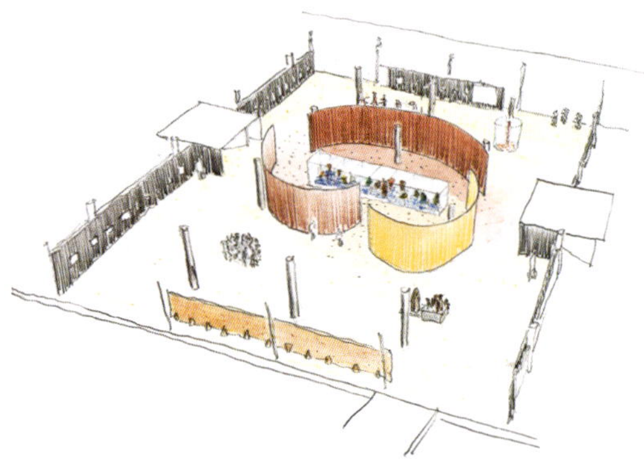

In the year 2000, during the celebrations of the 500th anniversary of the discovery of Brazil, the Brazil 500Years Association, whose directors were originally from the staff and board of the São Paulo Biennial Foundation, held a set of thirteen simultaneous exhibitions, all held in Ibirapuera Park buildings, in São Paulo. Each module was dedicated to a different chapter or theme within the vast retrospective panorama of Brazilian culture, from pre-history to contemporary art. The Afro-Brazilian module, occupying part of the top floor of the Biennial pavilion in São Paulo, focused on the influences of African art and culture, which arrived here with the African slaves brought to work on the plantations and in domestic and urban services between the 17th and 19th centuries.

The curators' project sought to explain the relations between the African-influenced Brazilian artistic production – the work of artists and artisans descended from the slaves – and its African matrix, represented by a nucleus composed of three sets of historical works corresponding to the three main African regions from which the slaves came: the Congo, Angola and Benin regions. The aim of the exhibition was to indicate the source of certain strands as well as the course of so many fusions and combinations which defined the particular character of African-influenced Brazilian art.

The museological project builds on this same tripartite core, translating it into a sort of threefold display that occupies the center of the gallery. It is defined by curved curtain surfaces, hanging from ceiling to floor, in three colors corresponding to the three types of soil belonging to the above-mentioned African regions; this reference is also alluded to in the flooring treatments of the three lobular areas. Inside the symbolically shaped and located nucleus the African works of art are exhibited, arranged on bases of deep *ultramar* blue, displayed along a single long window of laminated crystal traversing the three regions and presented as a synthesis of the ancestral references.

Starting from this memorial invocation, a variety of Afro-Brazilian works are distributed throughout the hall, enclosed by a mantle of black curtain, which serves as an exhibition backdrop at once neutral and racially coded. Playing against the curtain, the floor takes on the aspect of white sand, representing a Brazil in which all the influences combine and fuse in the construction of a specific identity.

The works of these Brazilian artists of African descent, either occupying the center of the space or suspended, levitating against the black curtains, tell the history of the multiple and varied forms of assimilation of the artistic values and ritual codices of tradition that were produced here in contact with other cultural influences of European and native origins. In this project, the Miesian inspiration (*Velvet and Silk Café*, Berlin, 1927) is clearly perceptible in the dematerialization of the supporting wall, achieved by the undulating ethereal curtains, as a stage scenery against which the objects are delineated, liberated from their concrete weight and thus granted their pure visual expressivity.

When necessary, a supporting wall as such makes an appearance as a symbolically recovered fragment of the adobe architecture of Benin, buttressed by rough surfaced conical elements: either as totems to display the exhibition's supporting text or as a long mural for the linear presentation of chronological references. Together with the other textures, colors and forms, this constructive and material reference contributes to the creation of a grave and respectful environment, simple and primitive, a scenario at the same time sacred and informal, where the fundamental sources of the black ethos regarding artistic expression reveal themselves in a simple way.

VC

Entrance to exhibition with audio-visual presentation; information totem; sculptures by Agnaldo.

- Sculptures by Mestre Didi
- Sculptures by Rubem Valentim
- Sculptures by Emanoel Araújo
- Grand display of African art

Revitalization of the area of the Monument to the Brazilian Indian Nations

Aparecida de Goiânia, Goiás state 2000

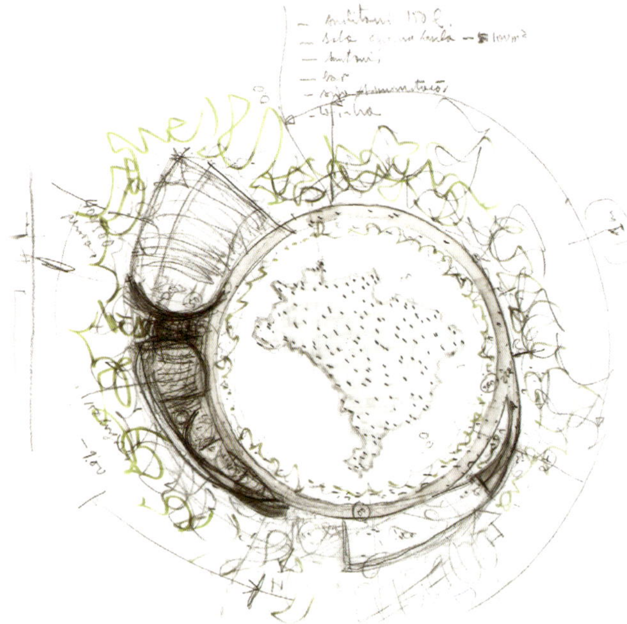

In 1992, the Goianian artist Siron Franco designed and built a memorial to the Indian peoples, in a region of *cerrado*, the resistant, low and tortuous vegetation of semi-arid Brazilian regions, close to Goiânia, capital of Goiás state. He named it the Monument to the Brazilian Indian Nations.

It consists of a set of 500 prismatic concrete blocks 7.5 ft high, planted within an empty, circular 4,500 sq yard area, covered by gravel. Each of these columns acts as support for elements related to native culture, such as replicas and petrified fragments of a range of objects, inscriptions, drawings, bas-relief designs, and feather art objects protected by glass enclosures. Like gray tombstones guarding old memories, they shape on the ground a striking map of Brazil, which can only be perceived from above.

With the goal of promoting the conservation of this sculptural work, which is subject to deterioration and depredation, and to refer it to the research and dissemination of the culture of the Brazilian Indian peoples, along with offering an infrastructure for the development of educational programs in the area of culture and the environment, the Brasil Arquitetura Studio set itself a challenge: to meet with the requirements of the program with a minimum of intervention, emphasizing the importance of the work of art erected there, amidst the *cerrado* landscape, and ensuring the conservation of the set.

The outcome was a design for a canopy as high as the prismatic blocks, to serve both as shelter to the path beneath it and as an elevated promenade, forming a large encircling ring, 115 ft in radius, made of pale concrete. This circular path highlights the floor designed by the artist, embraces the monument and allows visitors to see the map defined by the arrangement of the columns, as well as encouraging them to walk round it, creating meaningful new ways of enjoying the work.

Set at a tangent to the ring, an organically shaped construction houses an open-air amphitheater and, at a lower level, a space for workshops, a shop and an auditorium, along with room for the necessary infrastructure. A large reflecting pool on the roof cascades into a second pool beside the amphitheatre. The design called for all the walls to be coated in paint pigmented with the different types of soil found in that region, therefore in various shades of color. This palette ranges from black to bright yellow, including different shades of red and brown, and helps the walls to blend into the *cerrado* landscape. This vegetation advances under the canopy, representing the desired communion of man with the environment.

CRS

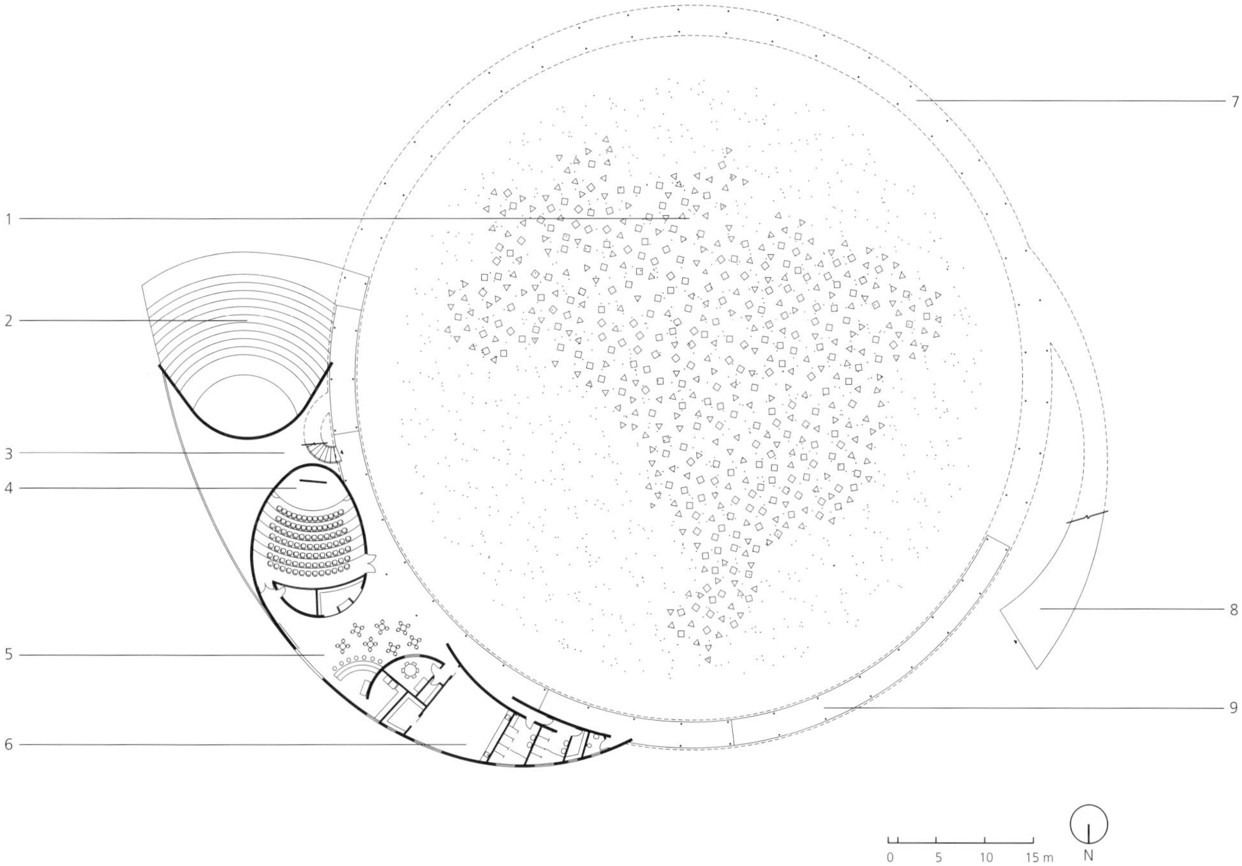

- Plan:
  1 Monument to the Native Brazilian Nations
  2 open amphitheater
  3 reflecting pool
  4 auditorium
  5 café
  6 workshop
  7 open space enabling vegetation to develop inside the circle
  8 access ramp to raised walkway
  9 covered walkway
- Elevations and sections

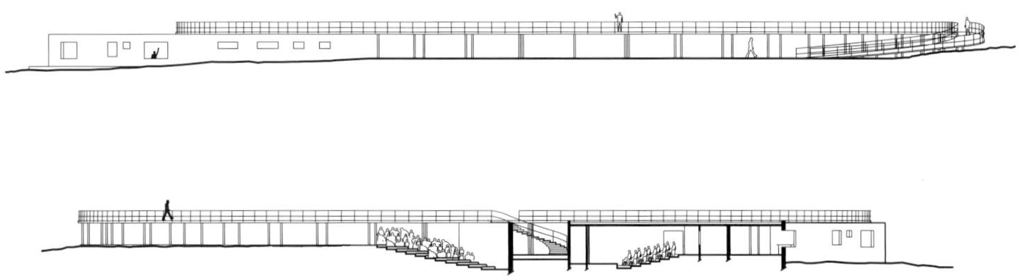

- General view denoting the monument's state of neglect
- The marquise (under construction, 2003): elevated circular walkway to enable a priviledged view of the monument, shaded path beneath allowing the *cerrado* vegetation to pervade the circle
- Panoramic view with the walkway/marquise already built

Headquarters of Instituto Socioambiental (ISA)

São Gabriel da Cachoeira, Amazonas state 2000

The design for the Instituto Socioambiental – ISA (Social and Environmental Institute) – headquarters, located in the heart of the Amazon region, on the bank of the Negro River, started with a rationalist statement – a white masonry cube, 52 ft to a side and three storeys high. The single block, like the huge *maloca* (spatious lodge built by the Indian peoples as a communal dwelling place) that embraces it, was built to house the annual meetings of the federation of 22 Indian peoples occupying the area of the region's reserve, and recovers ancient local construction techniques. The *maloca*, like the white cube, also represents collective work and celebration.

The integration of the project with the region was accomplished, first and foremost, by the incorporation of the traditional knowledge and techniques of the region's inhabitants. This is reflected in the attention to environmental comfort and the tropical climate, safety regarding the forest, and especially, in the choice of construction techniques that use locally available materials and labour, resulting in savings in time and costs and in environmental and cultural integration. The cube is thus encircled by a sheltering terrace that protects it from the weather and offers a view of the Negro River and the forest. The parapet rails and stairways, protected by trellises made of wood and vines which mark the horizontal and vertical circulation routes, provide shade for the white walls, which are deliberately pushed back.

The ground floor is for work and meeting areas, while the first floor consists of six apartments for research residents and visitors. The top floor has a meeting room, kitchen and restrooms, along with a large open veranda. Occupying more than half the area, the veranda, equipped with hammocks, is a space for relaxation and social gatherings, protected by an impressive roof. The timber structure of this unique element rests on slender lateral timber posts, which also structure the timber terraces, as if 'clothing' the central white cube. Its framework is designed to support itself by way of a traditional native system bound by vegetal cords, and is covered with *caranã* leaves, a traditional Brazilian palm tree. The initial calculations made by engineering specialists based on the architectural designs were later submitted to the local Indians who would eventually build and bind this roof using no fitted joints or nails. The overall design was approved with only a few adaptations, combining the sophistication of the proposed structure with the local construction techniques, a fusion which once again confirms the traditional dynamics of Brazilian culture.

CRS

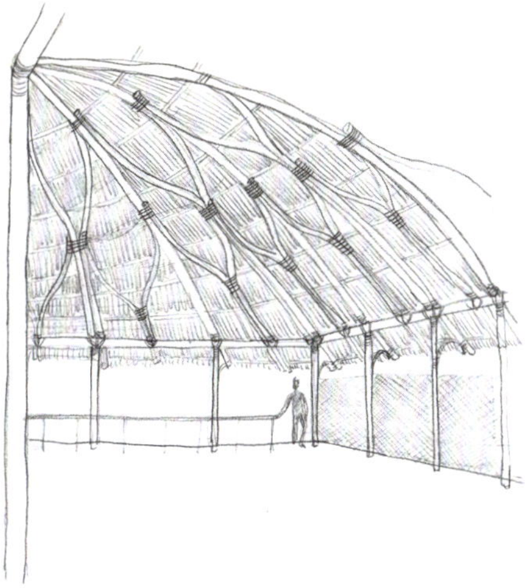

- Scenes from the Negro River and view inside the native Brazilian *maloca* (lodge) from the village of Camanaus
- Study
- Digital model of the project
- Roof structure

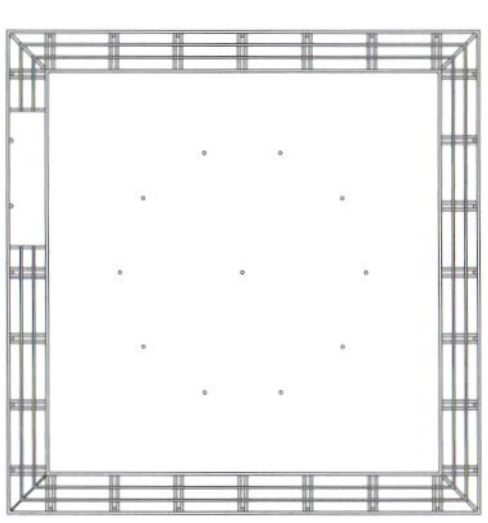

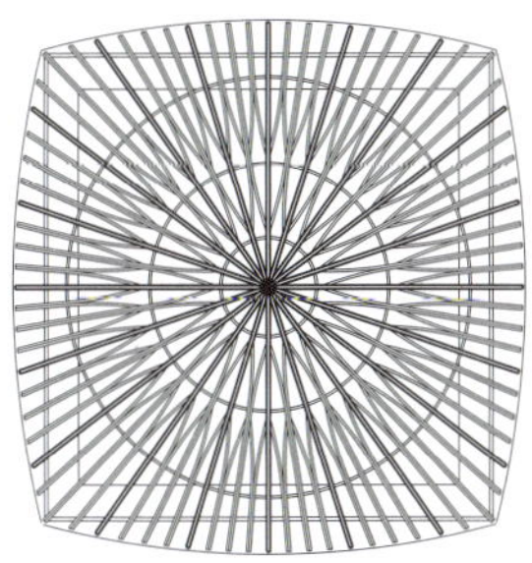

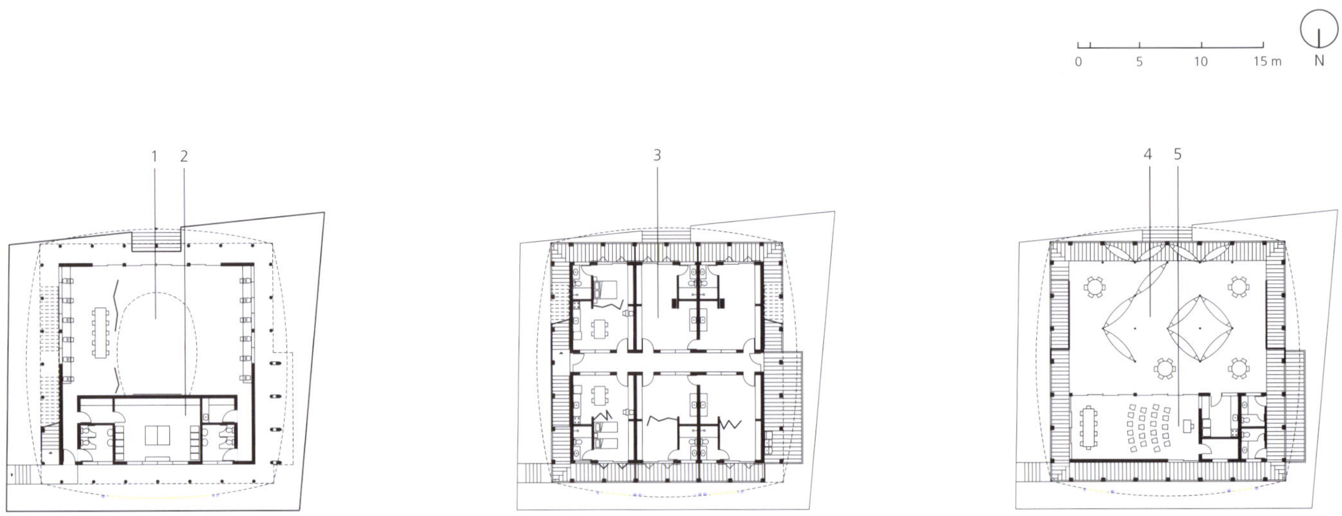
0
5
10
15 m
N
1
2
3
4
5

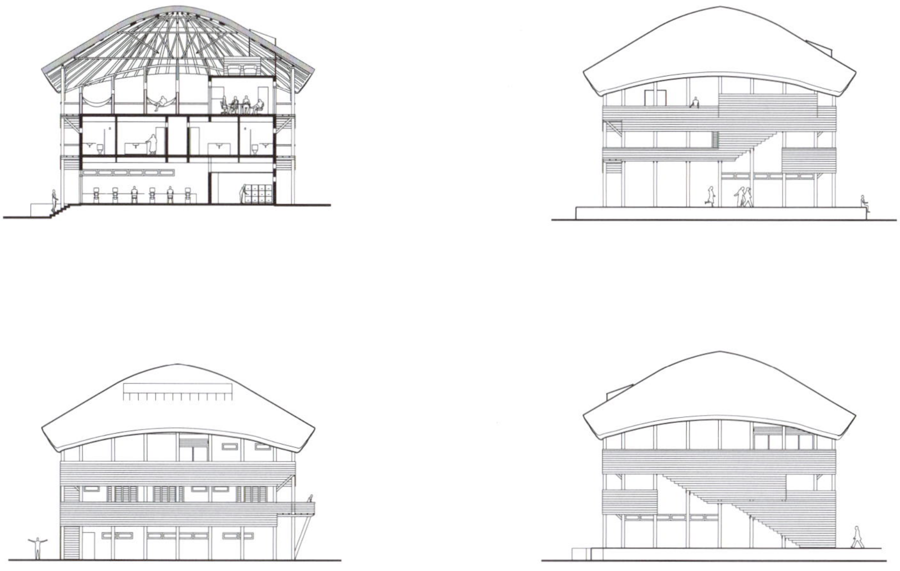

- Model
- Plan, ground floor:
  1 hall for general meetings and/or exhibtions
  2 File keeping room
- Plan, first floor:
  3 lodgings for researchers
- Plan, second floor:
  4 leisure
  5 meetings
- Section and east, north and west elevations
- Digital model with view of Negro River

Office Building

Brasília, Federal District 2001

To build in the city of Brasília will always pose a special challenge for Brazilian architects, even in the case of an office building on Avenue W3, among so many others built since the city's inauguration, bearing witness to the variety of contemporary approaches to architecture, to a greater or lesser extent removed from Lucio Costa's and Oscar Niemeyer's interpretation of the Corbusian ideas of the *ville radieuse* and *ville verte*.

The design for this office building, the team's first project for the country's capital city, sought to identify with the city's architecture not exactly by pursuing a formal match, but rather by aiming at the commended and equally modern true expression of materials. Built of exposed reinforced concrete, the building tends towards the more brutalist *Paulista* strand of modern architecture, although it seeks to explore the plasticity of concrete inspired by Niemeyerian curves to design the indoor terraces.

From outside, the building appears as an orthogonal box with its two main façades protected by continuous panels of trellised woodwork. In order to control luminosity and shield from the direct sun, the façades are covered by this curtaining, composed by juxtaposed two-dimensional modules, both of treated pinewood blades attached by bolts to the metal structure. These huge *brise-soleil* panels evoke both the tradition of colonial trellises and their adoption by modern architecture, notably in the work of Lucio Costa. They also refer to the Venetian blinds, used in the windows and in internal partitions. This time, the trellised panels have become the central element of design, and have conquered the façades.

The building's basic idea is the integration of spaces within the building and with the surrounding city. The atrium, five stories high, presents itself as a continuation of the street, with its shops alternating with vistas to the external landscape. On the four floors destined to office space, the access to the office units is made by the winding terraced corridors overlooking the atrium, converting the circulation scheme into a formal element of design and a life-enhancing factor for the building. When observing the atrium from above it is impossible not to be reminded of Niemeyer's Biennial pavilion in Ibirapuera Park, São Paulo, a felicitous quotation.

The key element of the project, in its structural and formal expression and in the generosity of the shared spaces, is a homage to the founding ideal of the city of Brasília and to its designers.

CRS

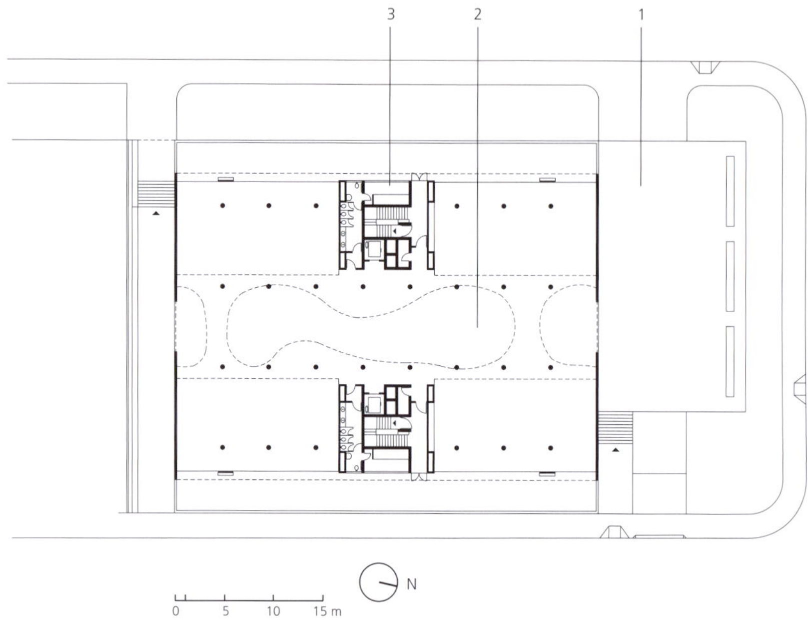

- Different angles of the central void (during construction, 2004)

- Ground floor plan, standard floor and roof terrace:
  1 main entrance esplanade
  2 central gallery
  3 vertical circulation system/ restrooms / utility rooms
  4 office spaces
  5 central void
  6 art gallery
  7 kitchen
  8 restaurant
  9 terrace
- Transversal and longitudinal sections

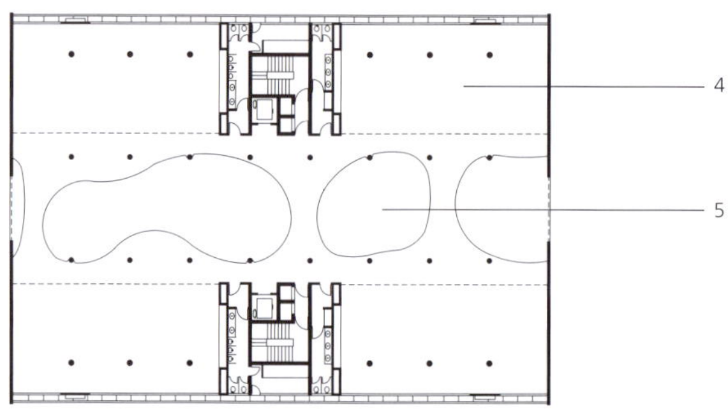

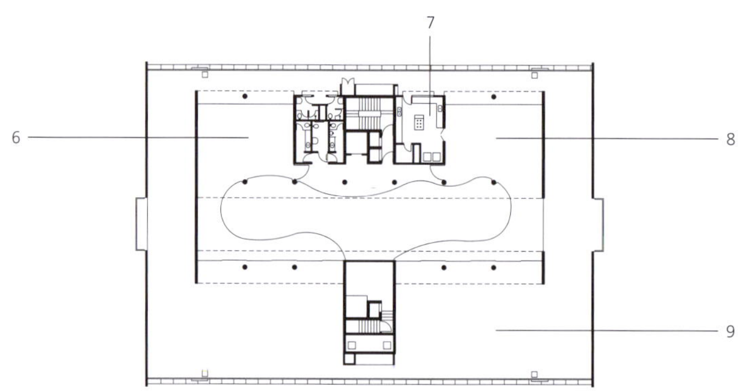

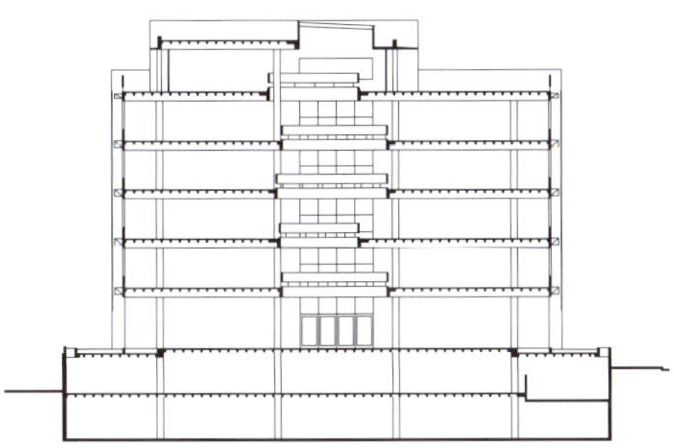

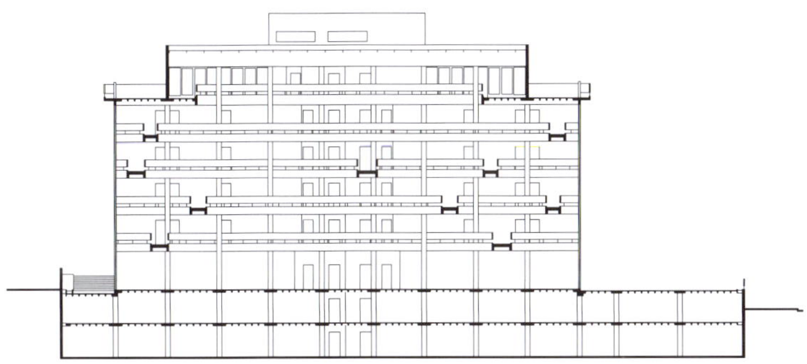

Tacaruna Cultural Center

Recife, Pernambuco state 2002

Inaugurated in 1896, halfway between the cities of Recife and Olinda, the installations of the Tacaruna factory constituted a reference to the industrial transformation of the sugar-producing Northeast in the early years of the Republic.

The building impresses for its scale, for the regularity of the openings – a series of colonial arched windows – and for the lack of symmetry of the set of three well-defined blocks. However, if it were not for the tall masonry chimney shaft planted to the right of the façade, it could be mistaken for a depot, a dockside warehouse or for the sugar refinery office that, earlier in the 19th century, occupied the main building. It does not display any of the characteristics that define the typology of the industrial buildings of English derivation so common in the Southeast, with their unrendered brick masonry and industrial shed roofs with rows of vertical openings, which could have been incorporated in the successive alterations promoted by the Tacaruna industries.

No longer containing industrial machinery, the building with its ancillary constructions and the surrounding area became the object of a competition. The idea was to revitalize the set by converting it into a complex capable of housing public facilities for leisure and culture, as well as a convention and commercial center.

The Brasil Arquitetura Studio's approach was to view the intervention as a wide-ranging project for the preservation of the existing vegetation and of the history represented by the building, which was to be integrated into the local cultural environment by a series of contemporary gestures. The main block, with its masonry walls and steel structure, was given prominence by the removal of superfluous renderings and claddings and the elimination of secondary structures which disfigured the original building. Improved in order to accommodate a Training and Documentation Center and an Exhibition and Interpretation Center, along with administrative sections and a cybercafé, the higher section of the building was granted a new system for vertical circulation, with panoramic elevators rising through the slabs of the first two storeys.

The main block limits one of the sides of a great esplanade (gained by the demolition of the old annexes and warehouses) and connects to the new building, which limits the opposite side by way of a 23 ft canopy. Both the canopy and the new extension form an interesting contemporary counterpoint to the dignified factory building.

The most striking element of the new building is a wall. A conventional wall 42 ft high and 650 ft long, interrupted in its extension only to embrace a smaller smoke stack (a remnant of the factory) and to meet the canopy. Built of rustic, irregular cyclopian masonry, its crevices are home to mosses, ferns, orchids and bromelias, watered by an embedded irrigation system. This hanging garden constitutes a background to the main building's façade and, at the same time, is part of the new extension, designed to provide space for external happenings such as fairs and meetings and for the administrative, commercial and maintenance services, besides housing the Third Millenium Institute.

Behind the garden wall, close but without touching it, an extremely sinuous and organic wall of white painted concrete winds its way along. Its extension defines an ample and free space, covered by a metallic structure with 8-ft high girders (the minimum height required for maintenance installations). Inside, an orthogonal and regular arrangement of 23-ft square modules defines work areas in independent environments, organized in two floor levels. The large exhibition area, with its mezzanine supported on columns and accessed by ramps, takes full advantage of this open and sinuous space. Strips of zenithal lighting and a system of reflecting plates capture the luminosity and block direct sunlight.

Also delimitating the esplanade are an acoustic shell, to the north, and a vertical block, a hotel, to the south. The esplanade itself contains an area of mangrove vegetation and concentrations of preexisting trees in addition to a mass of coconut trees proliferating on beach sand. The varied and contrasting vegetation of the complex accommodates two important cultural references: the Memorial to the Integration of the Arts – a composition consisting of thirty timber poles, each painted by a Brazilian artist, representing the tradition of Northeastern and Brazilian popular festivities – and the *Árvore Resistente* (Hardy Tree), a great fig tree wedged tightly in the remaining 20-ft of masonry of one of the old warehouses, preserved as a symbol of the strong and symbiotic integration of cultural man and his landscape.

CRS

The historic building and model.

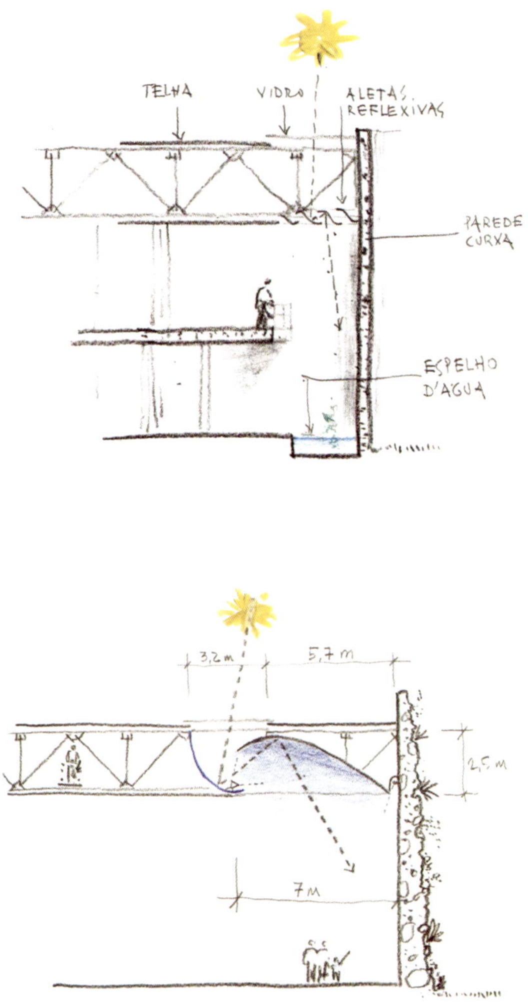

Studies for the natural lighting of the curvilinear wall and of the garden-wall.

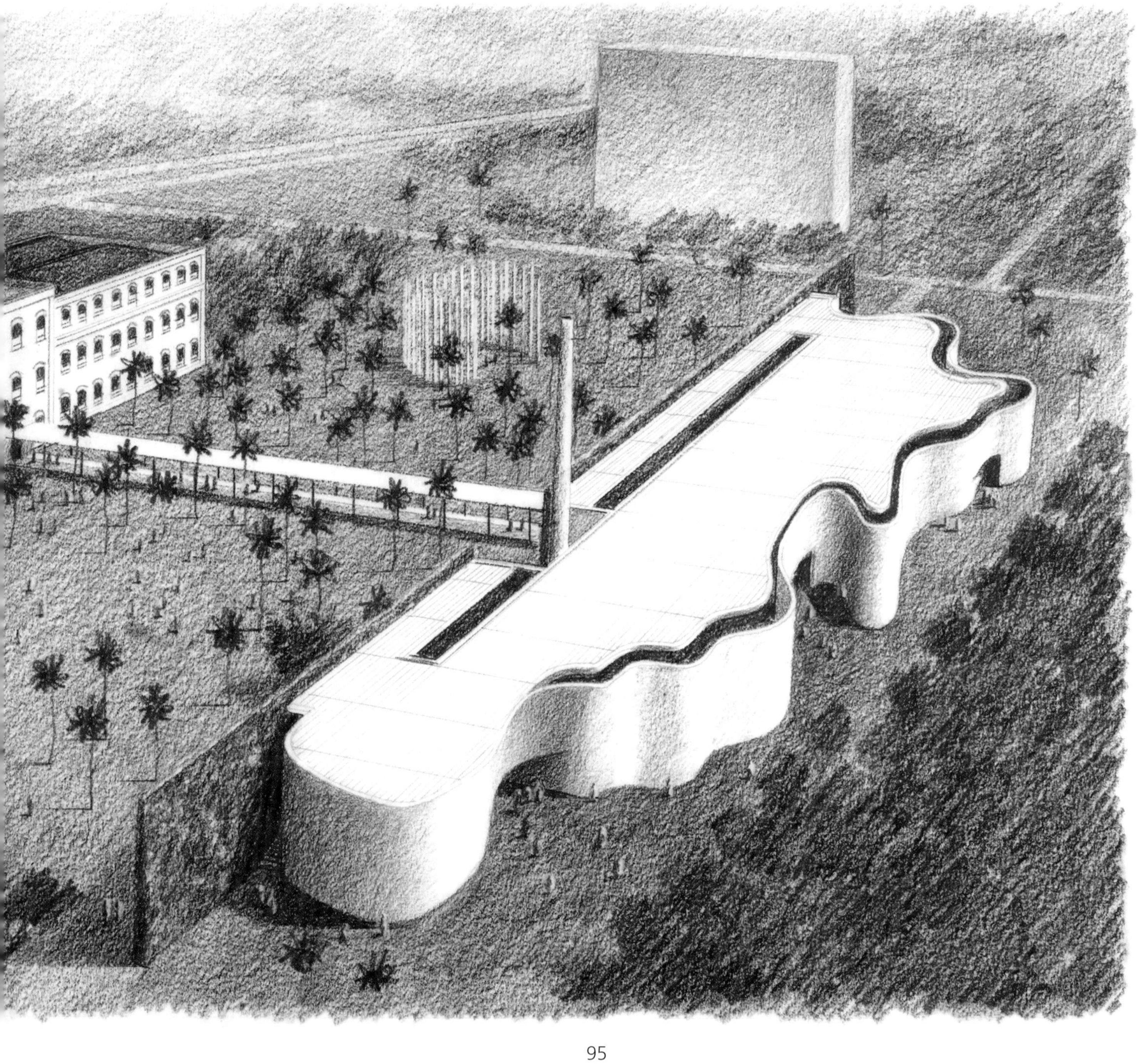

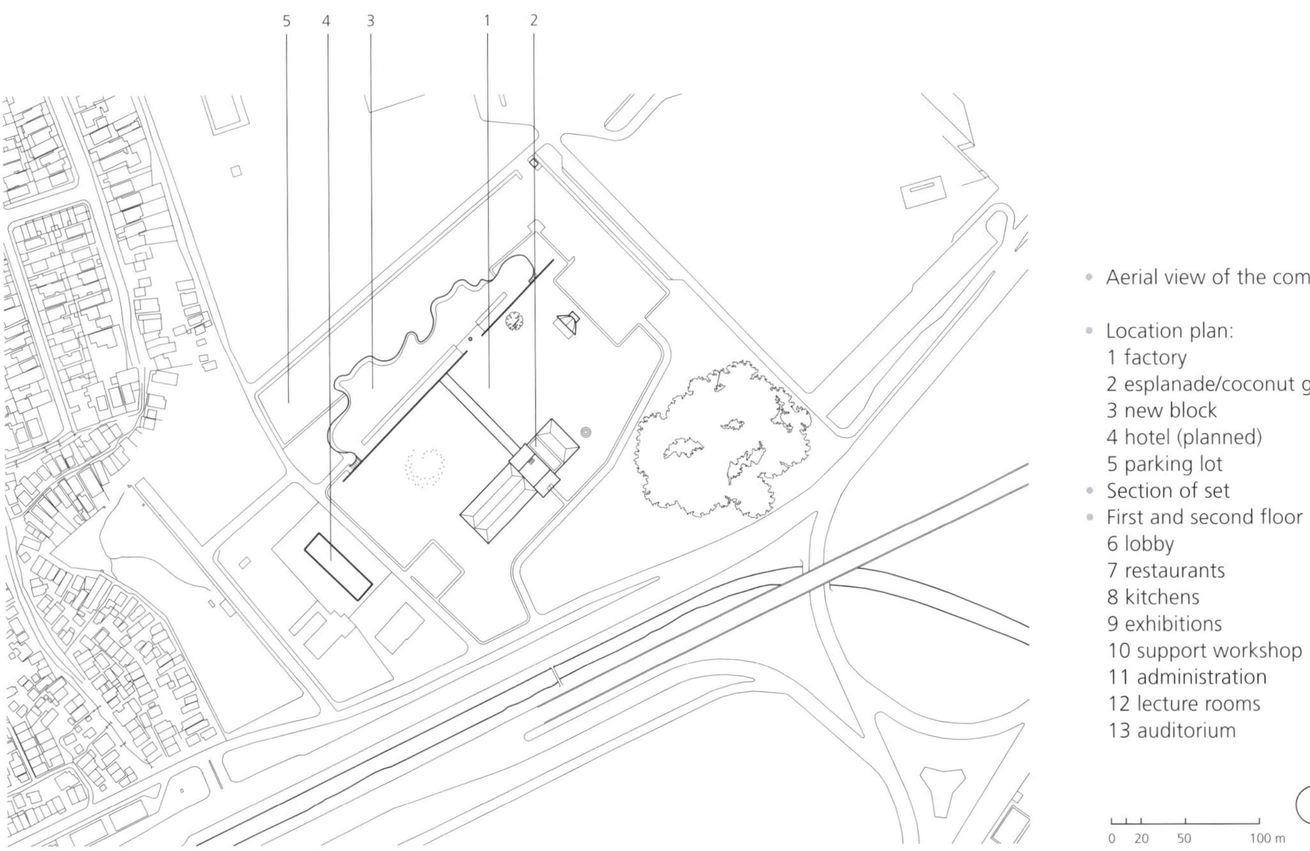

- Aerial view of the complex, c. 1920
- Location plan:
  1 factory
  2 esplanade/coconut grove
  3 new block
  4 hotel (planned)
  5 parking lot
- Section of set
- First and second floor plans:
  6 lobby
  7 restaurants
  8 kitchens
  9 exhibitions
  10 support workshop
  11 administration
  12 lecture rooms
  13 auditorium

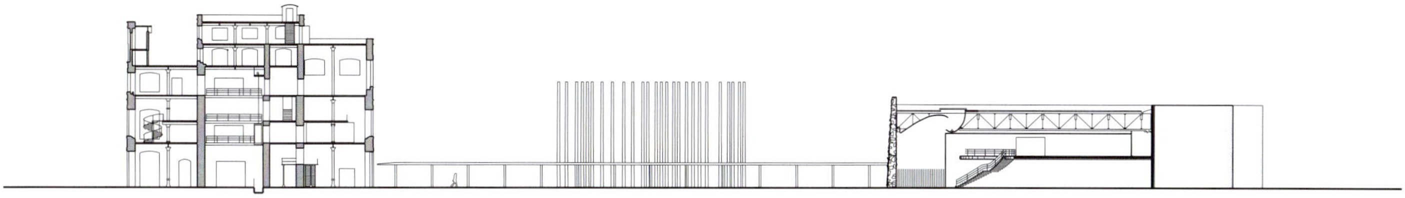

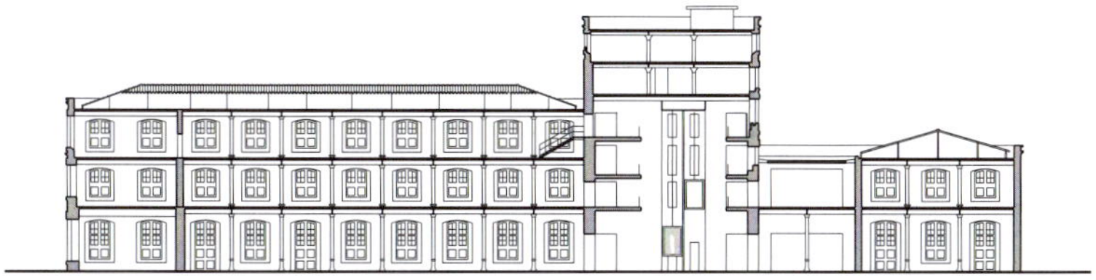

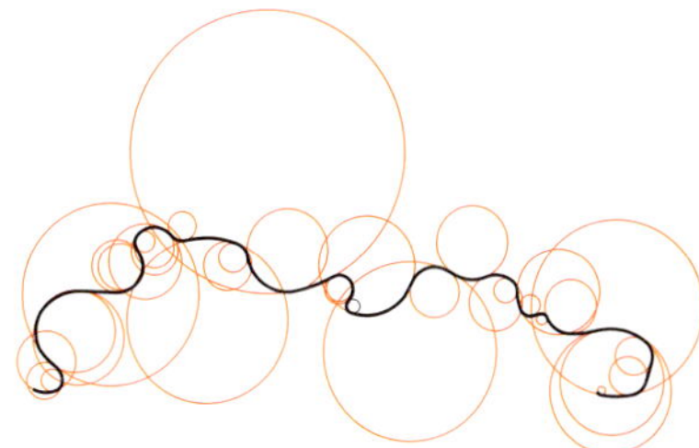

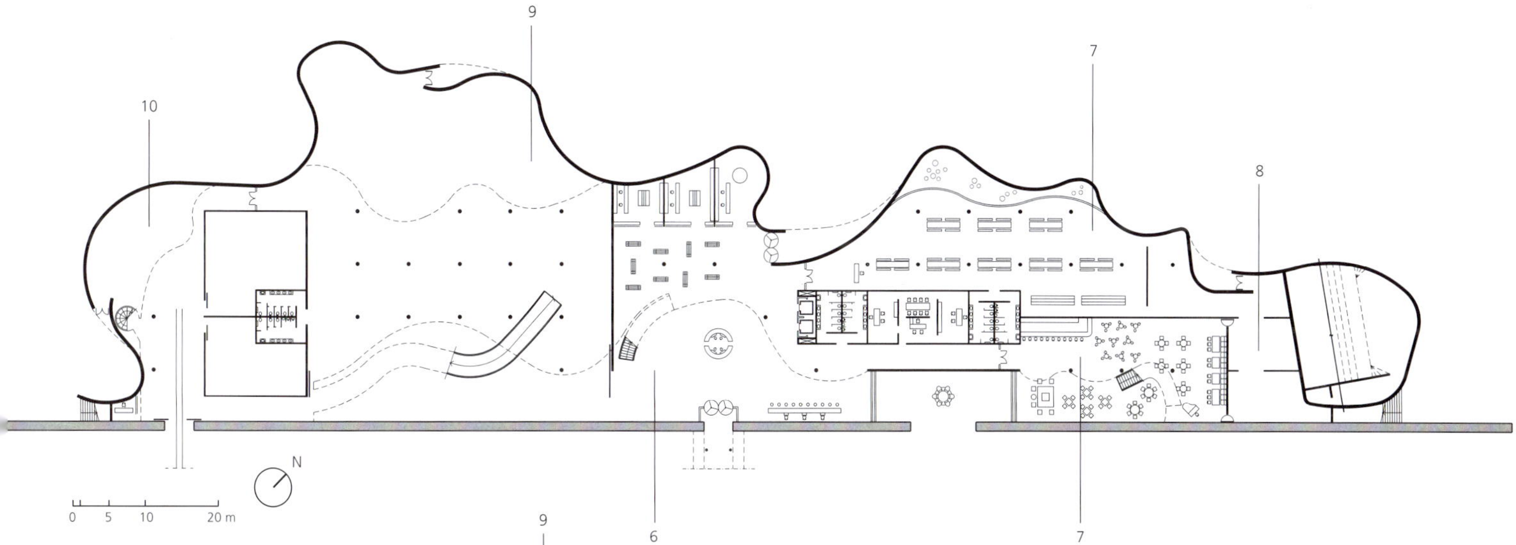
9
10
7
8
N
0 5 10 20 m
6
7

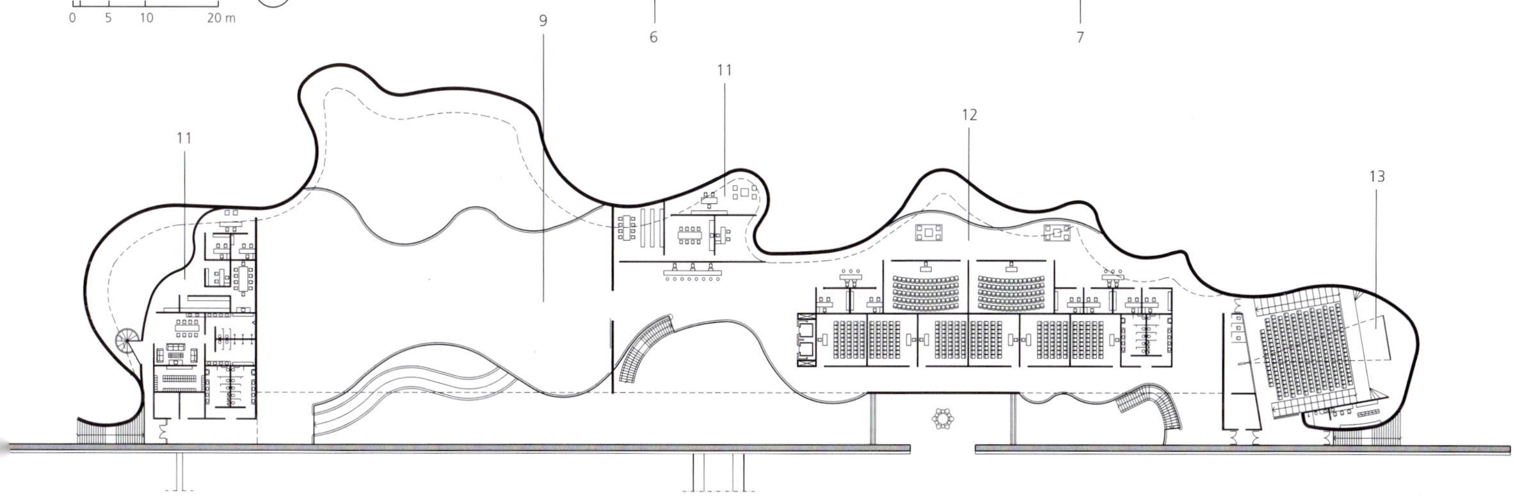
9
11
11
12
13

Rodin Museum

Salvador, Bahia state 2002

The kiss, by Auguste Rodin.

Creating the first affiliate out of France of the Rodin Museum, in Salvador, state of Bahia, meant meeting a number of prerequisites. The first was to find a site with cultural relevance to the city and that met all the technical requirements to house about seventy original plaster pieces, part of the collection of the Museum in Paris.

The chosen site was the eclectic style Comendador Catharino mansion – built in 1912 with cocoa money, and located among centenarian trees in the district of Graça. The adaptation of the spaces to the new use and the construction of an annex to expand them were the two operations that needed to be carried out in harmony with the building's architecture, protected as heritage property because of its importance and meaning to the history of the city. In addition, all the centenarian trees on the grounds were to be preserved.

The objective of both the restoration of the building and the new interventions was to provide the necessary infrastructure, adapting the spaces to the activities of the museum. Educational activities and the reception area, were located on the ground floor; the exhibition areas for the pieces from the Rodin collection in the two floors above; and administrative activities in the attic, restored for this purpose and accessed by a new stairway. A prismatic shape of exposed concrete attached to the rear façade of the building encloses the new stairway and elevator which provide access to the museum for the public and staff.

In order to provide storage area for the museum's collection and a place for temporary exhibitions and a café-restaurant, the plans called for an annex as big as the main building. The design for this extension represents a compromise between the limitations of the site and the architects' resolve to preserve the existent trees and respect the scale of the historic building, while affirming the contemporary identity of the new building and creating physical solutions of continuity and fluidity for the set. The result can be read as a situation of confrontation and harmony between the two distinct historical moments.

The main solution to offer continuity to the set is represented by the prestressed concrete elevated walkway. Extending unsupported towards the new building, it will provide a privileged view of Rodin's sculpture *Gates of Hell*, to be installed in the garden. The walkway runs to a discreet, bare concrete building, where it is enclosed by a timber trellised shield – a protective "outer skin" that veils part of the façade – then it peeks inside and goes out the other end to convert into an external lateral stairway. Inside the building, walls and floor slabs are intersecting concrete blades that interact to close and open exhibition spaces on different planes. The structure defines the space, which turns out to be an effective reflection of the program. The central space – a large area on the ground floor, two storeys high and illuminated from above – opens out to the garden by way of large glazed sliding doors. This space can be viewed from the walkway and from three other smaller spaces that encircle it on the first floor.

Two buildings, two historical moments that dialogue in a centenarian garden defining a cultural space intended as a meeting point, a place for social interaction that adds value and life to the urban environment.

CRS

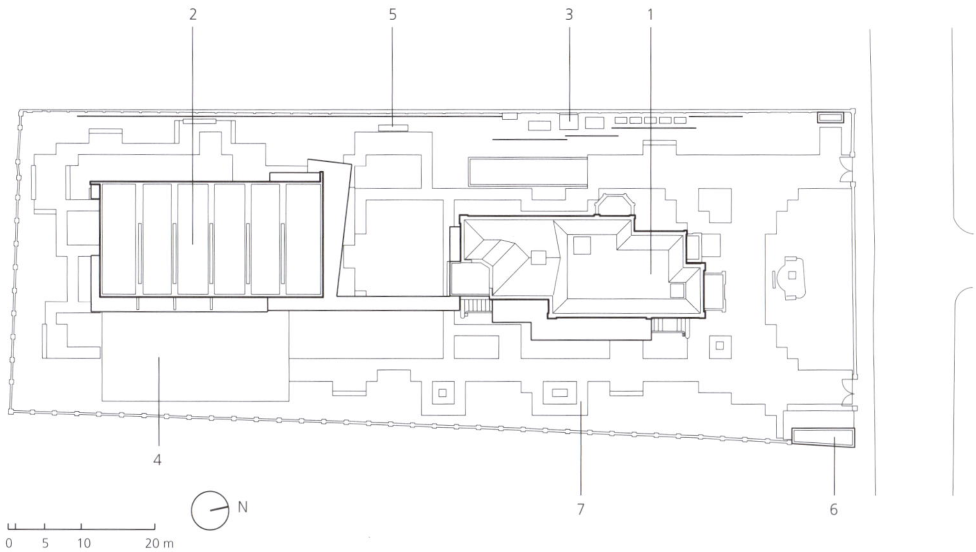

- Location plan:
  1 Comendador Catharino's mansion
  2 new block
  3 utility room
  4 patio
  5 *The Gates of Hell* sculpture
  6 entrance
  7 sculpture garden
- Digital model: overall view of the set

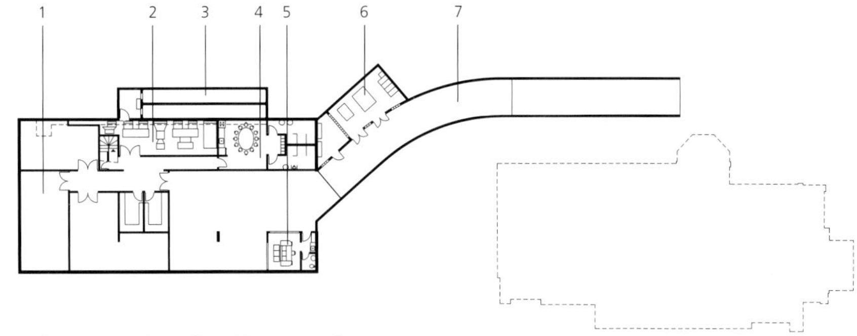

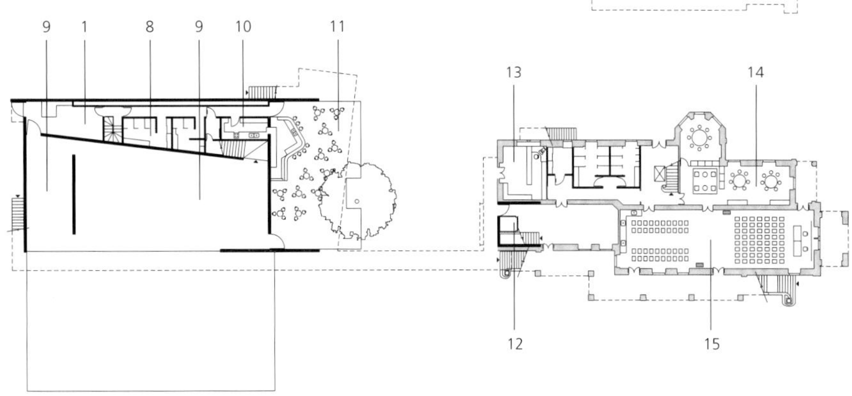

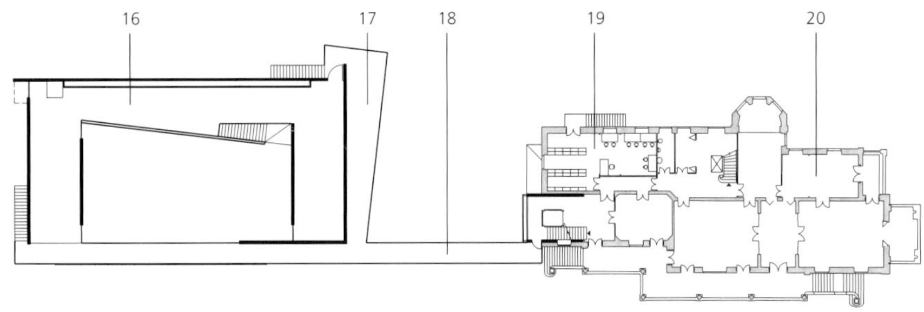

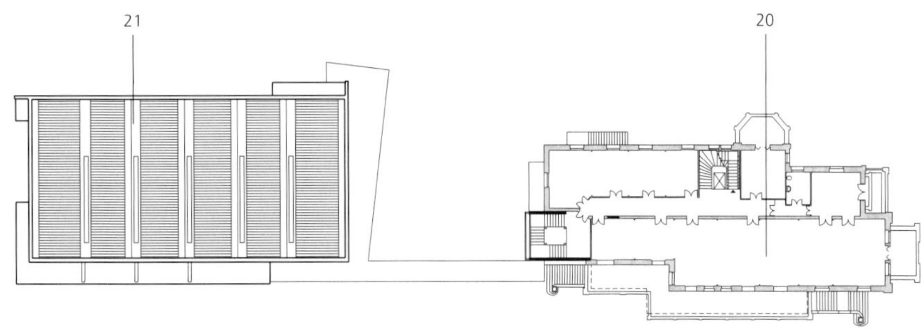

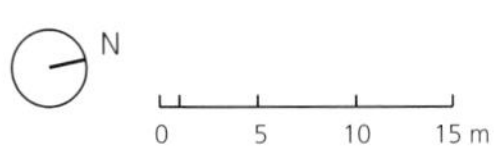

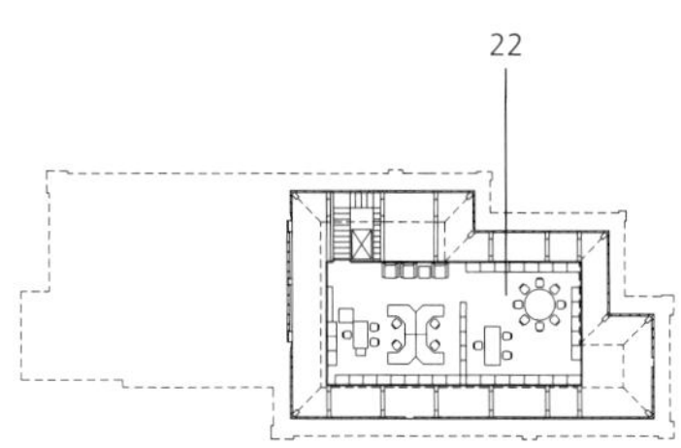

- Basement floor:
  1 storage/support area
  2 machine room
  3 water tank
  4 staff
  5 control center
  6 primary cabin
  7 ramp isolating/leading to basement
- Ground floor plan:
  8 restrooms
  9 halls for temporary exhibitions
  10 kitchen
  11 café
  12 system for vertical circulation
  13 shop
  14 instructors' room
  15 retreat/workshop
  16 mezzanine/temporary exhibitions
  17 observation point for *The Gates of Hell* sculpture
  18 raised walkway
  19 library/research
  20 exhibition hall for collection
- Roof plan of new block and third floor plan
  of original building:
  21 controlled zenithal lighting
  22 administration area

- Studies
- Digital model of walkway connecting the blocks

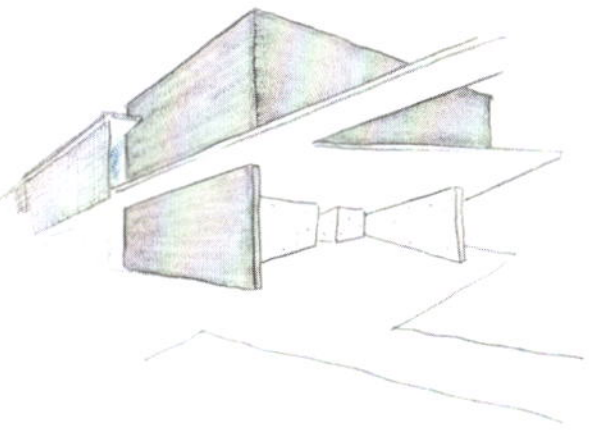
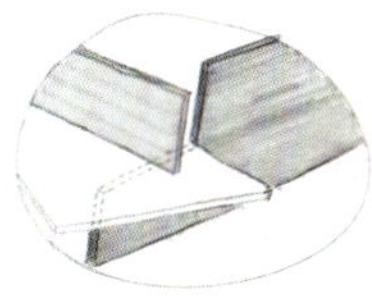
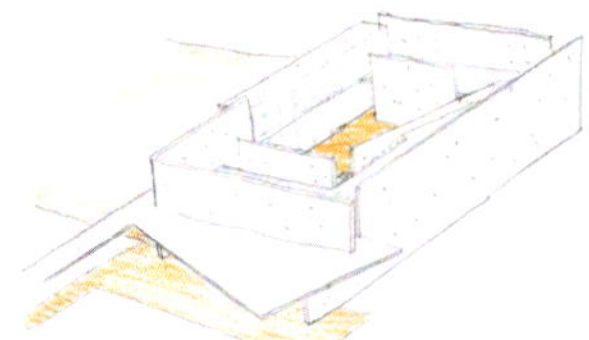

- Views of the set under construction (2005)
- Longitudinal section
- Digital model: southeast elevation showing vertical garden backdrop to Rodin's monumental sculpture, *The Gates of Hell*.

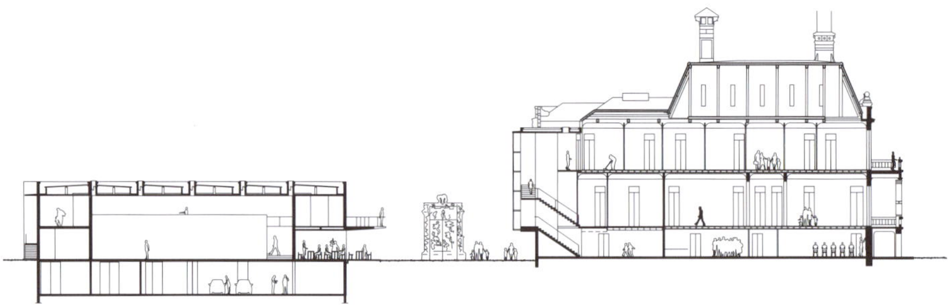

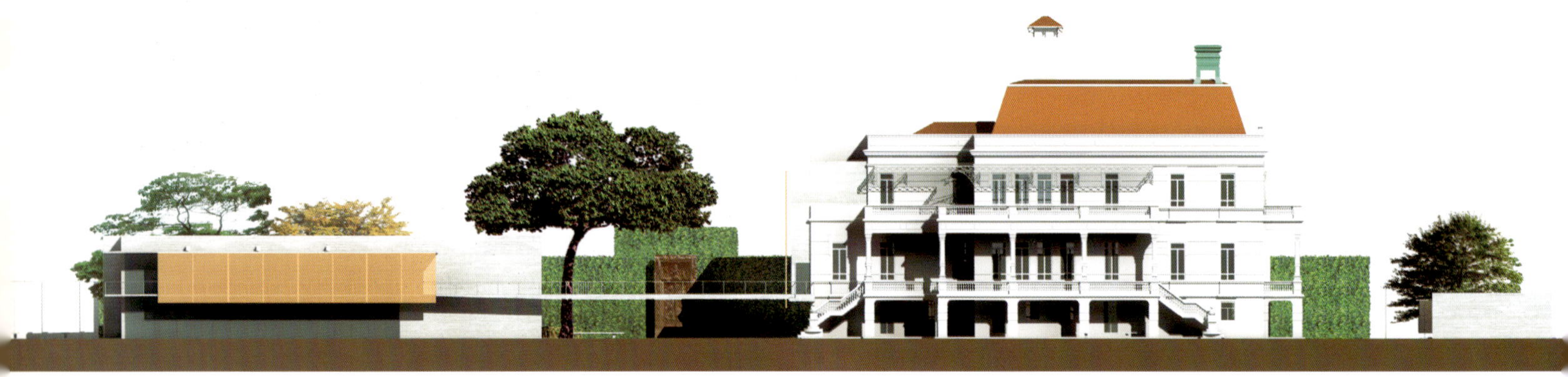

Saavedra House, Petrópolis, RJ,
Lucio Costa, 1942.

Park Hotel São Clemente, Nova Friburgo, RJ,
Lucio Costa, 1944-45.

Casa Brasilis: the Brazilian House

Vasco Caldeira

A house ought to be like a soul, open to the matters of life, and not a cave-dwelling, a jaguar's den. More than anything, a house ought to be a spiritual and moral entity, without resembling a stage set.
Lina Bo Bardi

The eight houses presented here – illustrating the particular vision of the Brasil Arquitetura Studio on a constructive program that is universal and, at the same time, interpreted in a diversity of ways – were designed over a space of eleven years and express permanent values along with aspects which are constantly being transformed. These values are more clearly perceptible in the house designs because the program is committed to technical and functional parameters which are less strict. They reveal inspirations and feelings, references and dialogues, generally in a more explicit way than do the institutional designs.

These houses, and others listed at the end of this book, are in no way garish. They do not constitute experimental works of awesome structural ingenuity, nor do they present themselves as fashionable consumer products. In no way are they proposed as exemplary solutions, be it in terms of construction techniques, or in the way they interpret a dwelling's basic requirements.

This does not mean that this architecture is excessively austere. It is neither especially aseptic nor unduly conscious of its formal or conceptual bearings, neither purist, nor rhetorical. The form varies; the integrity does not. The language exudes the scents of the materials that are used and which are given such a prominent role. Their manners evoke the multiple references that inspired them, collected methodically and attentively in different parts of the planet. The sensitive way they combine, merge, and recreate is revealing of the disposition and personal universe of the designers.

These designs do not constitute an intellectualist architectonic expression; though they do provide us with ample ground for reflection. They do not pursue simple or complex forms for their own sake, though both are accepted as expressions of the syntony between the ideas and their convenience.

The concepts and practices embodied in them evidence the commitment to a cultural project of an identity-building nature. The Brasil Arquitetura Studio houses aspire to be read as Brazilian architecture, which they achieve by their genuine incorporation of the national and popular experience and by the clarity with which they define themselves methodologically, in a permanent dialogue with the other, the diverse, the universal.

There is an Architecture that imposes itself immediately and to many, whether it pleases or not. It may be large or small scale. It may relate to its surroundings – the built and

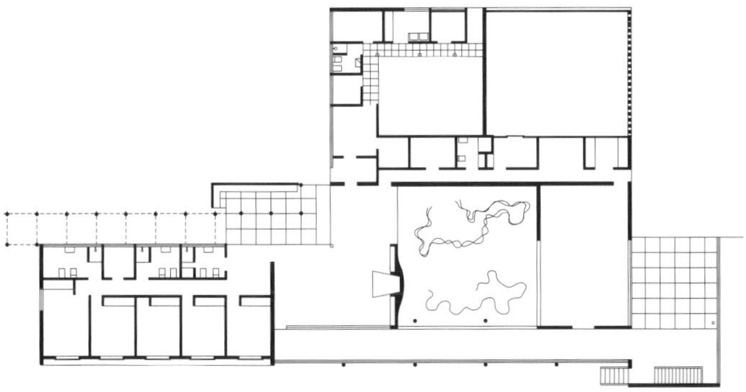

Country house of the ambassador H. Accioly,
Petrópolis, RJ, Francisco Bolonha, 1950.

natural environment – or not. A reasonable photographer captures what it appears to be. It may be of quality or be merely gratuitous. [...]
There is another Architecture that impresses less, and fewer people.
It may be large or small scale. It relates to everything which surrounds it, although this may not be apparent, or evident, or by reason of form. It may be of quality or not, though it is rarely, if ever, gratuitous. It may be modest, if nothing compels it to be otherwise; or difficult, but not due to immodesty.
Álvaro Siza

In its twenty-five years of existence, the Brasil Arquitetura Studio has carried out numerous designs for houses, mostly in the metropolitan capital of São Paulo state or along the coast. On the other hand, the team's experience with apartment buildings or housing developments has been rare.

An exception to this was their intervention in the housing estate of Gelbes Viertel in Berlin, having won an international competition directed to Latin American architects, the specifications of which converged with the nature of much of the team's work in the institutional area: the re-qualification of pre-existing sites or buildings of historic interest. Despite the fact that the intervention in question involved an architecture typical of post-war Europe's darkest phase of quantitative urbanism, there is no denying that these constructions and the surrounding urban landscape also constituted an historically significant subject, though a negative one. The action carried out, though superficial in terms of constructive modifications, takes into account and alters important elements of this rationalist severity, from which the architects had been seeking to distance themselves for many years.

For this reason, it would be interesting to examine the house projects in the light of the intervention operated in Berlin, on that schematic and crude rationalism – taken as point of departure – and an entire repertoire of forms, materials, colors and textures selected and combined in such a manner as to point to a Latin American and Brazilian identity. What they produce in their new designs reflects the same pursuit of cultural affinity, the same sensibility for the nature of the place, developed from an equally rationalist training which is still subjacent to many aspects of their work.

The nature of the team's work does not lend itself to a real estate market that demands relatively standardized products conforming to average tastes, as happens with many of the best and worst professionals. As a result, they have aimed at, and been sought by, a specific kind of client and situation which requires a more particularized approach, where the pursuit of individuality and due recognition of the artisan *modus faciendi* prevail, culturally identified with Brazilian traditional and popular manners.

The commissions most frequently undertaken by the practice relate to cultural equipment – the KKKK complex, the Rodin Museum, Teatro Polytheama, the Monument to the

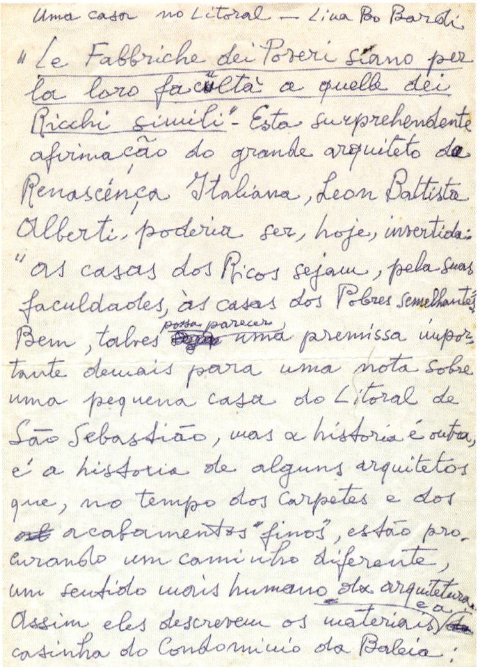

Uma casa no Litoral — Lina Bo Bardi.

"Le Fabbriche dei Poveri siano per la loro facultà a quelle dei Ricchi simili". Esta surpreendente afirmação do grande arquiteto da Renascença Italiana, Leon Battista Alberti, poderia ser, hoje, invertida: "as casas dos Ricos sejam, pelas suas faculdades, às casas dos Pobres semelhantes". Bem, talvez possa parecer uma premissa importante demais para uma nota sobre uma pequena casa do Litoral de São Sebastião, mas a história é outra, é a história de alguns arquitetos que, no tempo dos carpetes e dos acabamentos "finos", estão procurando um caminho diferente, um sentido mais humano da arquitetura. Assim eles descrevem os materiais e a casinha do Condomínio da Baleia:

"Le Fabbriche dei Poveri síano per la loro facultá a quelle dei Ricchi simili." This surprising statement by the great Italian Renaissance architect Leon Battista Alberti could be inverted today: "The houses of the rich are, in their properties, like those of the poor". Well, it might seem too important a premiss for a note on a small house on the São Sebastião coast line, but the story is quite another, it is the story of a group of architects who – at the time of carpets and "fine" finishings – took a different course towards a more human architecture.

Lina Bo Bardi, *Arquitetura e Urbanismo* magazine, n. 32, São Paulo, 1990.

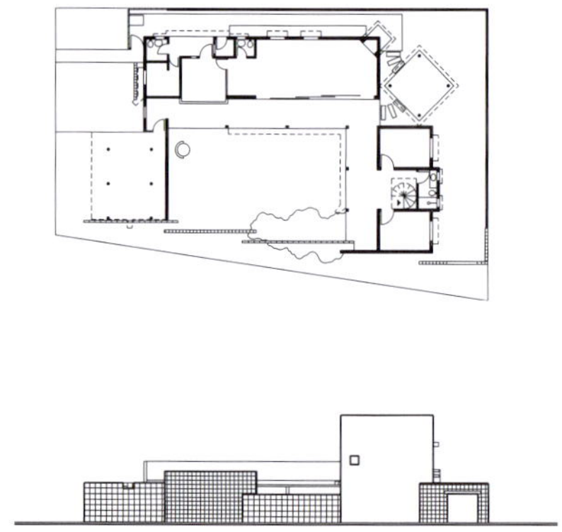

Baleia House, Brasil Arquitetura, 1985.

Brazilian Indian Nations, and the Instituto Socioambiental, to mention only a few – where there is invariably a need to construct a dialogue between the contemporary language of the new interventions and the uprooted references of architectonic remains belonging to the past.

The challenge of designing houses depends on the intensity with which the characteristics of the place and the ideas linked to the space and materials are developed. Experiencing the poetry of light and space is a confirmation of the stimulating potential of architecture as a recipient for everyday life.
Steven Holl

Their designs for residences, on the other hand, almost always entirely new constructions on vacant sites, constitute a privileged field for a freer exercise of the fundamentals of a method of architectonic composition attentive to the concreteness of the site (planimetrics, topography, light, landscape), to the individuality of the purposes contained in the client's requirements and to the particularity of the all-encompassing geographic and cultural environment.

The family for whom the house is destined has its constitution, its tastes, its economic circumstances; the site has its form, its vegetation [...] nearby there are buildings with their own proper tonicity; on the other side of the river, not far away, there is granite and schist; the labor force is not specialized; the Architect has his cultural, plastic and human education [...], knows the meaning of terms such as organicism, functionalism, neo-empiricism, cubism, etc., and, parallel to that, feels an unbounded love, which can be traced way back, for all the spontaneous manifestations of his country's architecture. It was by giving everything and everyone a chance to speak, in a magnificent and unforgettable dialogue, attempting at a true composite, that we achieved this realization.
Fernando Távora

Based on a particular conception of empiricism, the approach of Fanucci and Ferraz to their housing designs privileges a phenomenological perception of reality, seeking in the difficulties and obstacles of each specific situation the essential inspiration for the development of the designs.
The solutions offered, deeply sensitive to the concrete nature of the future users, and to their habits and the structure of their family and social relations, reveal a special ability for the invention of unique forms and tailored arrangements. These, unpretentious while playing an essential role, submit consciously to the rationality of modular construction and to other compositional regularities when convenient and, at the same time, confer humanity upon them. Thus emerges a compromise between the norm and spontaneity: in a delicate balance and by mutual comprehension, they reciprocally justify each other, becoming indissoluble.

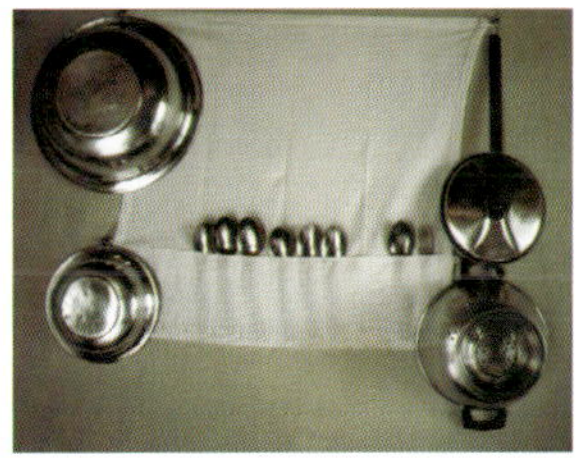

Architecture in the Mantiqueira mountains.

To design is to capture, at the exact moment, a disturbing and errant idea; and to restore serenity.
Álvaro Siza

The Brasil Arquitetura Studio's design strategy evolves dialectically between the analysis of the properties of the site, the program and the conditions of production (budget, schedule, availability of labor force and materials) and the construction of a unity of form and meaning, achieved by negotiating between very different factors such as the perceptive quality of the space, the nature and malleability of the materials and the meaning of the place to be created or transformed. All this is done without losing sight of the functional principle which guides the distribution of activities and their respective areas; this principle, while not a determining factor of the formal arrangement, is viewed as a point of departure for the construction of more complex spatialities, the result of an empirical accommodation between reason and sensibility.

Rather than a typological response involving the imposition of standards justifiable for their constructive and structural logic, for their implicit reproducibility or their exemplary form, resulting from an idealized understanding of real situations faced, the residential projects of the Brasil Arquitetura Studio propose a design strategy based on privileging perceptive experience and construction crafts, in an attitude of liberty in relation to the evolution of knowledge and to the discovery of the unexpected.

Reason and skepticism must yield to the horizon of discovery.
Steven Holl

The houses presented here express a rejection, one could say methodical, of the unitary case, of the single block building so dear to the *Paulista* school of architecture: "a shadow over the plot". They refute, in an analogous manner, the isotropic spatial continuum, without forsaking the concern for fluidity and the dialogue between the internal and external spaces.

On the one hand, the program is first translated into functional blocks, individualized in their volume and plasticity, varying, next, the degree and quality of their interrelation, which is reestablished, in a controlled way, among the distinct, imagined bodies. On the other hand, the spaces are designed in order to contemplate and to explicitly state the particular nature of their use, rather than having their essential characteristics subordinated to any factors of a constructive or formal nature. One cannot exactly talk of a "free plan" – for the interior space is generally more compartmentalized. The spaces are treated as particularized entities and their integration will constitute a subsequent stage of the process, when the connective elements are to be constructed with a gradual realization of the space in mind, mediated by physical and temporal parameters of the perceptive experience.

The experience of *phenomena* – sensations in space and time as distinguished from the perception of objects –

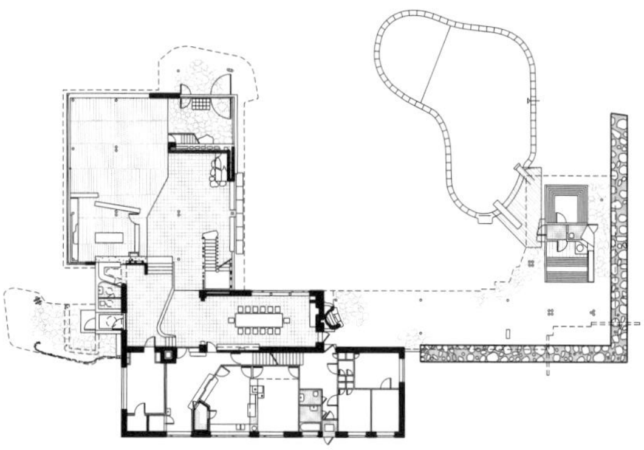

Villa Mairea, Alvar Aalto, 1938-39.

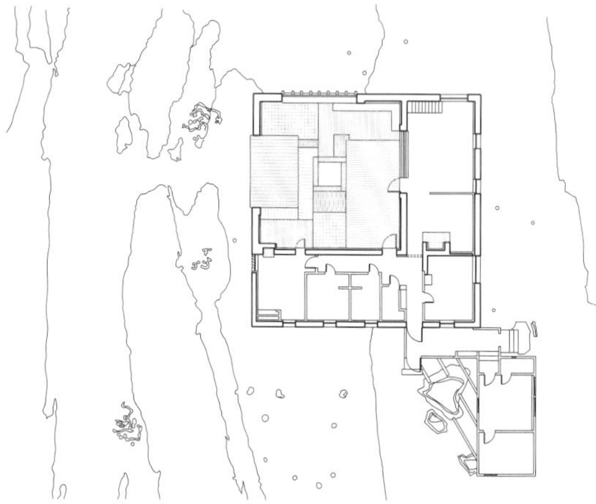

Muuratsalo summer home, Alvar Aalto, 1953.

provides a "pre-theoretical" ground for architecture. [...] Phenomenology, as it deals with questions of perception, encourages us to experience architecture by walking through it, touching it, listening to it. [...] As a way of thinking and seeing, it becomes an instrument of architectonic conceptualization.
Steven Holl

Owing to reasons that are not directly related to the forms, the materials or the architectural devices used, the houses designed by the Brasil Arquitetura Studio reveal, above all, a strong reverence for the sensibility and intelligence of Portuguese/ Brazilian vernacular architecture, understood as a culture born in the villages of Northern and Central Portugal, regions that supplied the majority of immigrants to Brazil during the colonial period. It is also the architecture that took place in Brazil, especially in Minas Gerais, in the 18th and 19th centuries and in the rural areas close to the coast, linked to the sugar-cane economy of the 17th and 18th centuries. After years of close academic and professional contact with ideas and professionals linked to the *Paulista* brutalism typical of the 1960s and 70s, the architects experience a rediscovery of profound Brazil, simple, ancestral, which in fact marks a reunion with the very biographical origins of both the architects, who come from the hilly, cattle-rearing areas in the south of Minas Gerais state.

Secondly, at the roots of this reencounter with more spontaneous expressions of Brazilianness, and also as a factor responsible for the opening of their hearts and minds to the range of disciplines that inform architecture – history, anthropology, cultural diversity and technology – is their meeting Lina Bo Bardi in 1977. This intense collaboration, which lasted for more than 15 years, drew the architects' attention to the wisdom of traditional, artisan and popular techniques – in architecture as well as in art and other domains – and also showed them the ways to the discovery of other creative universes beyond the genealogy of the modern movement and the European vanguards, the core of their academic learning. New geographies are included in their world vision, while they transcend the reductionist limits of a rational language which had long become just an accent. If the rational and functional criteria are never to be renounced, it is certain they are to be reinserted in a new hierarchy of values, in which the material, cultural and affective nature of phenomena becomes the central concern.

The new openness to the world of things and ideas which they acquire in this period of intellectual effervescence, at the end of the 1970s, allowed them to rediscover contributions which had been left at the margins of the main current of the modern movement, frequently in regions of the world that were in some way also peripheral, by such people as: Luis Barragán, Hassan Fathy, Sverre Fehn, Geoffrey Bawa and Fernando Távora. Representatives of the so-called "third generation" of modernism, each in their own way, they shared the same interest of recuperating real man, with the concrete elements of his social life and with his particular sensibility, to the center of architectonic motivation and purpose. The methods used by

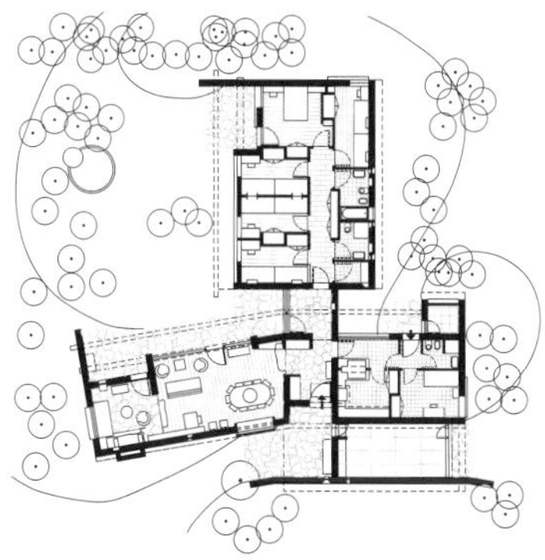

Ofir holiday home, Fernando Távora, 1957-58.

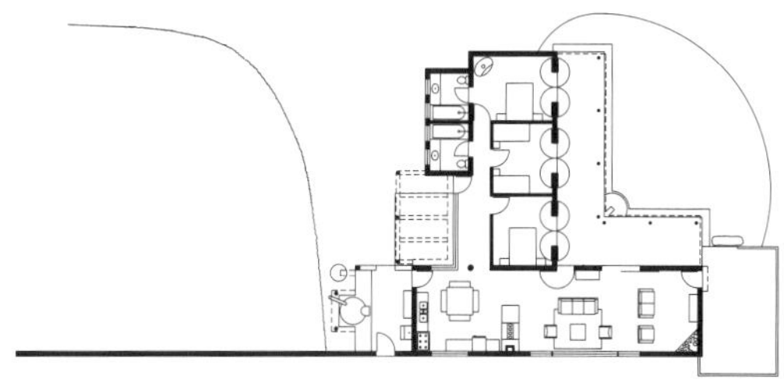

Mantiqueira House, Brasil Arquitetura, 2000.

each are different and their formal language even more so. What connects these disparate references collected outside the Brazilian context, in a period subsequent to that of their academic training, is the understanding of architecture as a territorialized cultural fact, a principle they would retain throughout their entire professional activity.

The same conviction and liberty leads them to the discovery, within the borders of their own country, of a new understanding of the contribution of Rio de Janeiro architects such as Francisco Bolonha, Alcides da Rocha Miranda and Carlos Ferreira, who, simultaneously, and under the influence of Lucio Costa, produce an architecture that proposes a synthesis of the contemporary principles of the local extroverted modernism and the qualities of the traditional Brazilian architecture of the colonial period, especially in regards to the adaptation to the physical environment, the constructive wisdom and the use of materials and techniques confirmed by tradition.

In the wake of the interest in the traditional and popular Brazilian culture present outside the big urban centers, stimulated since the 1930s with the creation of the National Institute of Historic and Artistic Heritage and by the work of the Brazilian writer Mário de Andrade as head of the Municipal Department of Culture of São Paulo, considerable attention was given in the following years to the study of urban and rural Brazilian architecture from the 17th and 18th centuries. The achievements of Lucio Costa in the 1940s and 50s influence a whole generation, and many of the designs for houses, hotels and holiday resorts of this period reflect the focus on the study of tradition and the advance of experiments combining modern technology and design with architectural materials and techniques recovered from the Portuguese-Brazilian architectonic heritage.

In designs such as the Marinho (1942), Saavedra (1944), Ferreira (1949) and Accioly (1950) houses, the Parque Hotel (1944) and the IRB holiday resort (1944), there is the usage, to varying degrees, of elements taken directly from the Brazilian colonial vocabulary; conversely, there is also the usage of contemporary techniques, such as that of reinforced concrete, in the reinterpretation of roof and traditional veranda stuctures. The fact that these are generally designs for large sites located outside the urban areas favours the decompaction of the program, by way of the creation of functional blocks connected by elevated walkways and galleries, defining patios and void transitional spaces. This circumstance, allied with the mild climate and the exuberance of the landscape, favours architecture with an outward orientation and allows the development of a varied repertoire of openings and integration expedients between exterior and interior.

If the layout of much of this architecture owes a great deal to the Corbusian and rationalist principles disseminated in the modernist Rio de Janeiro milieu, there is an undeniable similarity between their usual manner of positioning the building in relation to site – halfway up a slope looking out at the interesting view, with the ground floor serving as base for the elevated main floor served by terraces – and the rural residential typologies typically found in the state of Minas Gerais, in the

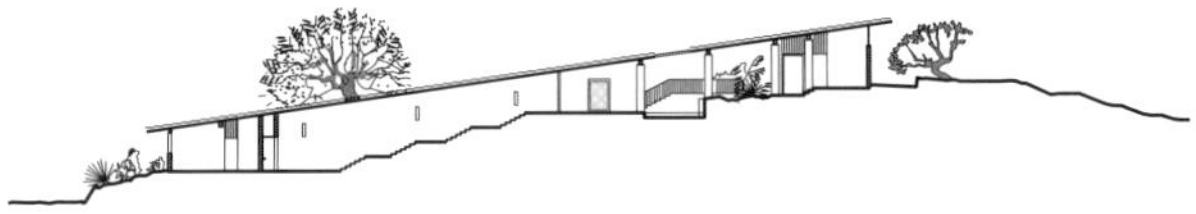

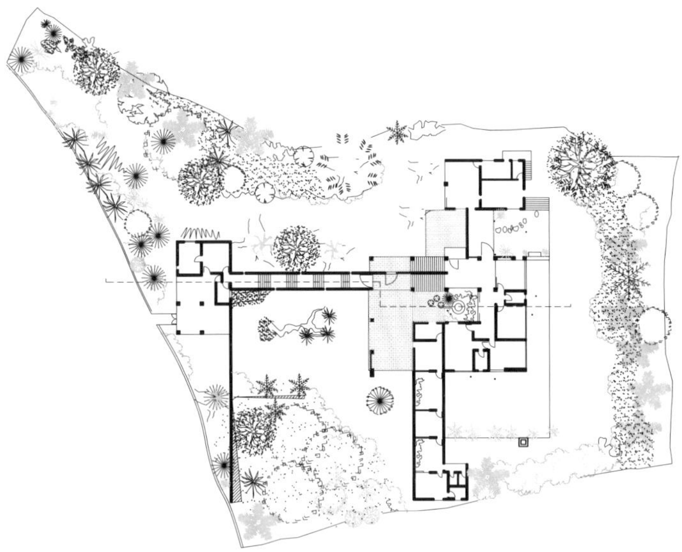

A. S. H. de Silva House, Geoffrey Bawa, 1960.

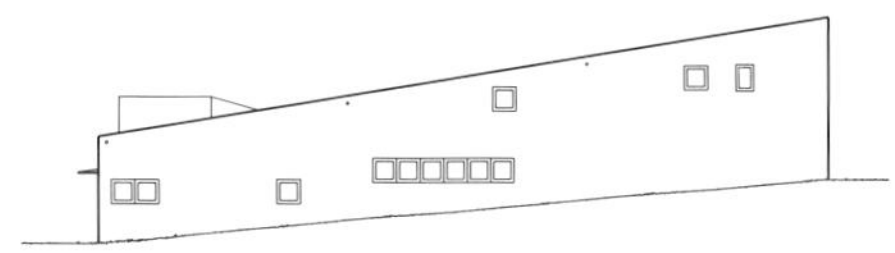

Cotia House, Brasil Arquitetura, 1998.

Zona da Mata, in the coffee growing region of the Vale do Paraíba and in northern and central Portugal.

In the case of the Portuguese context, so important for its ancestral aspect as for the mutual influences which occur in the golden age of modernism, as well as in the more recent period of prominence of the so-called Porto School, it is important to recall the effort carried out between 1955 and 1961 by the Portuguese National Association of Architects to organize an inventory of vernacular architecture in Portugal, creating a repertoire of the anonymous and traditional expressions from north to south of the country. At the same time, Fernando Távora, one of its organizers, carried out the paradigmatic projects Quinta da Conceição (1956-60) and the holiday house in Ofir (1957-58), in an effort to define a modern and geographically situated architectural identity, which so much resembles the cultural project of the Rio de Janeiro group in the same period. These projects, as well as the first houses of Álvaro Siza, reclaim the traditional cover and canal ceramic tiling for roofs and the rustic stone walls, which acutely contrast with the massive white masonry walls. At the same time, due to deflexions empirically grounded on discreet geographic accidents, a more intuitive and organic version is proposed for the resolution of the plans into interdependent functional blocks.

In relation to the work of Barragán – another reference perceived and acknowledged, in the houses designed since the time architect Marcelo Suzuki was part of the team –, what calls attention, more than the deference to his program resolution or formal repertoire, is the team's respect for his sensibility in relation to materials, his convincing subordination of technology to the authenticity of artisanship, which exudes humanity, and the intuitive and spontaneous ability with which he integrates elements from different cultures – Spanish-Mediterranean, North African and Arabic – to the rational central European vocabulary of his training.

Finally, if it's true the residential projects of the Brasil Arquitetura Studio make no apologia for the massiveness of the *Paulista school* approach – already present in the studies conducted by Luís Saia in the 1950s and 60s, which define the typology of the first dwellings built by the *Bandeirantes* (16th century pioneers), which was reclaimed in the suspended and introspective boxes of the most emblematic projects of Vilanova Artigas, Carlos Millan and Paulo Mendes da Rocha – it is also true that the team maintains this special ability for the controlled and inventive design of openings and for the dynamization of internal spaces contained in simple, prismatic volumes, by way of experimenting with multiple planes, scale variations and the inclusion of landscaped voids, the use of carefully placed stairways, *jiraus* (Tupi word for mezzanine or balcony) and walkways.

The ideas and circumstances described above are among the ones that most strongly influenced the creative process of the projects presented here. From one house to another, over the years the designs were implemented, one perceives reccurrences, reworkings and innovations as well as differences imposed by external factors, by the natural diversity of

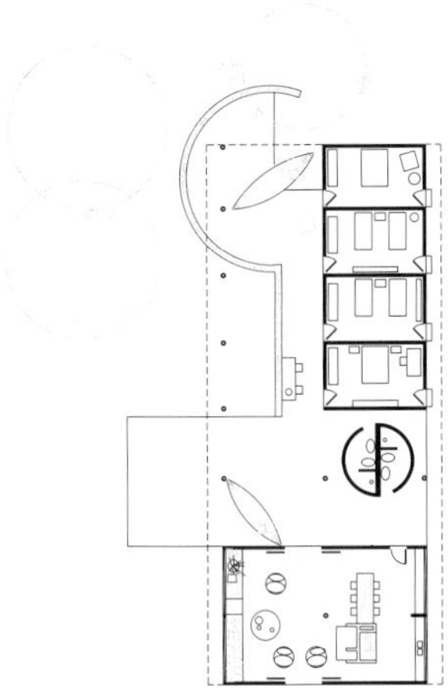

Lagoinha House, Carlos Millan, 1964-66.

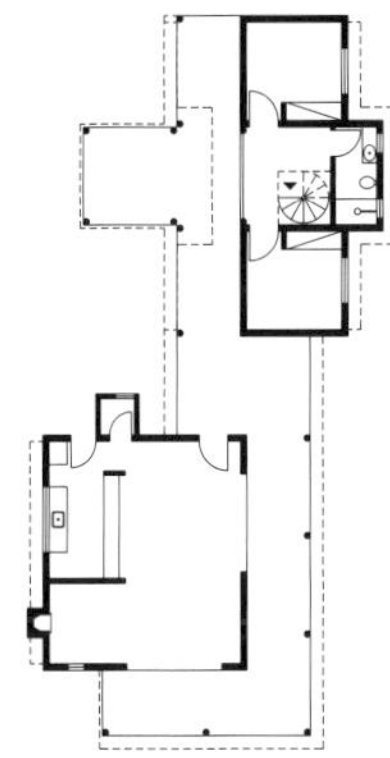

Paúba House, Brasil Arquitetura, 1986.

situations: the size and location of the plot, topography, neighborhood, scope of the program, etc. Be that as it may, what we see is a body of work in transformation, displaying some significant trends that are worth dwelling upon.

Among the permanent occurrences, two key interrelated aspects are noteworthy. All the houses have their main blocks placed comfortably on their terrains. The houses accommodate themselves to the land, at times transforming it, even recreating it, always with a view to appropriating it as an extension to the interior spaces. Alvar Aalto's lessons make themselves felt in the team's special sensibility for taking advantage of the slightest particularities of the site, incorporating them so they may dynamically interact with the design. A tendency of modern Brazilian residential architecture which is absent here is that of raising the buildings off the ground in order to liberate space for circulation and landscaping. Even when the built volumes gain a certain lightness and transparency due to the insertion of choice structural elements that either section or project from them, creating more radical openings or prominent canopies – such as the overhanging concrete blades of Casa Tamboré, which project the environments of the main floor towards the landscape – these are accessory devices which qualify particular situations, without denying the general principle of placing the building directly on the ground.

Partly because of the previously mentioned aspect, one notes that the structural system is almost always subordinated to the conception of space, which means that technology does not play a main role here. The architects use conventional reinforced concrete as essential support for the configuration of their built volumes, only occasionally resorting to – not for expressive purposes, but functional and structural ones – complementary metallic elements, such as steel rods, columns, etc. As with Le Corbusier's first houses, posts and beams of reinforced concrete blend with the rendered masonry, and usually have no prominent role in the formal expression. This way, an interesting expressive dynamic is created by the contrast between the relatively compact masses of the main volumes and these occasional irruptions of more athletic constructive and structural elements – canopies, slender columns, bladelike slab projections, etc. – which frequently work as elements of integration between the interior and exterior space: the verandas on pilotis of Casa Cotia (Cotia House) and Casa Morumbi (Morumbi House), for example.

Another important aspect, constantly featuring in the set of residential designs presented here, has to do with the volumetric fragmentation of the buildings. An omnipresent theme, it denotes the intention of creating interaction between the built forms and the environment – be that the topography, landscape, climate or the urban scene – rather than the rhetorical intention of decomposing the program by reconstructing a formal unity of greater complexity, based on the functional principle as a value in itself. In spite of that, one ought not disregard the example of American post-war residential architecture – especially that by Marcel Breuer – and the influence it had on Rio's architectural scene.

But formal and programatic decomposition also corresponds to more internal operations, such as that of

Houses in Alter do Chão,
Alentejo, Portugal.

Carré House, Alvar Aalto, 1956-61.

dynamizing the fruition of space by diversifying and interlacing the routes of space perception, and so constructing a rich web of relations directed to attend to the variety and wealth of situations present in domestic and social life. This way, it conceptually brings architecture closer to life experience. The succession of built volumes thus arranged in space allows us to discern the temporal nature of its necessarily gradual perception.

The fragmentation of the volumetrical arrangement is operated in different ways according to the density of occupation. On larger plots, as with the Tamboré, Aldeia da Serra, Mantiqueira and Cotia houses, where the overlapping of plans is rare and the functional identification of the blocks is more obvious, these easily become autonomous regarding their location on the site and the technical and formal treatment of the roofs, enclosing walls and openings. The multiplication and particularization of the constructed volumes give the whole an almost urbanistic quality.

In sites of a more urban nature, everything is concentrated in such a way that the necessary overlapping and compaction do not compromise the architects' sensibility in the reading of the site and the construction of place. On the contrary, the spatial restrictions seem to require from the compositional gesture a more acute development (outward) and a deepening of its awareness (inward).

In the projects carried out on more conventionally shaped plots, such as Casa Ubiracica (Ubiracica House), the challenge is to construct a sequence of variations, an alternation of contrasting spatial characteristics and a rhythm, in spite of the limited contextual references. On exotically shaped plots the shrewdness of the design is put to the test in other ways. The ability to make the logical criteria resulting from conventional constructive techniques compatible with the chance opportunities provided by the concrete situation of the site and the intended purpose of the buildings produced the instigating experiences of the Muro Azul and Morumbi houses.

These projects are eloquent examples of how, in contrast with the relative neutrality of the larger sites, the more confined ones can present difficulties that are easily converted into a system of suggestive variables. Based on the "convenient reason principle", these designs illustrate some important transformations in the team's design method. They start from rationalized schemes for organizing the plan, with the aim of transcending and enriching them every time they become inadequate to responding to the real situation's incongruities. They then carry out a controlled bending of the rule, deflecting the circulation axes, rotating the orthogonal fabric in specific places, upon which other sinuous lines are superimposed and incorporated – drawn from a diversity of formal repertoires – whose design accommodates arrangements as intrinsic and justifiable as those following the regular segments of structural grids. Everything combines, fuses, and interacts in a geometrically and constructively new manner, revealing, at the end, new solutions that are not in the least affected or rhetorical.

The residential designs of the Brasil Arquitetura Studio have been privileged construction sites for experimentation

Kharga, reference to Nova Baris, Hassan Fathy, 1967.

Studio-house, Luis Barragán, 1947.

with rustic construction materials and traditional techniques, many of them reclaimed from the Portuguese-Brazilian tradition, often modified and adapted, or combined with elements taken from modern learned culture. Instead of the didacticism of the preceding decades – which can be observed especially in São Paulo – in which the concern with the "expressive truth of materials" meant electing materials compatible with the expression of certain modes of construction considered truer than others, that is, closer to the proposed universalist social and political project – the choice of materials, as the Brasil Arquitetura Studio views it, has a more cultural bias, an attachment to the land and the Brazilian way which does not exclude a subtle evocation of equally telluric expressions originated from other parts of the world. One can sense the manifestation of an Ibero-American – or perhaps broader – fraternity implicit in the use of vivid coats of color, of stone exterior walls, of rustic wall renderings, fine timber trellises, irregular stone pavements, woven straw panels for ceiling claddings and Alentejo-style chimneys.

The appropriation of rustic materials, of craftsmanship production techniques, and of anthropologically identified motifs and hues gradually make way for a sort of new internationalism of peripheral cultures – a "world architecture". The poetry they have been weaving little by little supplants the pursuit of an image of Brazilianness for consumer use – national or international. It aims to find its place in contemporaneity.

The houses presented here – from the dominant compositional rigor of the Tamboré and Aldeia da Serra houses to the dissonance of the denaturalized stone towers of Casa Cotia, to the abstract vernacular syncretism of Casa Mantiqueira or the polyphonic nature of the superimposed geometries of Casa Morumbi – reveal this contemporary and Brazilian condition which enables the architects to have an equally attentive view of the particular as well as of the more universal elements of human experience. This stance towards creative architectural activity signals new perspectives of freedom, far beyond the 'isms' and within a universe of possibilities still to be discovered with patient investigation, authentic curiosity and legitimate pride in one's own identity.

BIBLIOGRAPHY

ARMESTO, Antonio; PADRÓ, Quim. *Casas atlânticas: Galiza e norte de Portugal*. Lisbon: Blau, 1996.

BRUAND, Yves. *Arquitetura contemporânea no Brasil.* São Paulo: Perspectiva, 1981.

JACQUES, Michel. *Steven Holl.* Basiléia: Arc en Rêve/Centre d'Architecture, 1993.

MINDLIN, Henrique. *Arquitetura moderna no Brasil.* Rio de Janeiro: Aeroplano/Iphan, 2000.

MONTANER, Josep Maria. *Después del movimiento moderno.* Barcelona: Gustavo Gili, 2001.

TRIGUEIROS, Luiz (Ed.). *Fernando Távora.* Lisbon: Blau, 1993.

Tamboré House

Barueri, São Paulo state 1989

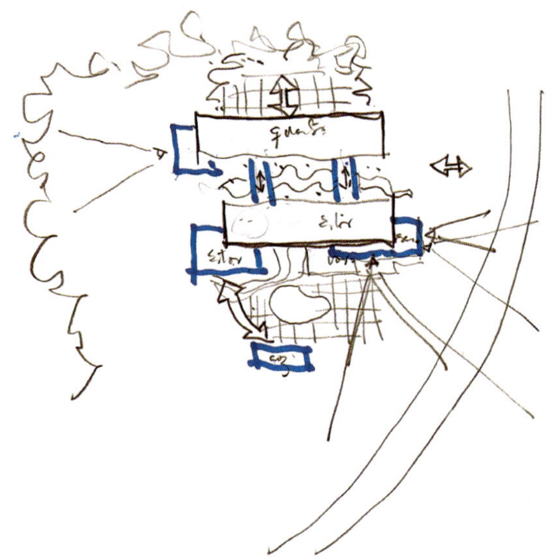

To start with, an ample and sufficiently sloped site with a generous view over interesting woodland surroundings. The specification of a quite extensive program immediately presented the challenge of avoiding a massive construction. On the contrary, the project attempts to occupy this vast available space by creating a concatenation of events in time and space, providing a range of paths that lead to their gradual discovery or perception.

Simplicity, clarity and functionality are the ideas that guide the first moves related to distribution and construction: two parallel main blocks interconnected at convenient points, concrete structural elements and masonry walls, with a conventional clay tile roof. In the front block the social areas overlook the pool and gardens; in the rear block the bedrooms, bathrooms, and dressing rooms.

From this initial distributive scheme the design undergoes successive distensions in shapes and location, every time the brief requirements and the pertinence of the rational plastic concept adopted here coincide. So that the outcome may convey the design experience, the processes of thought are made all the more explicit by characterizing the two main blocks by painting them white, in counterpoint to the blue of the secondary ones, which are aggregated to the white ones in order to better accommodate specific developments of the program. Similarly, the technological excellence of the critically calculated exposed concrete, the wide spanning quality timber window frames, the bladelike canopies either overhanging or suspended by steel rods attached to the structure, the curving timber cladding of the ceiling only mark their presence when justified by spatial or programatic exceptionalities.

VC

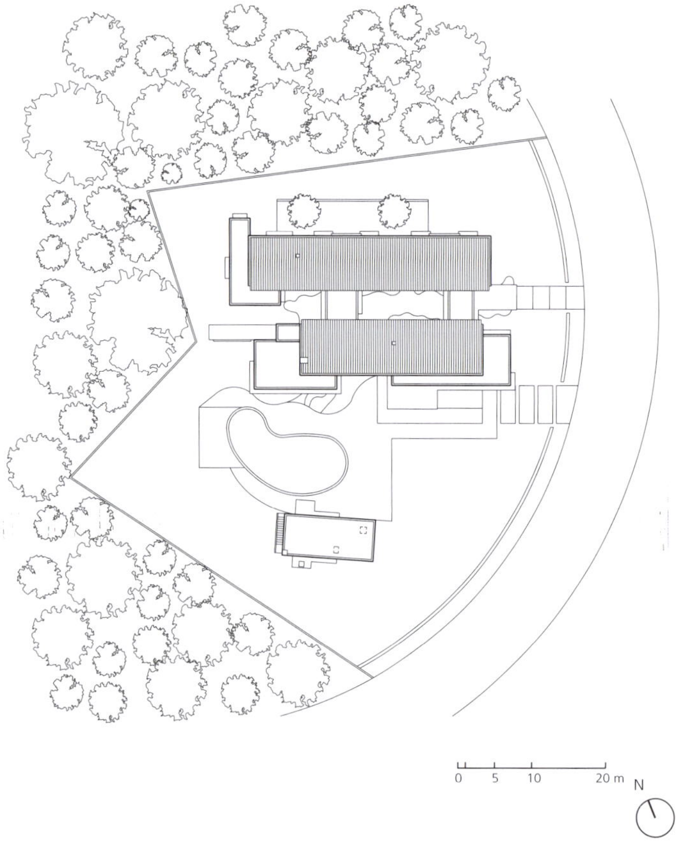

• Location plan

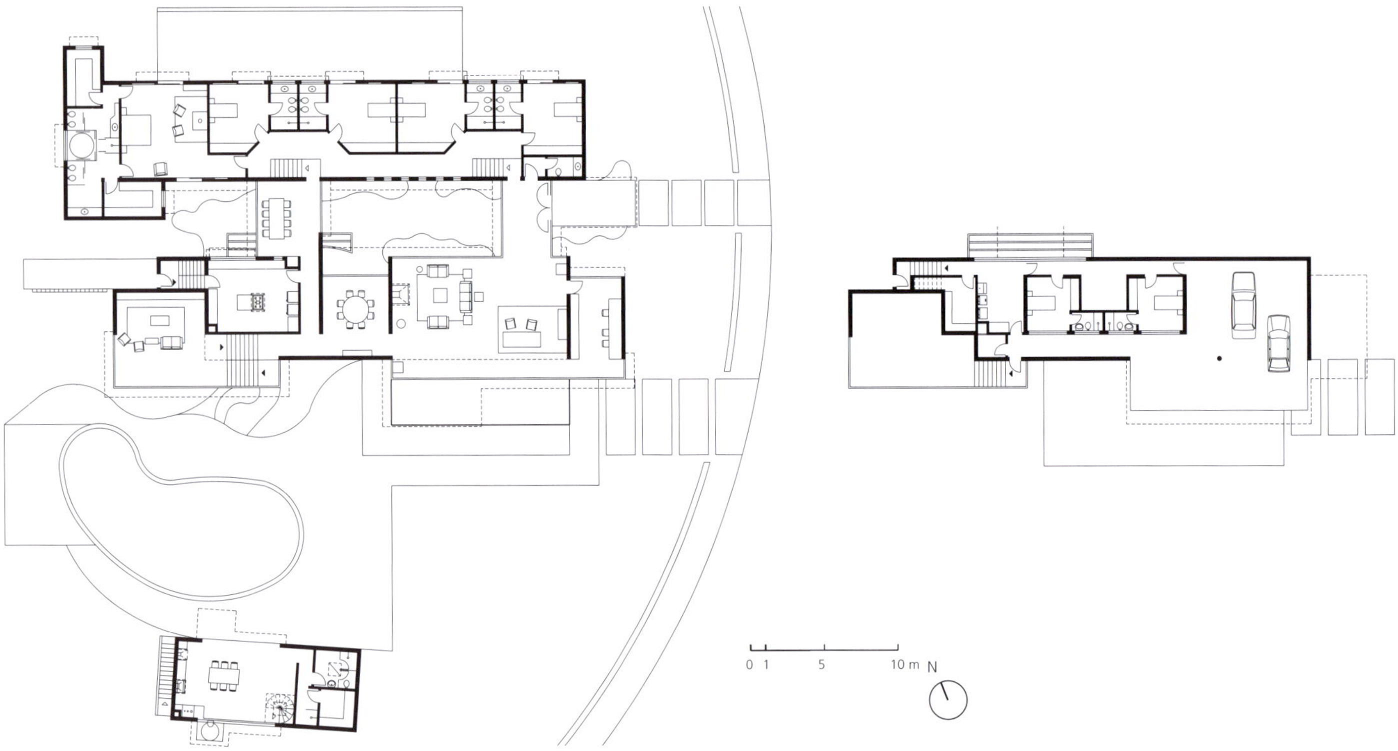

- First floor plan
- Lower floor plan

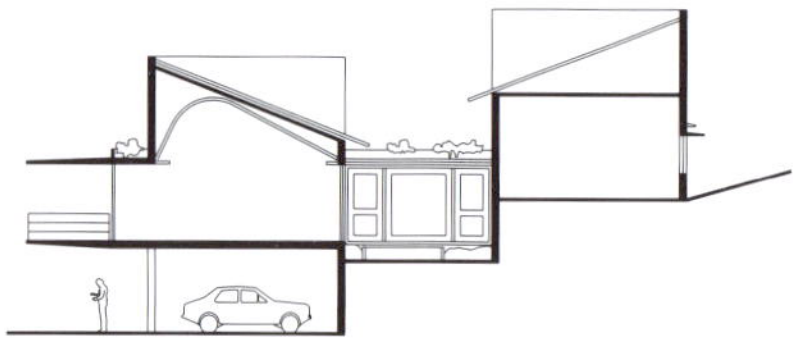

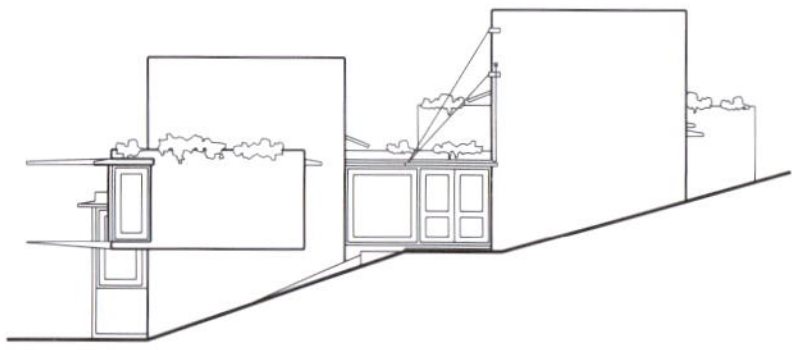

- Transversal section
- East elevation
- South elevation

Aldeia da Serra House

Barueri, São Paulo state 1989

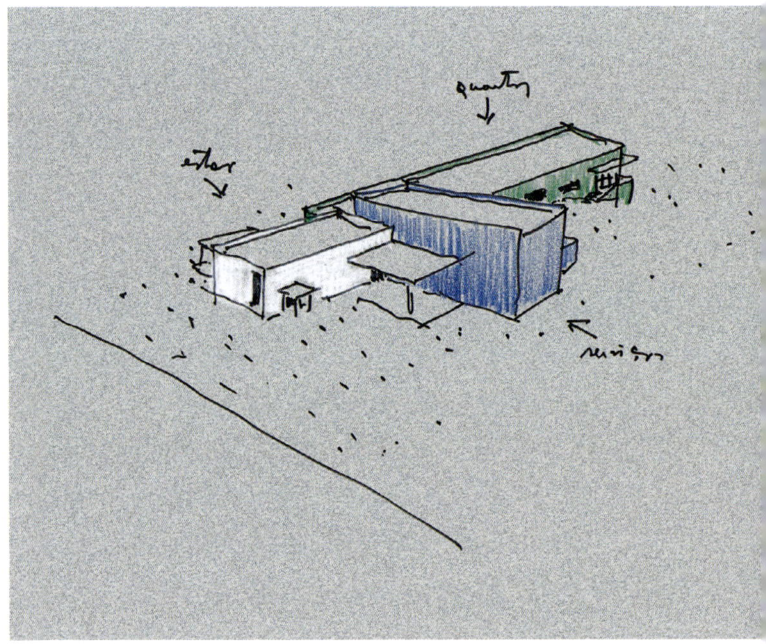

This house, built on a regular 1,800-sq yard site with a slight inclination in Aldeia da Serra, near the city of São Paulo, responded to a relatively extensive program – three bedrooms, library, studio and office, along with the usual living and service areas – and strong recommendations for a restricted budget and time schedule. This project was thus an ideal occasion for exercising the virtues of simplicity, for the pursuit of the essential, for a dignified use of elementary building techniques.

The subdivision into three functional ground level blocks, in this case, results from a decision to radically simplify the construction by a decompacting approach. The simple volumetric arrangement and the massive and textured aspect of the walls, rustically rendered, give subtle prominence to simple features such as openings, sunshades, jutting water pipes and canopies, among others. They are modest elements in the quantity, cost and utter simplicity of their design. Here, given the parsimony of the architectural move, color does not intervene to distinguish between first and second order volumes, but rather to characterize the different uses of the three sectors of the residence: white for the social block, green for the private one, and blue for the service block.

The plan layout proceeds according to a strict orthogonal, yet natural organization, not subordinated to decisions of a formal nature. The arrangement of the blocks on the plot organizes its present and future occupation, as it ensures ample garden space surrounding the social block, plus a generous area in the rear for future landscaping and leisure additions, while isolating the access and parking area. The connection of the three blocks is based on subtle opportunities of the plan and shape of the blocks. On one hand, there is the long longitudinal axis of circulation, which at the same time connects and separates the intimate and social areas, locating them at opposite ends, mediated by the transversal interposition of the service block. On the other, the height differences between the three blocks, emphasized where they meet at the center of the composition, create a visual dynamic of abstract quality that conveys in a simple, yet expressive manner the specificity and interdependence of the parts.

VC

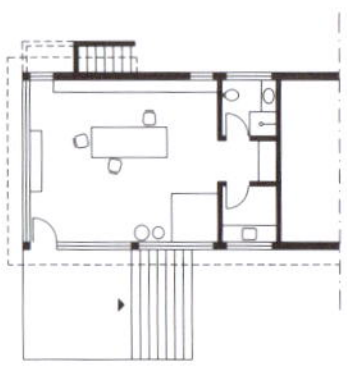

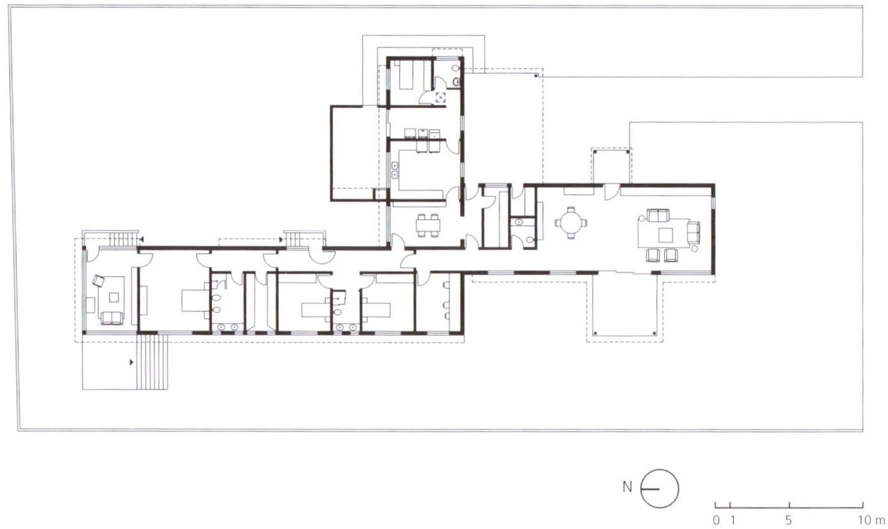

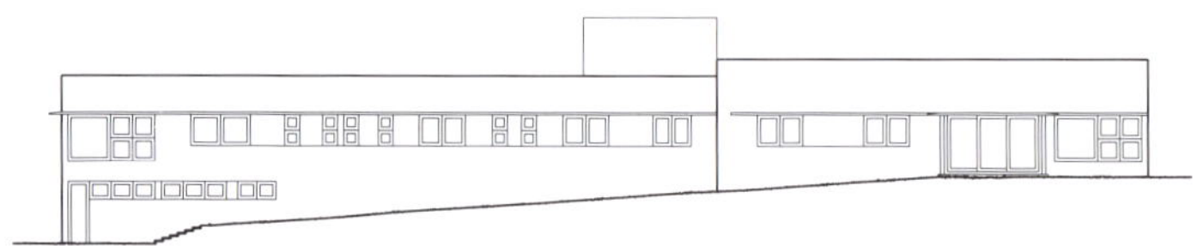

- Plan of basement level
- Ground floor plan
- East elevation

Blue Wall House

São Paulo, capital 1994

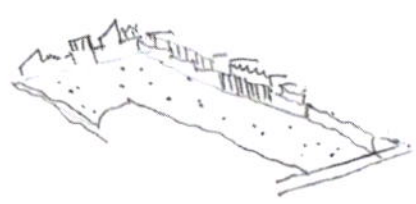

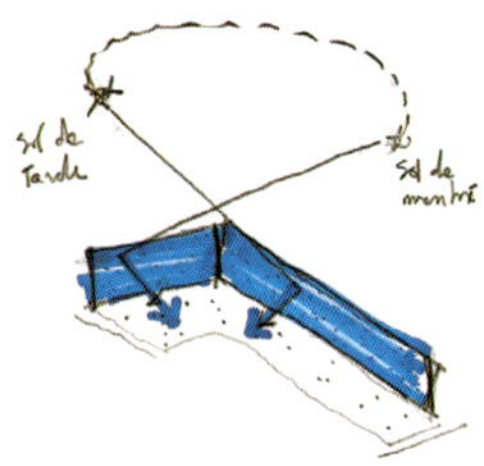

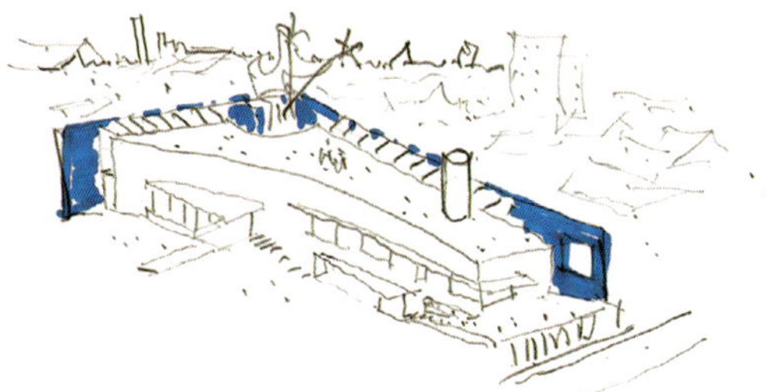

The plot for this residence in the capital of São Paulo presents many difficulties and suggestions. Here the narrowness and unique nature of the plot are the sources of inspiration for symbolic and functional criteria: the heavily built, palpable and noisy neighborhood, the indefinitely urban horizon; the plot with no marked front or back, irregularly shaped in the format of an open 7, linking perpendicular streets and having a slight inclination, a sort of broken passageway. Any move in order to reestablish continuity and fluidity must necessarily veer, twist or rebound. And that is what indeed happens.

The long external lateral boundary wall is designed to neutralize the possible interference from adjacent buildings. The blue 20 ft high wall acts as a background, thus providing a primary continuity, unifying the environments under its visual omnipresence with bluish sunlight reflections filtering through the void space between house and wall (a building code stipulation). The corner of the plot is reverted by the bending in the opposite direction of the building's glazed wall, creating an internal garden that illuminates and integrates the social and circulation areas as well as the two sides of the plot.

The essential points of the program are satisfied by the linear block where private living spaces are superimposed on dining, kitchen and domestic maintenance areas. Unfolding alongside gardened areas, the main façade also adjusts to the blue wall's deflection by a continuous and very subtle curving and proceeds to the plot's other end, defining the building's main space: an ample, two storeyed, living room.

VC

- Location plan
- Plan of basement level
- Ground floor plan
- First floor plan

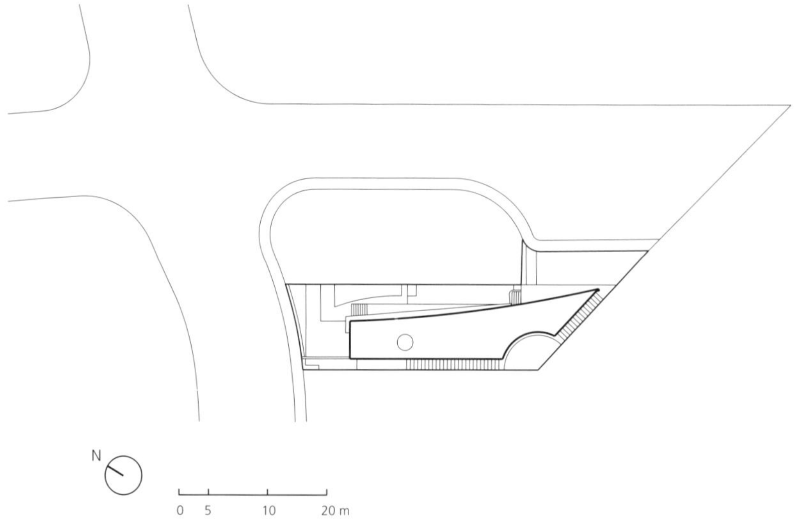

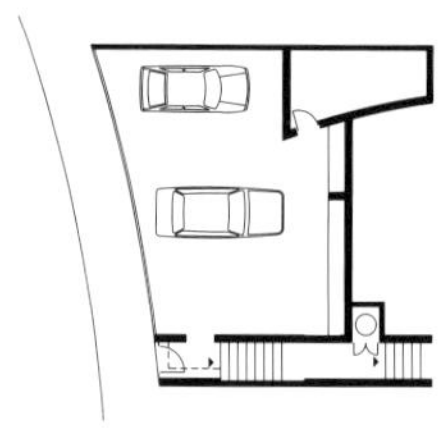

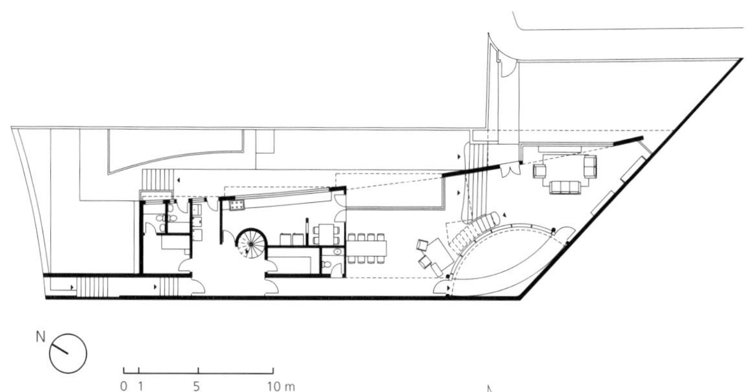

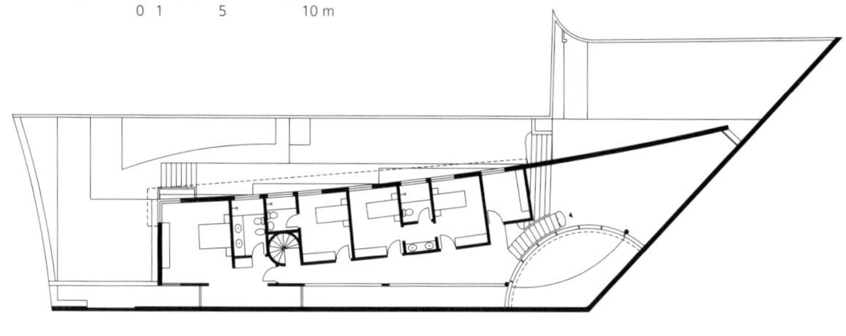

- Longitudinal section
- North elevation

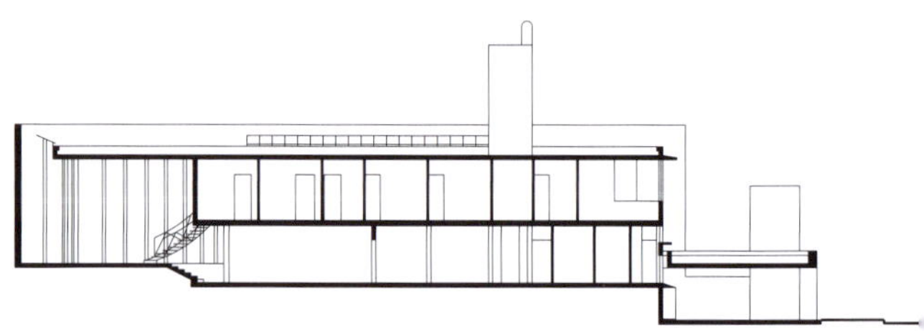

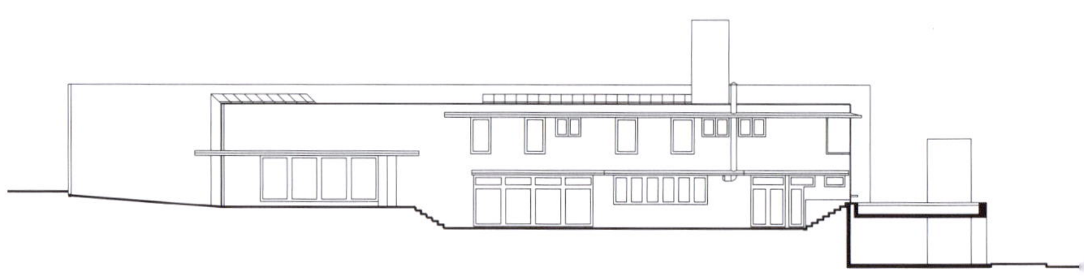

Ubiracica House

São Paulo, capital 1996

With the exception of the metal stairs and the Alentejo-style fireplace with its black stone floor cladding, there is not a single line in the design for this house in the city of São Paulo that deflects from pure and simple orthogonality. Even the roofs are flat and become reflecting pools which, in addition to protecting from the weather, are inhabited by carp. This antiformalist austerity, no doubt a tribute to some of the remarkable aspects of the so-called *Paulista* school, under whose disciplinary rigor both partners were trained, is, however, tinted in a very particular way by irruptions of lyricism and vernacular evocations. Strict cooperation between functional subordination and spontaneous traditionally Brazilian solutions from popular memory characterize a style of its own that, allied to a great sense of convenience and a deep appreciation of construction techniques, refutes the formalist and culturalist rhetoric.

The program is organized according to functional blocks differing in size and shape and distinguished according to the nature of their uses, with a view to a public/private gradient without lacunae: living room and library as social areas, office and dining room intermediate, and bedrooms, kitchen and veranda as private areas. This succession of spaces is arranged linearly along the longitudinal axis of the plot, which presents a slight acclivity. They are aligned along the longitudinal axis of a slender bladelike slab, which defines itself, in succession, as canopy, walkway, gallery and corridor. This element constitutes a practical means of functional integration and works, at the same time, as a symbolic representation of the progressive discovery of the spaces, with their qualities and surprises. As it evolves, it sections planes and spaces, integrating the different environments in an unequivocal but controlled manner.

From front to back, the itinerary starts off with a sort of shop window beside the main access to the house. This turns out to be an aviary, which foretells other vernacular ingredients still to come. Then, the concrete blade laterally intercepts the compact volume of the double height living room at first floor level, converting into a jirau (mezzanine), or elevated interior walkway. The high living room wall along which it runs houses bookshelves from floor to top. Before reaching the bedrooms the slab converts itself into a glazed gallery, producing a kind of hiatus between the front and back blocks, as it runs alongside a small terrace (from which one accesses other enjoyable spaces on the roof top). In the heart of the domestic intimacy, from the entrance to the guestroom to that of the master bedroom, the circulation route converts into a window-lined corridor, completing the progressive interiorization.

If on the first floor the axis predominates over all, on the ground floor and in the external green areas the spaces communicate in a fluid manner, by means of a visual integration controlled by subtle shifts, pauses and the distinctive treatments of surfaces and openings, always aimed at an empirical accommodation of the living experience, a characterization of the environments that rejects the isotropic spatial continuum of more dogmatic rationalisms.

VC

• Ground floor plan
• First floor plan

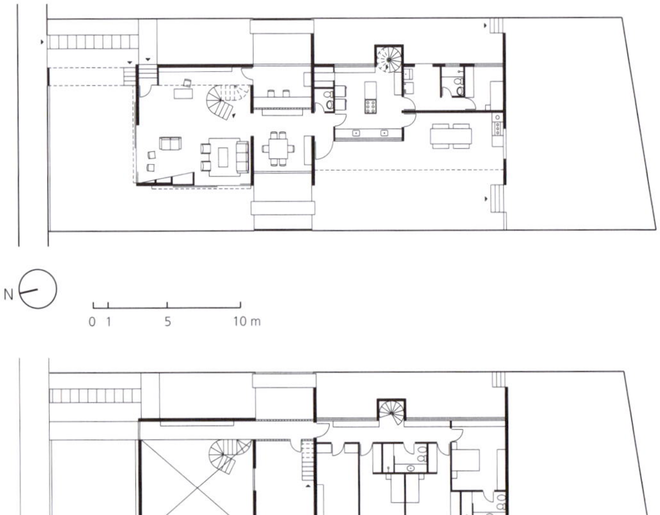

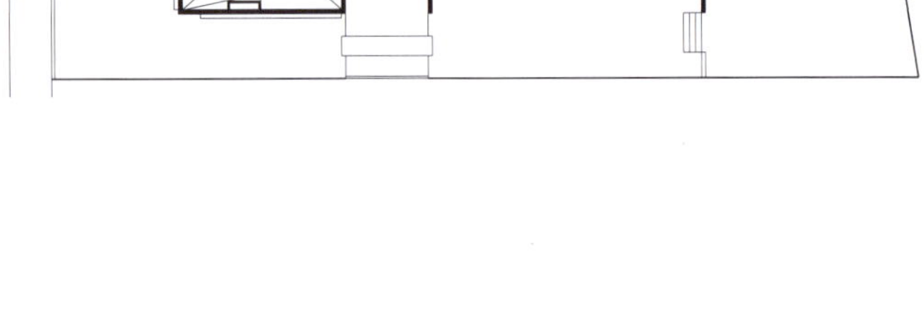

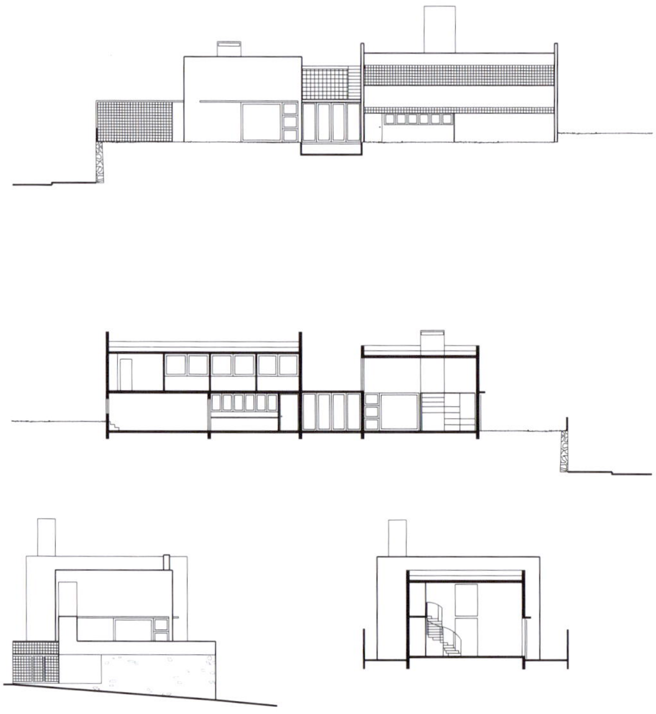

- West elevation
- Longitudinal section
- North elevation
- Transversal section
- South, east and west elevations

Alto de Pinheiros House

São Paulo, capital 1996

This is one of the most compact of all the houses designed by the practice in recent years. The design is influenced by the conventional nature of the urban site, but also results from a combination of other factors related to the building process. Two aspects are immediately apparent: first, the conciliation between a swimming pool running alongside the boundary wall and a landscaped area to be enjoyed by all long stay environments; and second, the maximization of the open area at the back, which emphasizes the privacy of this space removed from the contextual references of the surroundings.

The compactness and simplicity of the distribution – a classical longitudinal block of superimposed floors, with the living, dining and playrooms and service areas downstairs; bedrooms, bathrooms and private circulation areas upstairs; a small block, at an angle, containing entertainment facilities on the ground floor and an office upstairs – do not prevent the dynamization of the internal circulation routes and the alternating of introversion/extroversion spaces according to convenience. The built volumes of the two main floors do not coincide, allowing the emergence of verandas and terraces. The mismatch is solved by the mediation of an angled canopy slab that challenges, and at the same time ensures, the integration of the blocks and floors: the top floor clearly more hermetic, with Venetian blinds to the bedroom windows, and the ground floor enclosed by glazed sliding doors integrating the interior with the landscaped outdoor spaces.

In the front part of the building, an opportune elevation of the ceiling gives the living room a special status that is confirmed by the blatant blind front façade, broken only by a simple and massive rustic timber doorway, and by the no less conspicuous presence of an alentajana chimney painted blood-red over a roughly textured rendering. This commanding symbolic element – which functions at the same time as a structural and formal element – articulates the various dislocations and scale shifts which operate, in this part of the building, as plan or elevation, the multiple transitions between public, social, semiprivate and intimate spaces.

VC

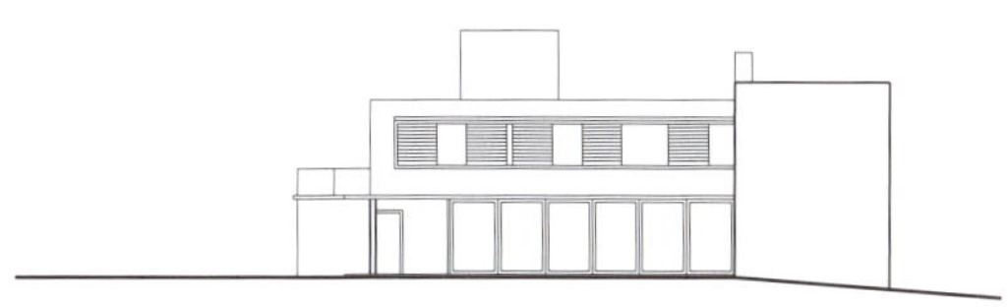

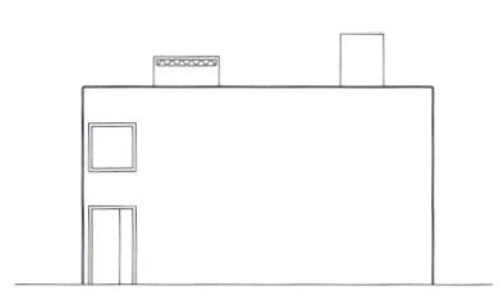

• South, east and west elevations

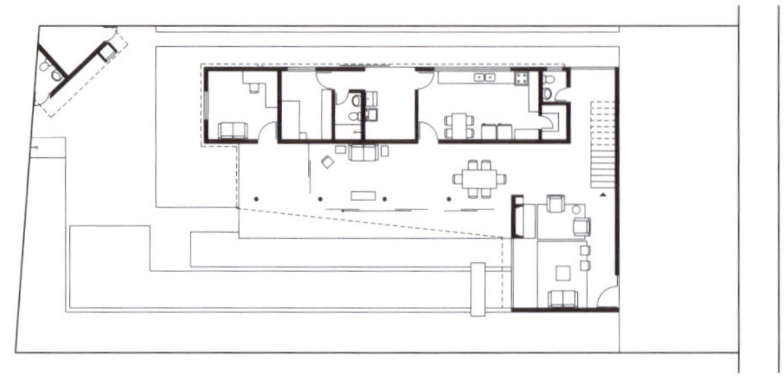

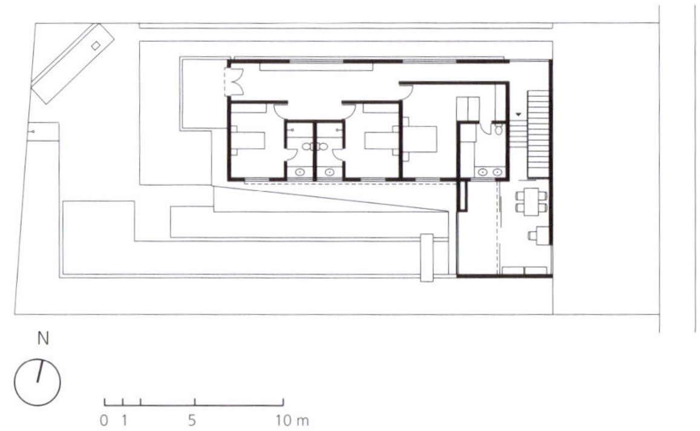

• Ground floor plan
• First floor plan

Cotia House

Cotia, São Paulo state 1998

This project, implemented on a spacious site that recalls the situation encountered years earlier with the Tamboré House, revisits the theme of program decompaction, but this time according to different composition principles and with a renewed formal repertoire. There are three blocks, arranged and oriented according to zoning and topography conveniences. Two of them are interconnected by an elevated, glazed walkway, and contain the essential activities of a house – kitchen, dining and living-room in one block, bedrooms and bathrooms in another, while a third, adjacent to the entrance, houses the service areas.

A cyclopian masonry wall limits the contours of the upper topographical level, close to the access, and at the same time introduces a striking plastic element, a fundamental reference, and organizes the disposition of the first two blocks. The long wall with its irregular course appears to be the pretext for breaking the orthogonal rigidity of the plan by the introduction of oblique virtual relations between the constructed bodies, as if they were lacunae in rational logic, or spaces for decisions containing a certain element of arbitrariness. Its role as inducer of liberties is further emphasized when its vigorous and telluric image rebounds on the neighboring pavilion in the form of isolated elements as a support for a stairway and fireplace chimney.

The constructivist logic of a geometry obtained from the perpendicular intersection of solids and planes combines with the inclination of the roofs and walls and with the resulting triangular and trapezoidal figures. The elevations receive a marked topical treatment in accordance with the needs dictated by the site plan and by the use of the environments. No attempts were made in order to obtain homogeneity in the disposition of the openings, which was defined by structural or construction requirements only. This new orientation is clear in the ambivalence of the social block: its completely glazed southern façade, looking out over a reflecting pool and internal garden, contrasts with the massive north-facing façade, sectioned by a low canopy that shields the living room from the sun, projecting the view from inside towards the lower part of the garden and to the swimming pool.

VC

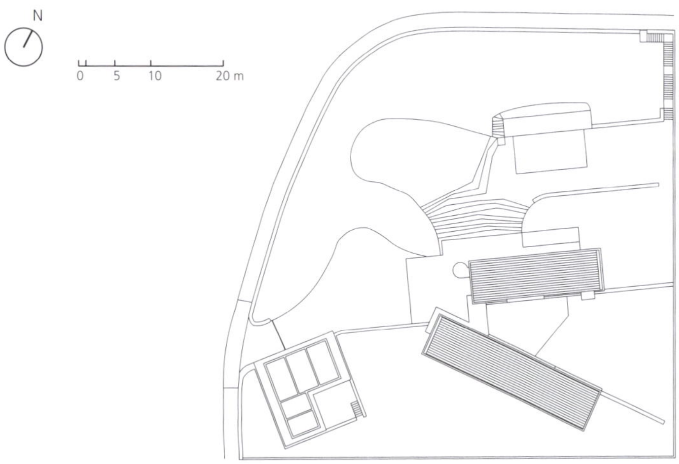

• Location plan

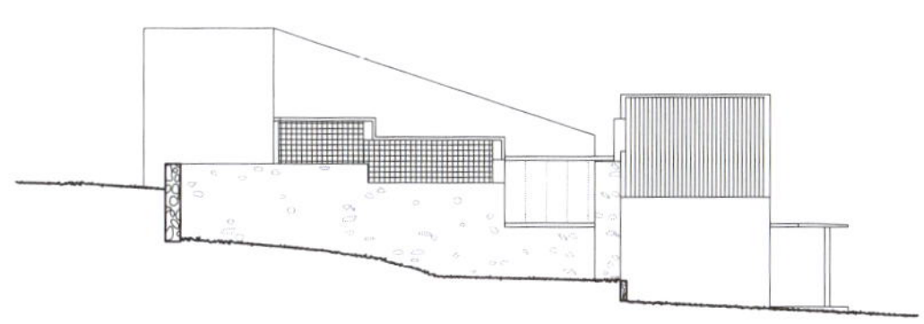

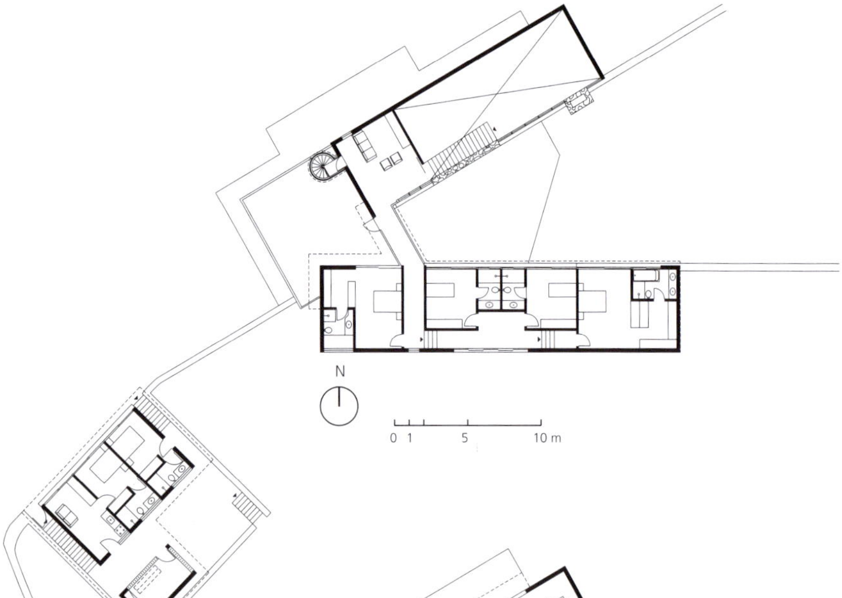

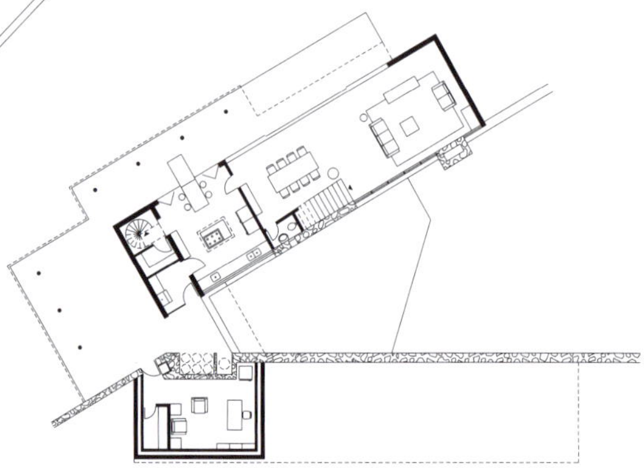

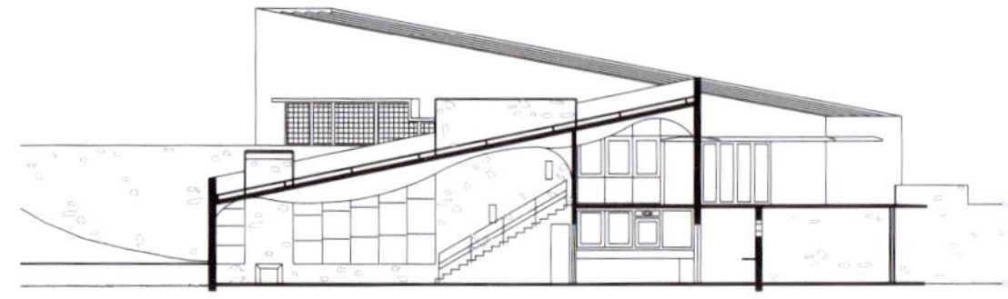

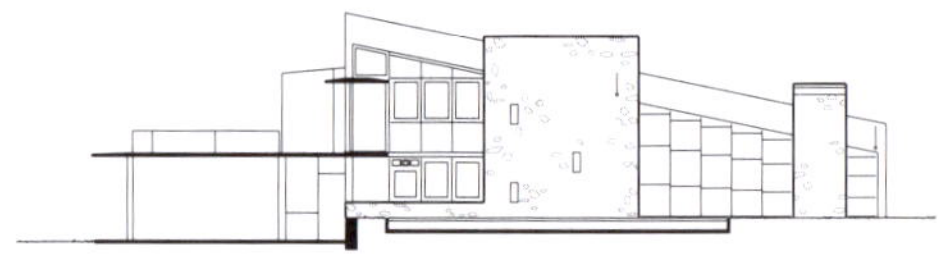

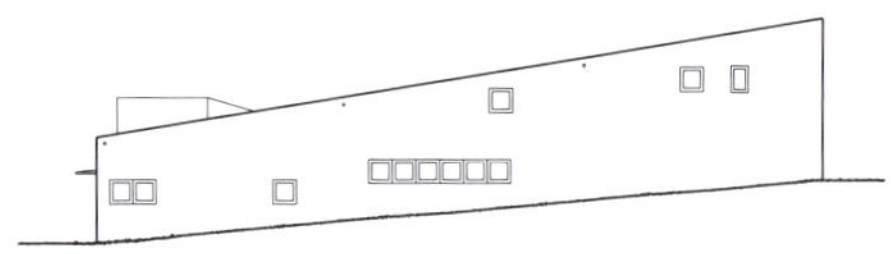

- Ground floor plan
- First floor plan
- Longitudinal section (living room)
- South elevation (bedrooms)
- Joinery scheme (living room)

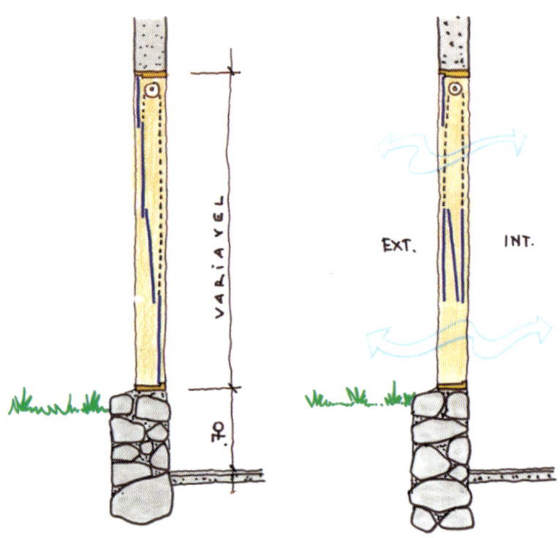

Morumbi House

São Paulo state 1999

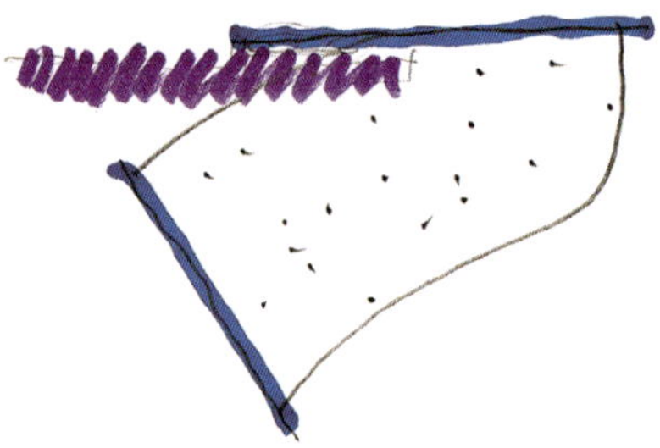

In an urban corner plot in São Paulo, facing southeast, this residential design illustrates the maturing of the liberties exercised for some time by the architects, related to the rupture with rationalist assumptions in terms of plan organization, of distribution and of site location. Here, more than in the Casa do Muro Azul and Casa Cotia projects, the transcending of the orthogonal grid suggested by conventional constructive logic – structural axes, the meeting of walls, standardized window/door frames, etc. – is accomplished in a way that goes beyond a looser arrangement of the different plan sectors internally structured in a more rigid manner. The dictates of concrete (rather than abstract) convenience, related to the living experience of the created environment and not to its constructiveness, come to markedly interfere in the conformation, the design of the spaces. The fluidity becomes more permanent and less syncopated. The operations that lead to these transformations of the basic rational and functionalist principle are not the products of virtuosity, caprice or formalism. They are operations guided by the pursuit of the adequate, of flexibility, of the adjustment of dispositions that at first sight look contradictory.

This time the general organization is more compact from the start, with the traditional superimposition of the bedroom storey over the ground floor (living rooms, kitchen, etc). However, it is necessary that the bedrooms face east in search of the morning sun, which they are made to do, though dragging along with them important parts of the social area located on the floor below.

Consequently, this pulls the office out of the confined space to which it looked condemned, and revitalizes a dead corner of the plot, enabling it to it participate in the play of transparencies and in the inter-penetrations of interiors and exteriors. With this rotation movement the predictable box is broken, in a manner no less logical for being unexpected, bringing the light of day into a previously closed off area of the house.

VC

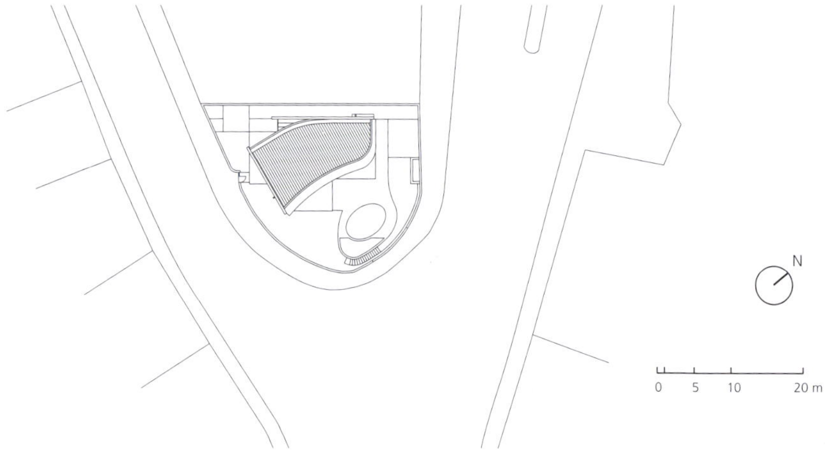
N
0
5
10
20 m

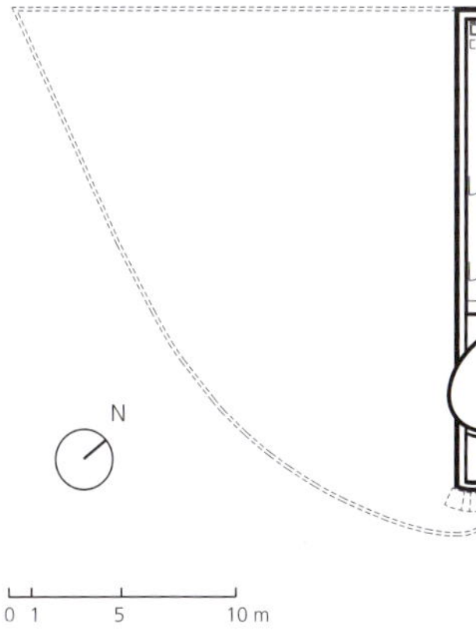

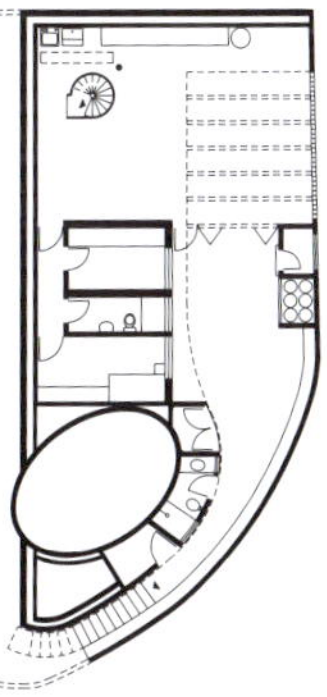

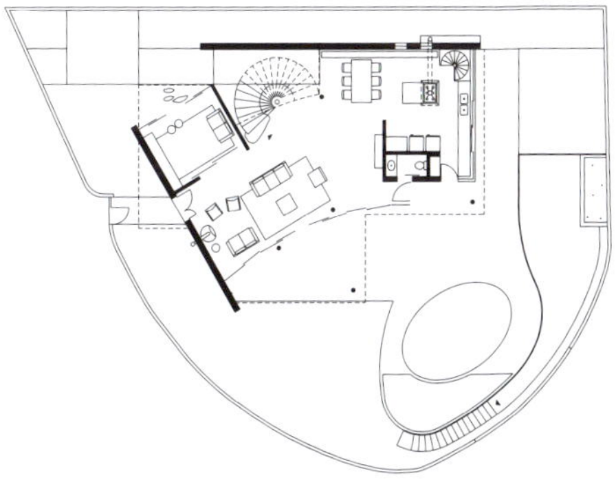

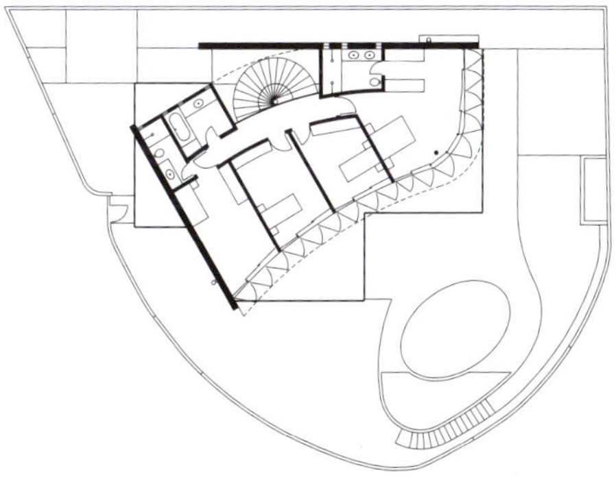

- Location plan
- Basement level plan
- Ground floor plan
- First floor plan

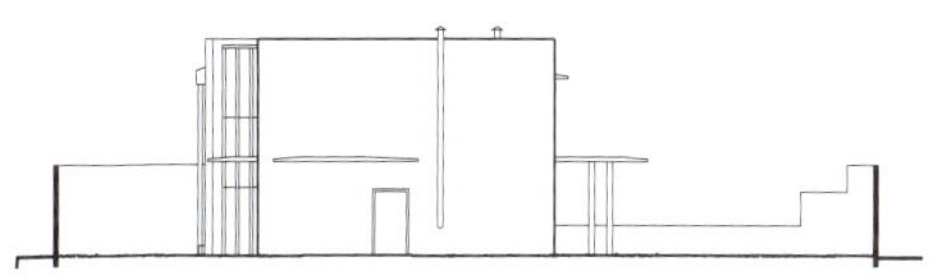

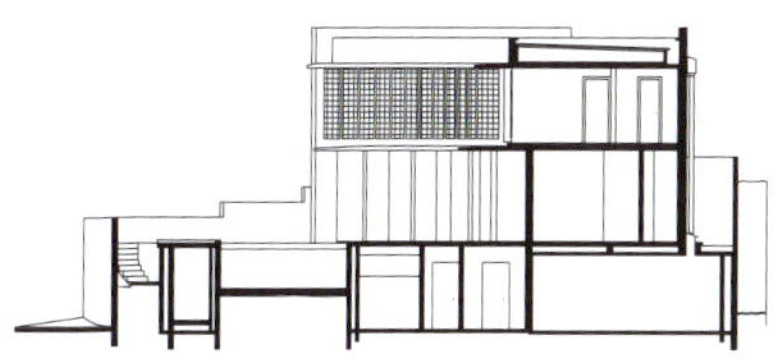

- Southwest elevation
- Transversal section

Mantiqueira House

São Francisco Xavier, São Paulo state 2000

The ambivalence already noticed in certain aspects of the design for Cotia House is here raised to the category of *parti pris*, a founding idea. The contrast between the image of a prismatic white shape critically perched over a riverbank – with which the design deceives the distant observer – and the bucolic appearance of the veranda-flanked pavilion, which internally unfolds into intimate retreats, is so sharp that it suggests a deliberate provocation. And so it is, and even more so because it results from very simple and objective motives and from choices that are all clear and fully justified. We are presented with a complexity entirely free of the rhetorical load that often accompanies difficult *assemblages*, blends and dialogues full of covert meanings.

In this design for a weekend home in São Francisco Xavier, in the Mantiqueira Mountains, there is a surprisingly natural accommodation between such disparate elements as the generous panoramic window set in the white wall of the living room – looking out over a vast expanse of mountains – the rustic stone fireplace, the traditional masonry oven and the twisted trunk post in the passageway leading to the bedrooms, which, all blended with the living room, announce other simplicities in the private areas, such as terraces with hammocks, a clay oven and an arbor.

Due to choice of site location, the house teeters on the edge of the bank rather than nestling at the center of the small plateau, where space abounds. In reaching the abrupt and concrete edge of the site, frontier between the seclusion of the shelter and the immensity of the panorama, the house takes the form of an incisive blade, inscribed with pure forms and monumental dimensions adjusted to the scale of the landscape. This symbolic barrier also constitutes the necessary functional protection against the actions of winds and storms coming from the south, and extends beyond the construction, lending its shelter to the terraces and gardens at the back. The thick wall, with its few openings treated as panoramic lookouts, relates to the limited light and broad view of its orientation as do the verandas and the Venetian blinds to the sunlit and enjoyable aspect of the plateau adjacent to the entire north side of the house.

Thus, the coexistence between the spectacular significance of a panoramic observation post and the introspection of this vernacular domesticity is ensured by a design stance in which the convenience of what presents itself to be experienced takes precedence over the normative vocation of typologies. It is a constructive rationality that does not deny itself structural rigor and careful detailing, and yet does not attempt to create an impression; nor is it bothered by the incorporation of elements from spontaneous architecture, carrying out these blends with a sense of practicality stripped of formalisms and therefore open to all there is to discover.

VC

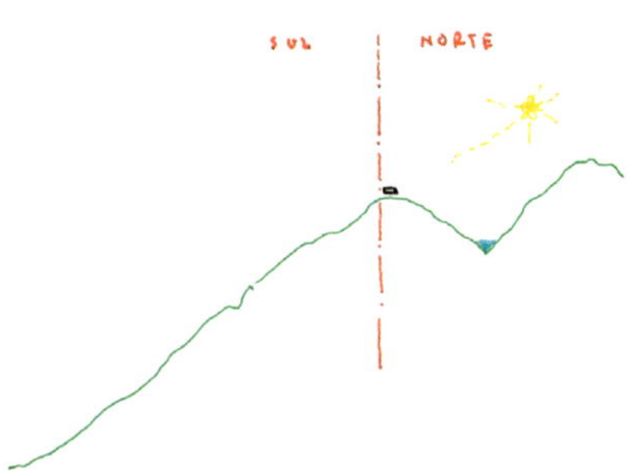

Sculpture by Richard Serra: *Pulitzer piece, stepped elevation* (1971, St. Louis, Missouri).

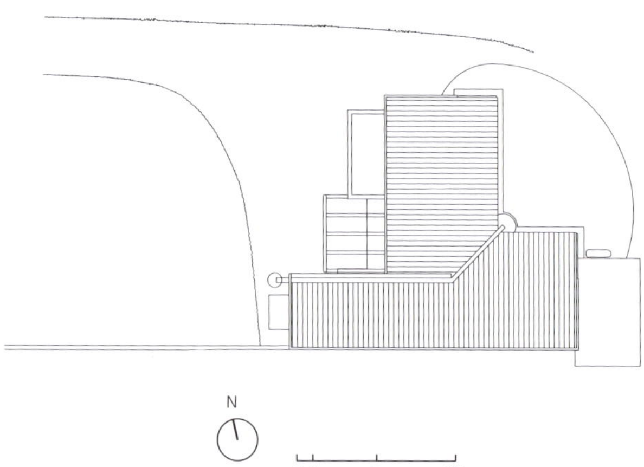

• Location plan

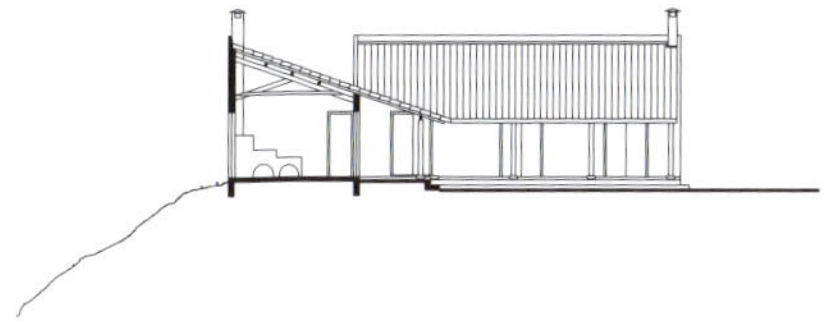

- Section through living room
- North and south elevations

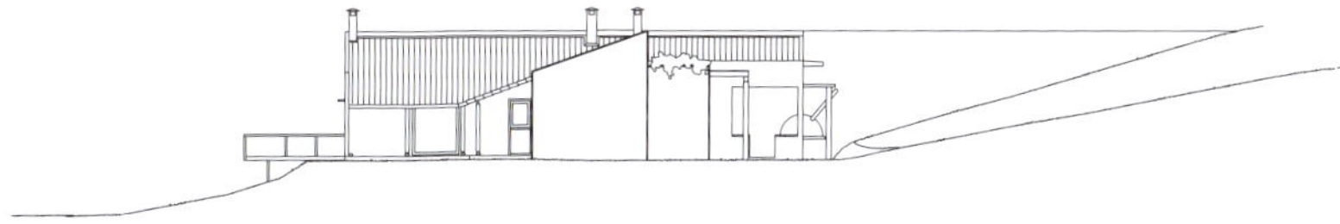

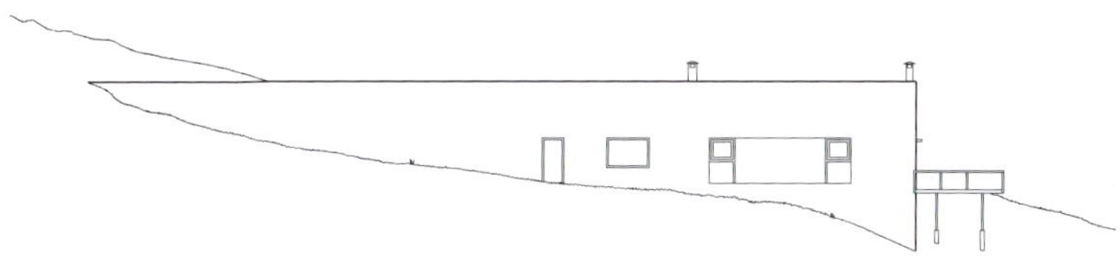

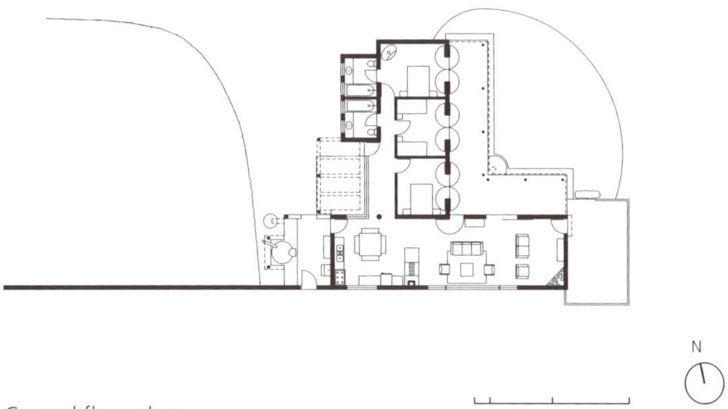

• Ground floor plan

Architecture and Furniture: Baraúna Joinery

Marcenaria Baraúna came into being as an extension of the practice Brasil Arquitetura Studio. In 1986, after some years of architectural activity, we summoned up the energy to set off on a new adventure, meeting a demand that had pulsated in us for some time: to manufacture our own furniture designs. Our partner at the time, Marcelo Suzuki, left in 1995, making way for the architect Paulo Alves in 1997.

We not only wanted to design furniture, but to be involved in the production as well, to experiment with different techniques, types of joints and finishes – we wanted to reduce the distance and time between the drawing board and the finished product. So we started working on another scale – with the obligatory *in loco* supervision – without, of course, abandoning the drawing board. On the contrary, we designed absolutely everything. And everything was architecture.

So it was and so it continues to be. At Barauna we design architects' furniture. The reasoning, the concepts, and the way of approaching each question are the same as those we adopt in our architectural projects or in urban planning. The logics of structure, balance, behavior and strength of materials, comfort, economy of means and inputs, essentiality, all of this draws us to render the constructive system explicit Furniture with nothing superfluous, subordinate to the same logic as machines and tools, which are only of worth if they function adequately, if they attend to their use. Furniture intended to last must be economic and beautiful while explicitly stating its purpose, which is to respond to the needs and aspirations of its time.

To dive into the world of wood is fascinating. It reveals textures, colors, smells and, most interestingly, different properties that make it suitable for multiple functions: weight, density, fiber length, flexibility, hardness and other variables guide to the most appropriate application. And in the specific case of the Brazilian flora, its diversity represents a vast field to explore.

As with our architecture, in designing furniture we reflect and seek inspiration in Brazilian colonial history, in the vernacular experience, in the modern pioneers, both national and international. We look around us, in time and space, though without making a routine of it, with no prejudice against novelty wherever it comes from, but averse to fashion or style-isms. We do not assume the role of inventors or original creators; we do not even call ourselves designers, since this word, full of meanings in the English language, has been extremely banalized in Brazil. We are architects who project furniture.

FF and MF

- *Caipira* (country folk) stool, designed by Francisco Fanucci.
- *Girafa* chair and *Frei Egídio* chair, designed by Lina Bo Bardi, Marcelo Ferraz and Marcelo Suzuki
- *Borboleta* stackable chair, designed by Marcelo Suzuki

• *Filó* chair and armchair, *Triângulos* table and PB armchair, designed by Francisco Fanucci

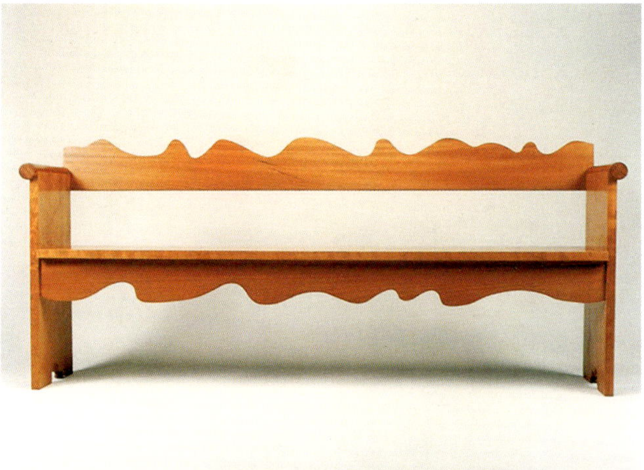

• *Marola*, H-40, and *Light* benches (with and without back), designed by Marcelo Ferraz

- *Cavalete* armchair, designed by Marcelo Ferraz
- *Parabiwa* armchair, designed by Cláudio Correa
- Line of modular office furniture, made of plywood and melamine laminate, designed by Francisco Fanucci, Paulo Alves and Marton Cyuricza

An interview

Passages from an interview conducted in May of 2005 by editor Denise Pegorim and Antonio Carlos Barossi (Tata), an architect and professor at the University of São Paulo School of Architecture and Urbanism and the Escola da Cidade.

Just an impression

MF: Once I was designing a country house for a friend just outside the city of São Paulo. It was to be a small house on a small plot of land. We were able to come to an understanding on the first draft I presented: the project addressed all of his concerns. That is, not quite. He thought one of the rooms should be larger because he would like space for a comfortable armchair to do some reading... I argued that if we enlarged one of the bedrooms, the living room would have to be smaller or something of the sort. He finally agreed. At the door, just as I was leaving, I said, "Don't worry, the drawing is one thing and the actual construction another; one can't get the exact three-dimensional picture from the drawing; the bedroom might seem small but that's just an impression." And he countered, "What is architecture if not pure impression?" Every time I remember this episode I think, That's it! Exactly! The phenomenology of architecture has helped us to see where we are moving. Many don't want to see it, or think it doesn't matter, but architecture is done in the realm of phenomena.

Modern? Not Modern? Does it matter?

FF: Theoretical and critical discourse is often based on assumptions that do not take into account certain essential elements of architecture, certain conditions which precede verbal discourse. For instance, for we architects, it may be important to identify wheter a project is modern or not. It happens that, for the user of the space, it's something that absolutely doesn't matter.

The rash presumption that verbal discourse – that it may be capable of comprehending the realm of architecture – is a huge mistake. Logical discourse is insufficient; poetry is insufficient... because architecture is a very specific way of talking about things, and a project is a way of talking about architecture. In the act of designing, there are many things we do we are not totally conscious of, the result at the other end, the effective use of the space, with all the effects generated in people's lives. To make architecture is, in a way, to run this great risk, that of penetrating the unknown and almost intangible territory that lies between thought and the action. And so we're back to phenomenology, which contemplates the universe of sensations, of the interactions of man with space.

Sound and silence, solid and void

MF: Architecture is the space we live in, which we experience this or that way, at a certain moment, with the people that happen to be there... With music on, the space has a certain quality; without music, there's another perception; illuminated or dark, day or night: everything interferes. People tend to think that only the built areas result from a particular organization of space, without realizing that what's in between them is an integral part of the set.

I believe that training one's eye to perceive this interplay is essential to the education of young architects. This is why it makes sense to compare architecture to music. Music only exists because there is sound and there is silence, which interplay this way and that. This is what architecture's about: constructed space, empty space, solid, void, solid, void.

A little irresponsibility

FF: An architect must be a bold professional. There comes a time in our work when we are called to infringe, so to speak. It has nothing to do with civic disobedience of any kind, of course, or of neglecting ethical standards in any way. This has to do with taking a gamble, based on an intuitive feeling, and of captivating people with the idea of it, winning their confidence to share the risk with us. It is a gamble, it could even be viewed as irresponsibility of a sort, in the sense that one can't be totally certain it is going to work. Once I mentioned this at a debate at the *Bienal de Arquitetura*, here in São Paulo, and it triggered a huge polemic, perhaps because I might not have expressed myself clearly, the term "irresponsible"... Sometimes we have a hunch, an educated hunch, of course, a feeling about the project, and my opinion is we must always pursue it. We may not always have a perfect logical argument to back us, nor technical reasons to justify a proposal, but we know something worthwhile is bound to result. That's the time for gambling. And here lies a point in common with the artist's work, for we're talking of intuitive knowledge.

Building dwelling thinking

FF: There's a really beautiful essay of Heidegger's, you must have read it, of course, entitled "Building dwelling thinking". It tells us that, in old German, the source of the term "inhabit" is the same as that of the term "build", and that, by tracing farther back, in the very beginnings of language and human communication, "to build" meant the same as "to be". The act of dwelling is, for humanity, a permanent learning process, and the architect is, in a way, a helping hand in this task. Man's first notion of shelter was to protect himself from the weather with animal hides. When he used the hide, or any other material, to shelter others but himself, he began making architecture. And he will never stop. This is perhaps the essential meaning of architecture.

A house is a poem

MF: An architecture that supposedly determines everything doesn't exist. The project may be replete with intentions, interpretations, but there is always room for the imponderable. This is where architecture compares with art – a comparison we should not refrain from. We're talking about poetry now. Obviously there are the social, civic, technical as well as economic requirements to be considered: the house must not collapse, must not kill anyone and so on and so forth, one can't spend too much money. But there is also the other side, and we keep moving from one to the other all the time: there's an indefinition in the proposed spaces, an opening for meanings. To design a house for someone is like offering this person a poem.

Hospitals, penitentiaries, bordellos

MF: Making architecture, in my opinion, urges that we dispose of our own selves for a while, and get under the wolf's skin, so to speak. To design a restaurant, for instance, one has to play the cook for a while, the waiter; for a hospital, the doctor, the patient, the nurse…

FF: We designed a hospital once, but we spoke with some of the doctors before we began. We then asked the nurses for their opinions, and this was fundamental, because they had a completely different reading, just as relevant as the perspective given by the doctors, of course.

MF: I'm very fond of a phrase by the Portuguese philosopher Agostinho da Silva, in which he says that the *world* is what we construct and wish to preserve, what we care about, the opposite of *worldly*, in its sordid acceptance. I think it is unnatural for an architect to design arms factories and prisons, for instance. To create spaces that negate life, freedom. Perhaps that is why we once didn't accept a comission to design a prison.

FF: It's a difficult subject. What kind of dignity can someone have in a place like that, a jail, a place for confinement? But to say that we would not design a prison is, perhaps, a bit cowardly on our part, for prisoners do exist in our society. One day, at the university, I suggested that the students design a bordello for the port of Santos. This caused two diametrically opposed reactions, one of excitement and one of protest. The idea was eventually shelved. Does it make any sense to refuse to improve the dignity of these people? I believe that I would never accept a comission to design an arms factory. But a prison? Actually, it is cowardice. Since there are so many people in there…

Space people share

MF: When you're going to present a project, you have to go with the will to defend something you believe in. By that, I mean, you only design a house you would live in, a building you would enjoy visiting, the same with a hospital or a school…

ACB: I don't think that you should necessarily design a house you would want to live in. The client might be a madman, for instance...

FF: You have a point. But I still believe that sometimes you have to try and imagine yourself as mad as your client. I'm not speaking of attending to people's idiosyncratic whims. We believe architecture is something more all-encompassing: to enable everyone, the mad included, to relate to light, to nature, to people. The thing we value most is space for people to share.

A shopping mall

MF: Can you imagine, we happen to be designing a shopping mall at the moment! For many years we wouldn't even consider the idea. It was our way of rejecting their presence in our cities. Almost invariably they oppose street life, they are gigantic walls built against the city itself. On the other hand they are here to stay and present us with a challenge.

FF: Why not create a space that is a continuation of the street or sidewalk and that would favour free interaction between people? Why can't shopping malls be a little more… permeable?

MF: ...like a trading space, the traditional market place, like urban life has always been throughout history? This is the "conversationable space" the Portuguese poet Fernando Pessoa talks about.

FF: To recover the role of the *gallerias* in downtown São Paulo, like the passages and alleys that run within blocks, linking streets – this could be an alternative to malls… We keep on trying.

To inhabit the city

FF: We inhabit the city. We spend quite a long time outside home, and an architect must consider the whole of a person's life. To inhabit, in this case, has a much broader meaning and denotes a double bond: "I live in this city, I belong to it, and it belongs to me". The town of Cambuí, where we grew up, in the state of Minas Gerais, perfectly illustrates this bond. It is a very festive town, and observes a full calendar of celebration dates; the commemorations are hardly ever private. Everybody meets at the square, it is there that everything takes place. To favour a greater social interaction, to celebrate, home becomes the city itself.

MF: But "the city no longer lives in me", as goes a verse from one of Chico Buarque's (Brazilian composer) songs. Would the city be more welcoming, had it proper sidewalks, pleasant squares, if one hadn't to spend so much time looking downwards to avoid the pot-holes, perhaps we might feel a little more at home. However, in Brazil, things are not like that. That is still utopia.

Useful and beautiful

MF: There is something I would have liked to have done. When I went to Greece and saw the traditional Greek architecture, I couldn't stop thinking: no one will ever come close to it, this level of perfection is impossible to achieve! Everything fits – the distances, the proportions, the places where one eats, the places one sleeps in. There is no distinction between what is useful and what is beautiful, no separation between esthetic and practical values. And this is how it is with every small house, in every village, on all the islands. It's an architecture that has nothing superfluous, no excesses. It's all an architect could wish to accomplish in life.

The utopia of everyday life

FF: I believe that two or three words mentioned in this book serve as key to our work, beginning with the idea of "everyday life utopia," which involves paying permanent attention to small things. For us, the ordinary may be above many theories; our direct relationship with things, concrete life, is what counts.

The world in the curriculum

MF: To look at architecture from all over the world, from every culture, from our closest sources to the most distant, the less immediate – this should be the basic core for curriculuae in architecture. It is essential to look as closely at Japan as at a Brazilian Indian village in the Amazon, to see how the people protect themselves from the sun, the rain, and to perceive what is private and what is collective in each place. In Greece my son slept in a bed that was nothing more than a hole in the wall with a curtain. It was the most valued sleeping place: "Who's going to sleep in this bed?" And how does one design a hole?

ACB: There is something I often notice in students: they think that the shapes associated with their lives are natural, that the formal universe they know, organized in that particular way, is part of nature and not of human history. If one placed a wash-tub just outside the bedroom, how would they react? They would be shocked and think it unnatural. However, if they saw an arrangement of that kind in Japan, where there are no bedrooms, where one sleeps in the living room, or if they knew that even in Europe there are apartments where one enters by the sleeping quarters and not by the living room, then they would begin to understand that spaces can present other meanings, other shapes and other kinds of beauty.

FF: Precisely. Perception is de-automated.

MF: You look around and assess whether it's OK or it's not. Then comes the shock, the surprise, and you start measuring. For me, to travel and to measure the world is essential to architecture.

Not just an additional concern

FF: As Brazilians, one thing we know about the history of architecture is that it's Eurocentric. There is a European perspective in charge of the history of the Western World. That is why, influenced by that approach, we learn architecture as a discipline we cannot recognize ourselves in, sometimes. To pay permanent attention to costs is a way of avoiding this perspective. The cruel persistence of our economic situation and our precarious city infrastructure influence the esthetic aspect, and this goes far beyond a simple "additional concern." Frank Gehry, responsible for the Guggenheim Museum, Bilbao, is known to say that he creates essentially economical projects. He is, in fact, economical, but this is an economic notion of little use to us. And perhaps the esthetics that he expounds, derived from the economic and technological possibilities at his disposal, are no good to us. They're part of another reality.

Rigour as pleasure or prison

MF: There is no such thing as architecture without form –form is the result of any architectural move. But it will always have to stand the long test of the phenomena. This brings to mind the *Neue Nationalgalerie*, in Berlin, a project by Mies van der Rohe, completed in 1968. You enter the bathroom, for example, and notice the lines of the floor tiling that approach from outside. If you're an architect, inevitably you begin to count: one large tile equals eight medium-sized ones, and eight of these equal sixteen of the small ones. The line comes by the floor, climbs the wall and takes over. It's impossible to not be influenced by the precision of this design. It's exciting.

FF: Also in Berlin, in a contemporary building, we shared the experience of another type of rationalism: the tiles formed sets of five, these sets were grouped with many others and interacted in a ruthlessly precise manner, forming a system that seemed to imprison us. We then began to walk "on a wrong step" till we discovered that to correct it we needed to stride four tiles at a time. I must admit that we were kind of guarded in relation to this place and had many expectations regarding the other; we were willing to keep an open mind in relation to both projects, but the fact is they stirred opposite sensations.

MF: We are used to viewing this rigour as typically Germanic, that this degree of order is a legacy of the Prussians, but why does it move us in one case and imprison us in another? Where does the difference lie? Why is it that in some places you feel as if there's a firing squad waiting outside and in others you get a sense of wisdom and a feeling of pleasure? This is the matter of poetry, which knows no nationality. It is the magic of architecture.

The artist's mark

MF: There comes a time when architecture must be subtle. It mustn't show. The architect's heavy hand reveals itself when he schemes: "It's my turn now! I'll leave my mark!" This absolutely ruins our cities. In Brazil, we're champions in that procedure. Architects, recently graduated or not, are always trying to create something striking. It may be a house, a shop, a small building... There's an example on every corner: the work of an architect unable to relate to the surroundings. There's a commitment to the city that ought to be respected. As there is in London, for instance, where houses on a street are basically the same size, where all streets have a uniform appearance, and all commercial centers are clearly demarcated. Here in Brazil the architect feels under no social obligations whatsoever. He doesn't realize that as he builds the tiniest part of a city, he is building a part of his home. That any piece he does is a piece of the city.

Heritage as a mirror

MF: Heritage is generally viewed as something frozen in time, as a document. However, if we view it also as an instrument, things become much more interesting. As an instrument, one can bring it to the present time. It's like a mirror that would say: "This was made in the 18th century. Good, isn't it? Fantastic! Shall we take it as a quality standard?" When we deal with heritage, there's always that little voice warning: "Be careful! This was made a hundred years ago, its importance lies in this or that!" But one also thinks: "I don't live two hundred years ago, I don't build with adobe, I build in the 21st century." This dialogue with the past is the same one ought to have with one's neighbor, with the sidewalk, with one's city, even if it's not a protected site. Our heritage is the city, and the respect and attention that are due to it demand that sometimes we should just blend in; at times it is only necessary to give things a little push, add just a little touch, and the architecture flourishes.

Past and present

MF: The generation of our masters, disciples of the first modernists, were not concerned about heritage the way we see it now. It was a time when it became imperative to refute the 19th century's legacy, to consider it all as trash; the immediate past was hampering the progress of man, industry was emerging and it was necessary to create an architecture suited to the machine age, to the new times. An architecture that would definitely make its presence felt.

FF: A complicating circumstance was that, in Brazil, modernism and the perception of the importance of architectural heritage were closely related from the very start. At the same time IPHAN (Institute for Protection of the National Heritage) was created by Mário de Andrade, while the architect Lucio Costa, our modernist pioneer, was evolving from neo-colonial to modern architecture. People tended to think that to build the new it was necessary to bust the block. The direct opposite of this belief is still active in Iphan's bureaucracy. Let's take an example: the fire that destroyed an historic building in Ouro Preto, a town listed as world heritage. What did they decide to do? The option was for the construction of a building in the Portuguese colonial style, identical in every respect to the one which was destroyed. It is hard to imagine a more disrespectful attitude towards the town of Ouro Preto than to adopt, in 2005, an architecture mimicking that of the 18th century. Modernism, in Brazil, generated misconceptions of this kind, radical stances one way or the other. Certain projects in which we dealt with historical heritage have taught us we must adopt a contemporary attitude, to discern the possible dialogue between our time and the past; we must relate the two but not attempt to imitate, never by copying the old.

Water mills of the South

MF: This story began with a friend of ours, Judith Cortesão, who insisted we visit the Italian water mills near the town of Ilópolis: "Those amazing buildings in the woodlands!" This was five years ago. Much later, I travelled south and decided to pass by Ilópolis and have a look. I never thought I'd find such striking architecture by Italian immigrants, dating from the turn of the twentieth century. I was fascinated. There were five water-mills. One of them was scheduled to be demolished because the mill owner had died and the family wanted to sell the land. A group was organized. What we lacked in terms of money we made up for in enthusiasm: "We must make the water mills work again! Create a path to the wind-mills and bring people to visit! And perhaps create a bread festival!" Well, we had an audience with the mayor and began our movement, involving more and more people along the way. With our contacts in São Paulo we managed to find a sponsor, Nestlé, which not only bought the water mill and donated it to the community, but also funded a baking school for the city. The Italian government, through the IILA (Instituto Ítalo-Latino-Americano), is sponsoring a fantastic course on wood restoration, with teachers from Italy and students of different ages and levels, from all over South America. The aim of the course is the restoration of the water mills.

FF: These are the really exciting projects, like the KKKK project in the city of Registro. You see, Ilópolis has 4,500 inhabitants. The water-mills are now operating again. The corn flour produced by the mills is now being sold in the region and even as far away as Porto Alegre.

MF: These form but a small sample of the innumerable possibilities that can be created by architectural intervention. The improvement attains such a scope that the architectural project becomes just a small part of it.

I've never been there

FF: There are buildings we haven't actually visited but are acquainted with by means of drawings, pictures or descriptions. Such is my case with the Convent of La Tourette. I always wished I could have designed it. I've read so much about it and friends have praised it; so it holds a powerful mystique for me. I think it's the best example of Le Corbusier's maturity. It allows innumerable interpretations and there's no better way to understand his lack of pretentiousness in relation to materials. There one can see the roughest, shoddiest, coarsest and most beautiful concrete imaginable. It makes us think anything can be done, achieved, even in the most precarious conditions. Sophistication does not require high technology. The picture I make of La Tourette may be somewhat idealized since I've never been there, but sometimes I have the feeling I could trace Le Corbusier's steps in accomplishing the design. Imagination often carries us away, doesn't it? Perhaps I'd better never go there.

On the drawing board

MF: Sometimes you avoid the issue, go to lunch, get back, and make yourself believe you're not really at work on the project. You try to fool yourself. Designing means looking beyond, trying to conceive how people will react to a certain space, certain materials, paths, objects, everything you have brought together. We are constantly devising different alternatives, for instance, one could come in this way, make one's way round that table or through that passage, nearer the windows or by the kitchen, and so on and so forth. Until the time comes when we feel the pressure of a deadline, or of a client, for instance, to make decisions. This is where commitment comes in. An artist, when he's not in the mood, doesn't work. Architecture brings us under tremendous pressures: it must be done. I'm amazed that some architects are able to spread a sheet of paper on the drawing board and ask: "What is the program?" and immediately start designing. How can it be that easy? It is certainly not easy for me. Often I begin with an absolutely purist reasoning, a logic that is strict in its use of proportions, for instance, only to dismantle it later. It may be torn apart during our conversations at work, for in our practice the architects are quite honest and outspoken. Provocation is a valid strategy, as well as talking nonsense, for one never knows when nonsense will turn out to be useful for the project. It ends up being an exercise in depuration. Actually, it's better if an idea is not readily accepted. When you propose something and it is criticized or refuted, it stimulates you to think harder, to strengthen your argument in order to make it hold up. This method really works. Our architecture has always been based on collaboration. I have never managed to design anything without exchanging ideas. Never. Francisco, I guess, can do that better than I can.

FF: Certainly not.

Chronology of projects

Selection of projects 1979-2005

Grisbi Worker Housing Estate
co-author: Marcelo Suzuki
project : 1979
description: 22 residential units for textile industry workers
area: 1.860 m^2 (2,224 sq yd)
location: Pirapora, Minas Gerais state

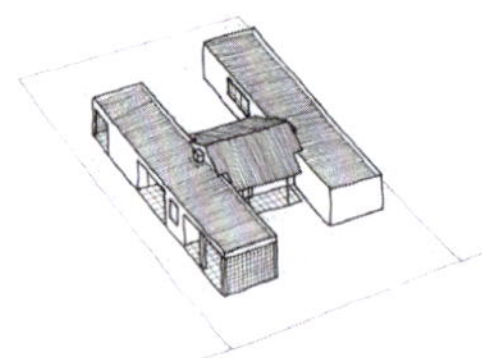

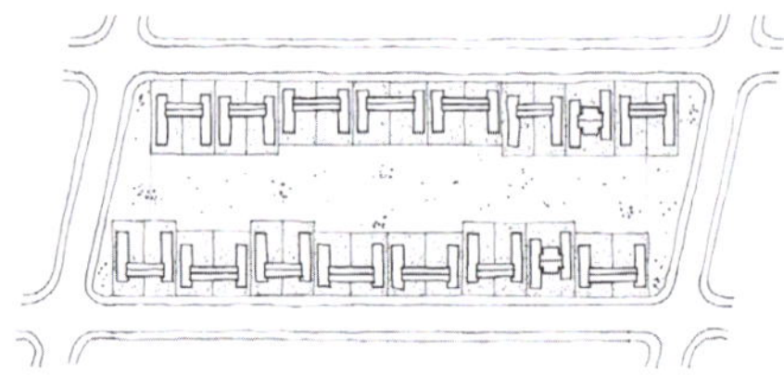

Cambuí House
project: 1979
construction: 1979/1981
area: 240 m^2 (287 sq yd)
location: Cambuí, Minas Gerais state

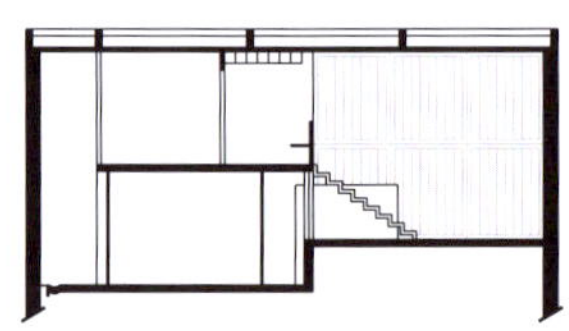

Grisbi Textile Industries (p. 24-31)
co-author: Marcelo Suzuki
project: 1980/1987
construction: 1980/1987 (unfinished)
description: polycondensation, spinning and texturization unit
area: 25,781 m^2 (30,834 sq yd)
location: Petrochemical Complex of Camaçari, Bahia state
Awarded prize at 2nd International Biennial of Architecture of São Paulo, in 1993

Itupeva House
co-author: Marcelo Suzuki
project: 1981
construction: 1982/1985
area: 387 m^2 (462 sq yd)
location: Itupeva, São Paulo state

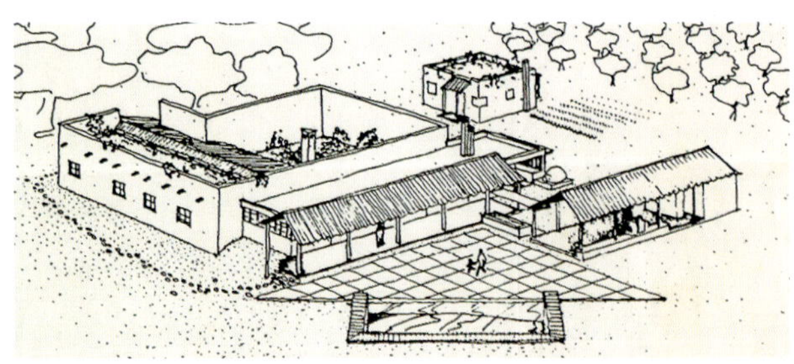

Jardim São Francisco House

co-author: Marcelo Suzuki
project: 1982
construction: 1982
area: 210 m² (251 sq yd)
location: São Paulo, São Paulo state

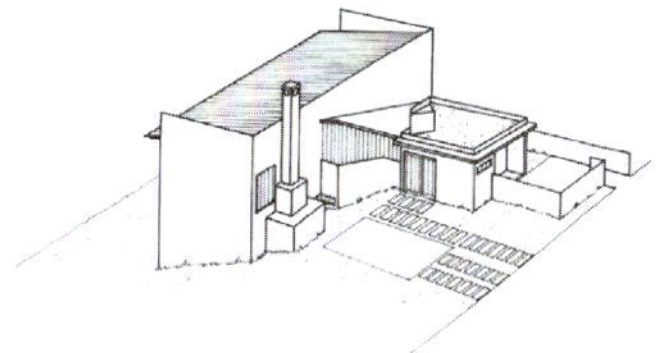

House on Island

co-author: Marcelo Suzuki
project: 1983
construction: 1984/1985
area: 800 m² (956 sq yd)
location: Guapé, Minas Gerais state

Ibiúna House

Co-author: Marcelo Suzuki
project: 1984
construction: 1984/1985
area: 54 m² (64 sq yd)
location: Ibiúna, São Paulo state

City Council Chambers and Cultural Center

co-authors: Eneida C. Ferraz Cruz and Marcelo Suzuki
project: 1985
description: City Council Chambers, Convention Center, Public Library and Museum of Image and Sound
area: 1,828 m² (2,186 sq yd)
location: Varginha, Minas Gerais state
Winning design in public competition

Baleia House

co-author: Marcelo Suzuki
project: 1985
construction: 1985/1986
area: 250 m² (299 sq yd)
location: São Sebastião, São Paulo state

Benedito Calixto Square
co-author: Marcelo Suzuki
design project: 1985
description: landscaping redesign, community facilities, child's playground
area: 4,712 m² (5,635 sq yd)
location: São Paulo, São Paulo state
Competition

Paúba House
co-author: Marcelo Suzuki
project: 1986
construction: 1986
area: 210 m² (251 sq yd)
location: São Sebastião, São Paulo state

Professor Dantés School
co-author: Marcelo Suzuki
project: 1986
construction: 1987/1988
description: restoration, renovation and expansion of school built in 1911
area: 1,250 m² (1,495 sq yd)
location: Igarapava, São Paulo state

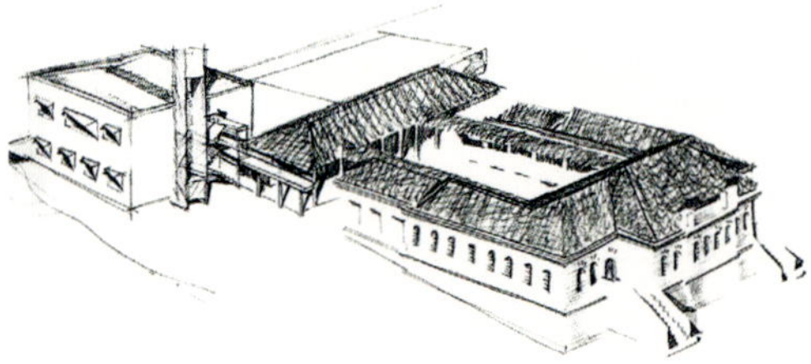

Star Point Store
co-author: Marcelo Suzuki
project: 1986
construction: 1986
description: renovation of surfing goods store
area: 354 m² (423 sq yd)
location: São Paulo, São Paulo state

Housing complex in Sahi
co-author: Marcelo Suzuki
project: 1986
description: three residential units and common area
area: 290 m² (346 sq yd)
location: São Sebastião, São Paulo state

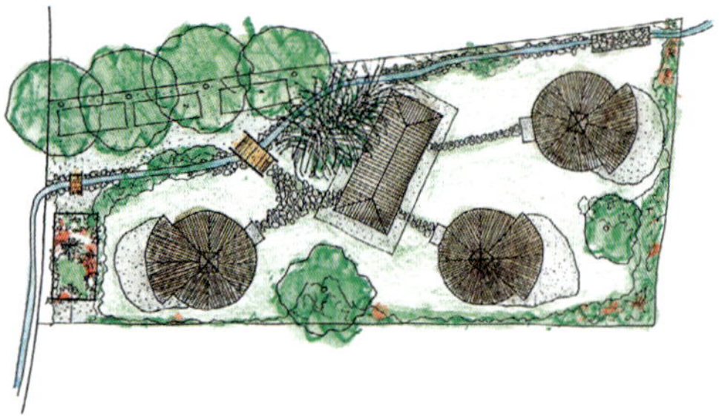

Tamboré House (p. 116-23)
co-author: Marcelo Suzuki
project: 1989
construction: 1990/1991
landscape design: Luciano Fiaschi
area: 910 m² (1,088 sq yd)
location: Barueri, São Paulo state

Aldeia da Serra House (p. 124-27)
co-author: Marcelo Suzuki
project: 1989
construction: 1990/1991
area: 517 m² (618 sq yd)
location: Barueri, São Paulo state

Cachoeira House
co-author: Marcelo Suzuki
project: 1989
construction: 1989
description: restoration and renovation of single family dwelling
area: 258 m² (308 sq yd)
location: Cachoeira, Bahia state

Superior School of Administration and Business (ESAN)
co-author: Marcelo Suzuki
project: 1990
construction: 1990/1994
description: classrooms, library, auditorium, chapel, snack bar, sports facilities and administration offices
area: 10,500 m² (12,558 sq yd)
location: São Paulo, São Paulo state

Santa Bárbara House
co-author: Marcelo Suzuki
project: 1990
construction: 1991
area: 467 m² (558 sq yd)
location: Santa Bárbara, São Paulo state

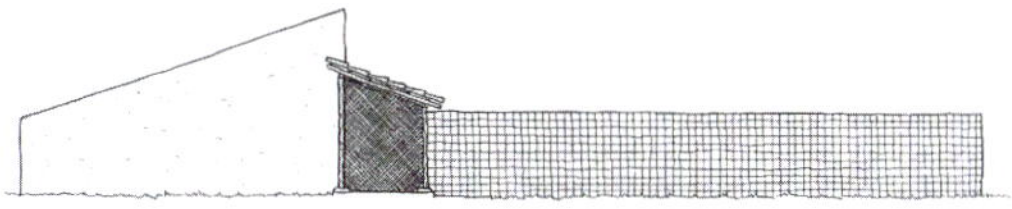

Home Hall of São Paulo Cemetery
co-authors: José Rollemberg de Mello Filho,
Marcelo Suzuki and Tereza Herling
project: 1990
construction: 1997
description: mourning rooms, reception, café and services
area: 840 m² (1,004 sq yd)
location: São Paulo, São Paulo state

Coronel Joaquim José School
co-author: Marcelo Suzuki
project: 1992
construction: 1994/1995
description: expansion and renovation of school
area: 2,520 m² (3,013 sq yd)
location: São João da Boa Vista, São Paulo state

Muro Azul House (p. 128-123)
co-author: Marcelo Suzuki
project: 1994
construction: 1994/1996
area: 400 m² (478 sq yd)
location: São Paulo, São Paulo state

Faculty of Odontology of Braz Cubas University
co-author: Guilherme Paoliello
project: 1994
description: classrooms, laboratories, 300 units/equipment,
library, snack bar and lounge
area: 4,900 m² (5,860 sq yd)
location: Mogi das Cruzes, São Paulo state
Winner in design project competition

Headquarters of the Federation of Indigenous Organizations of the Upper Negro River (Foirn)
design project: 1994
construction: 1994/1995
description: offices, lodging facilities, crafts workshop
and a large typical Indian "hut" for meetings
area: 1,000 m² (1,196 sq yd)
location: São Gabriel da Cachoeira, Amazonas state

House for researchers of the Instituto Socioambiental (ISA)
co-author: Ricardo Caruana
project: 1994
construction: 1995
description: lodging facilities and office
area: 160 m² (191 sq yd)
location: São Gabriel da Cachoeira, Amazonas state

Polytheama Theater (p. 32-41)
co-authors: André Vainer, Marcelo Suzuki and Roberval Guitarrari
project: 1995
construction: 1996
description: restoration and extension of historic building, and construction of support building
area: 3,158 m² (3,776 sq yd)
location: Jundiaí, São Paulo state
Brazilian Institute of Architects/IAB-SP Best Built Project — Rino Levi Award of Architecture, 1996.
Representative of Brazil as finalist in the 1st Ibero-American Biennial of Madrid, 1998
Grand Prize for Restoration at Quito's 11th International Biennial of Architecture of Quito, Ecuador, 1998

Ubiracica House (p. 134-41)
project: 1996
construction: 1996/1997
area: 300 m² (358 sq yd)
location: São Paulo, São Paulo state

Alto de Pinheiros House (p. 142-147)
project: 1996
construction: 1997
area: 292 m² (349 sq yd)
location: São Paulo, São Paulo state

KKKK Complex (p. 42-51)
project: 1996/1997
construction: 1998-2001
description: restoration and expansion of historic building and adaptation to provide space for museum of Japanese immigration, social center and teacher training center
area: 10,870 m² (13,000 sq yd)
location: Registro, São Paulo state
IAB/SP Best Design 2002 — Building Revitalization Award

Expeditionary Forces' Square
co-author: Lina Harumi Shimuzu and Kunihiko Takahashi
project: 1997
construction: 1998
description: renovation and expansion of square, with space for concerts and restaurant
area: 4,356 m² (5,209 sq yd)
location: Registro, São Paulo state

Vera Cruz Cultural Center
project: 1997-2001
construction: 2000/...
description: theater, cinema, exhibitions and workshop spaces
area: 3,685 m² (4,407 sq yd)
location: São Bernardo do Campo, São Paulo state

Revitalizing of Gelbes Viertel (p. 52-65)
collaborators: Pedro Moreira and Nina Nedelikov
project: 1997
construction: 1997/1998
description: redesign of buildings, squares, patios and streets in the Hellersdorf district
location: Berlin, Germany
Winning design in international competition

Brazil Pavilion at 1998 Lisbon Expo
project: 1997
description: amphitheater, central square and mezzanine for permanent exhibition, hall for temporary exhibitions
area: 1,930 m² (2,308 sq yd)
location: Lisbon, Portugal
Competition

Riverside Park (p. 42-43)
project: 1997
construction: 2004
landscape design: Koiti Mori
description: urban park on the bank of the Ribeira de Iguape River
area: 150.000 m² (179,400 sq yd)
location: Registro, São Paulo state

Pedra Branca Ranch Hotel
project: 1997
description: social center, chalets for lodging,
recreational area with stable, corral, sports facilities and swimming pool
area: 3,635 m² (4,347 sq yd)
location: Mantiqueira Mountains, Das Pedras River, Minas Gerais state

Vila Mariana House
project: 1998
construction: 1998
description: renovation and extension of single family dwelling
area: 250 m² (299 sq yd)
location: Cambuí, Minas Gerais state

Bank Boston Branch, Avenida Paulista
project: 1998
construction: 1998
landscape design: Raul Pereira
description: renovation and adaptation of residential building
area: 590 m² (705 sq yd)
location: São Paulo, São Paulo state

Rico Lins Studio
project: 1998
construction: 1999
description: building alteration and adaptation to
provide for artist's studio and home
area: 300 m² (358 sq yd)
location: São Paulo, São Paulo state

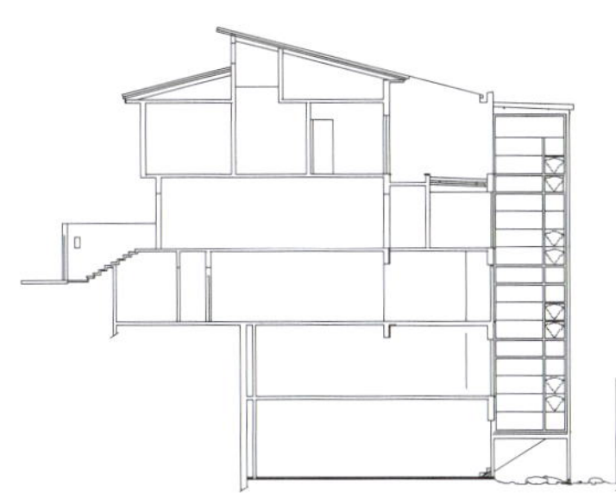

New headquarters of Fundação de Amparo à Pesquisa do Estado de São Paulo — Fapesp (São Paulo Research Support Foundation)

project: 1998
description: square, auditorium, library, laboratory, management, executive and president's offices
area: 11,755 m² (14,058 sq yd)
location: São Paulo, São Paulo state
competition

Sagarana House

project: 1998
construction: 1998/2000
description: renovation and extension of single family dwelling
area: 250 m² (299 sq yd)
location: São Paulo, São Paulo state

Cotia House (p. 148-53)

project: 1998
construction: 1999/2000
landscape design: Raul Pereira
area: 400 m² (478 sq yd)
location: Cotia, São Paulo state

Bus and Train Terminal (p. 66-75)

project: 1998
construction: 1999
description: intermodal terminal for public transport
landscape design: Henrique Banetta
area: 8,653 m² (10,348 sq yd)
location: Santo André, São Paulo state
IAB/SP Best Built Project Award, in 1998.

São Francisco Xavier House

project: 1999
construction: 1999
area: 225 m² (269 sq yd)
location: São Francisco Xavier, São Paulo state

Lookout Shelter
project: 1999
construction: 2000
area: 24 m² (28 sq yd)
location: São Francisco Xavier, São Paulo state

Morumbi House (p. 154-59)
project: 1999
construction: 2001
area: 420 m² (502 sq yd)
location: São Paulo, São Paulo state

Tamboré III House
project: 1999
construction: 2001/...
area: 460 m² (550 sq yd)
location: Santana de Parnaíba,
São Paulo state

Cine-Teatro de Variedades Carlos Gomes (Cultural Center)
project: 1999
description: restoration of historic building,
movie theatres, theatre and exhibition areas
area: 1,900 m² (2,272 sq yd)
location: Santo André, São Paulo state

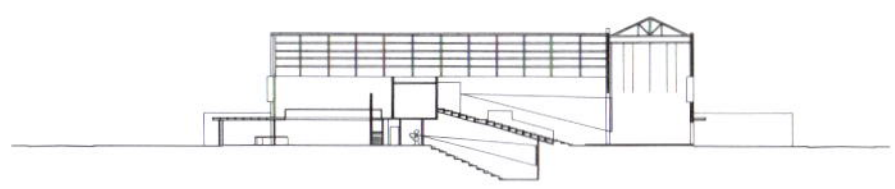

Darcy Ribeiro Foundation
project: 1999
description: renovation and expansion of residential building
area: 583 m² (697 sq yd)
location: Rio de Janeiro, Rio de Janeiro state

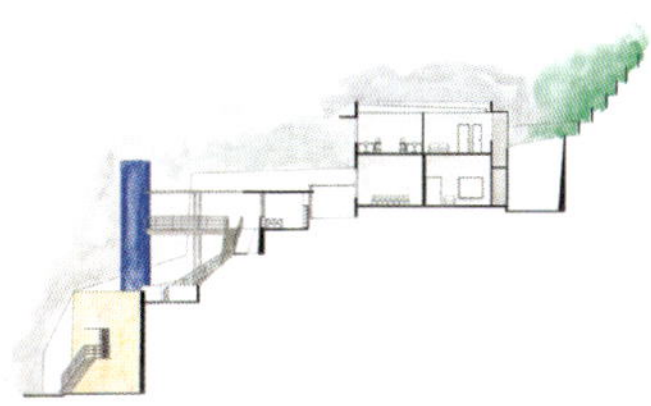

City Showcase (Infobox) (p. 75)
design project: 1999
description: exhibition and dissemination of urban projects center
area: 660 m^2 (789 sq yd)
location: Santo André, São Paulo state

Mantiqueira House (p. 160-167)
project: 2000
construction: 2001
area: 178 m^2 (212 sq yd)
location: São Francisco Xavier, São Paulo state

Revitalization of the area of surrounding the Monument to Indigenous Nations (p. 80-83)
project: 2000
construction: 2001/...
description: supporting infrastructure for the monument built by Siron Franco
area: 2,150 m^2 (2,571 sq yd)
location: Goiânia, Goiás state

Headquarters of Instituto Socioambiental (ISA) (p. 84-87)
project: 2000
construction: 2004/...
description: offices, auditorium, apartments for researchers, living space and terrace for celebrations
area: 1,083 m^2 (1,295 sq yd)
location: São Gabriel da Cachoeira, Amazonas state

Afro-Brazilian Exhibition—Brazil: 500 Years/Visual Arts (p. 76-79)
project and execution: 2000
description: exhibition area of Afro-Brazilian art
area: 2,000 m^2 (2,392 sq yd)
location: Biennial Pavilion, São Paulo capital
IAB/SP Honorable Mention — Interior Architecture

Exhibition *A Estética do Cangaço* (*The Aesthetics of Cangaço*)—Brazil: 500 Years/Visual Arts
project and execution: 2000
description: itinerant exhibition about the *Cangaço* Movement (civilian armed militias)
area: 810 m² (968 sq yd)
location: Postal Service Cultural Center, Rio de Janeiro, Rio de Janeiro state

Popular Art Exhibition—Brazil: 500 Years/Visual Arts
project and execution: 2000
description: itinerant exhibition about popular art
area: 600 m² (717 sq yd)
location: Cultural Center of the Bank of Brazil, Brasília, Federal District

Museum of the Telephone—Telemar
project: 2000
description: exhibitions hall, research center and auditorium
area: 1,743 m² (2,084 sq yd)
location: Rio de Janeiro, Rio de Janeiro state
Competition

Monument to the Immigrants and Migrants of the State of São Paulo
project: 2000
description: monument, exhibition hall, café and administration
area: 386 m² (461 sq yd)
location: São Paulo, São Paulo state
Honorable Mention in public competition

Exhibition *Trajetória Ayrton Senna*
project and execution: 2001
description: curatorship and design of exhibition about the life and career of Brazilian racing F-1 driver Ayrton Senna (1960-1994)
area: 1,200 m² (1,435 sq yd)
location: Manoel da Nóbrega Pavilion/Ibirapuera Park, São Paulo, São Paulo state

Tamanás House
project: 2001
construction: 2001
description: renovation of single family dwelling
area: 355 m² (424 sq yd)
location: São Paulo, São Paulo state

Atibaia House
project: 2001
area: 330 m² (394 sq yd)
location: Atibaia, São Paulo state

Office Building (p. 88-91)
project: 2001
construction: 2002/...
description: suites offices, restaurant and exhibition gallery
area: 5,500 m² (6,578 sq yd)
location: Brasília, Federal District

Anima Building
project: 2001
description: medical clinics and laboratories for clinical tests
area: 11,625 m² (13,903 sq yd)
Local: Brasília, Federal District

Das Antas River Park and Urban Expansion Plan
project: 2001
description: urban design
area: 600,000 m² (717,600 sq yd)
location: Cambuí, Minas Gerais state

Cultural Institute and Museum of the City
project: 2001
description: multi-use hall, galleries, bar/restaurant, video rooms
area: 500 m² (598 sq yd)
location: Cambuí, Minas Gerais state

Market Square
project: 2001
construction: 2004
description: snack bar, public washrooms and square
area: 1,576 m² (1,884 sq yd)
location: Cambuí, Minas Gerais state

Escola da Vila (School)
project: 2001
description: renovation and expansion of school
area: 1,500 m² (1,794 sq yd)
location: São Paulo, São Paulo state

Headquarters of Corpo Dance Group
project: 2001
description: theater and cultural center for dance group
area: 9,931 m² (11,877 sq yd)
location: Belo Horizonte, Minas Gerais state
Competition

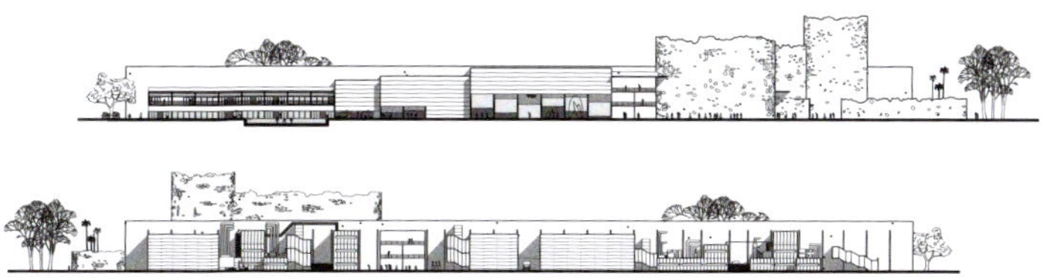

Tacaruna Cultural Center (p. 92-97)
project: 2002
description: renovation, adaptation and expansion of old sugar mill to house training, documentation and exhibition center
area: 15,500 m² (18,538 sq yd)
location: Recife, Pernambuco state
Competition

Takano School
project: 2002
description: graphic arts school, auditorium and laboratories
area: 2,873 m^2 (3,436 sq yd)
location: São Paulo, São Paulo state

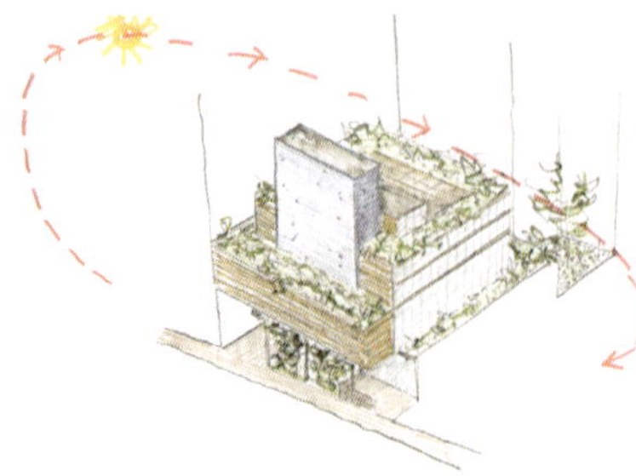

Federation of Indigenous Organizations of the Upper Negro River (FOIRN)
project: 2002
description: coordination offices, exhibition area and stores
area: 785 m^2 (938 sq yd)
location: São Gabriel da Cachoeira, Amazonas state

Emanoel Araújo Studio
project and construction: 2002
description: house alteration and adaptation to artist's studio
area: 450 m^2 (538 sq yd)
location: São Paulo, São Paulo state

Oscar Niemeyer Museum
participation on the team of architect Oscar Niemeyer
project: 2002
construction: 2002
description: renovation and adaptation of the Castelo Branco Building to house the museum
area: 30,000 m^2 (35,880 sq yd)
location: Curitiba, Paraná state

Exhibition *Uma História do Sentar (A History of Sitting)*
project and execution of museum display: 2002
description: architectural design of exhibition
area: 600 m^2 (717 sq yd)
location: Curitiba, Paraná state

Rodin Museum of Bahia
(p. 98-103)
project: 2002
construction: 2003/...
description: renovation, adaptation and expansion of a historic building to house the affiliate of the Rodin Museum of Paris
landscape design: Raul Pereira
area: 3,000 m² (3,588 sq yd)
location: Salvador, Bahia state

Museum of Porto Seguro
project: 2002
construction: 2003/2004
description: renovation and adaptation of the old City Council Chambers and Jail
area: 500 m² (598 sq yd)
location: Porto Seguro, Bahia state

Central Sugar Mill of Piracicaba
project: 2002
description: renovation; adaptation and expansion of the old sugar mill for the installation of the Museum of Science and Technology; Paper, Printing Industry and Graphic Arts Museum and Center for Conventions, Leisure, Fairs and Events
area: 20,000 m² (23,920 sq yd)
location: Piracicaba, São Paulo state

Space in V Bienal Internacional de Arquitetura
project and execution: 2003
area: 120 m² (143 sq yd)
location: Fundação Bienal de São Paulo/Ibirapuera Park, São Paulo, São Paulo state

Jardim Santo André Educational Center (CESA)
project: 2003
description: public school for one thousand students from four to ten years of age
landscape design: Vera Lucia A. Paiva Ribeiro
area: 3,113 m² (3,723 sq yd)
location: Santo André, São Paulo state

Afro Brazil Museum
project: 2004
construction: 2004
description: renovation and adaptation of the Manuel da Nóbrega Pavilion to house museum
area: 12,000 m² (14,352 sq yd)
location: Ibirapuera Park, São Paulo, São Paulo state

Bixiga Commercial and Cultural Center
project: 2004
description: arena theater, film theaters, commercial area and parking lot
area: 57,336 m² (68,573 sq yd)
location: Bela Vista, São Paulo, São Paulo state

Multiplex Pavillion/Pavilhão de Tudo
project: 2004
description: atelier, living room, leisure area with swimming pool, sauna, changing rooms, kitchen and soccer grounds
area: 441 m² (527 sq yd)
location: São Paulo, São Paulo state

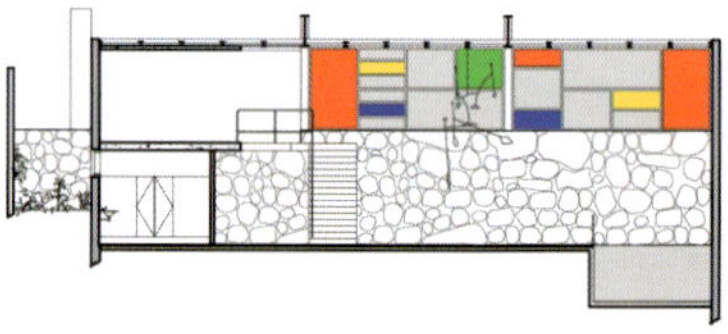

Cambuí Municipal Market
project: 2004
description: restoration and renovation of the old market building
area: 200 m²
location: Cambuí, Minas Gerais state

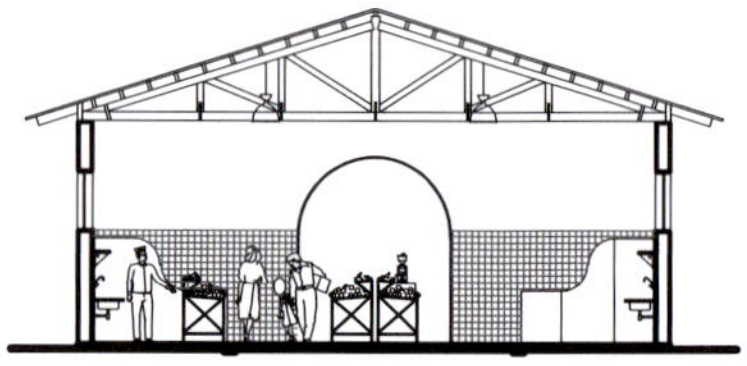

Judaic Museum
project: 2005
description: renovation, adaptation and extension of the Beth El Temple to house museum
area: 3,117 m² (3,728 sq yd)
location: São Paulo, São Paulo state
Competition

Bacopari House
project: 2005
construction: 2005
description: renovation of single family dwelling
area: 270 m²
location: São Paulo, São Paulo state

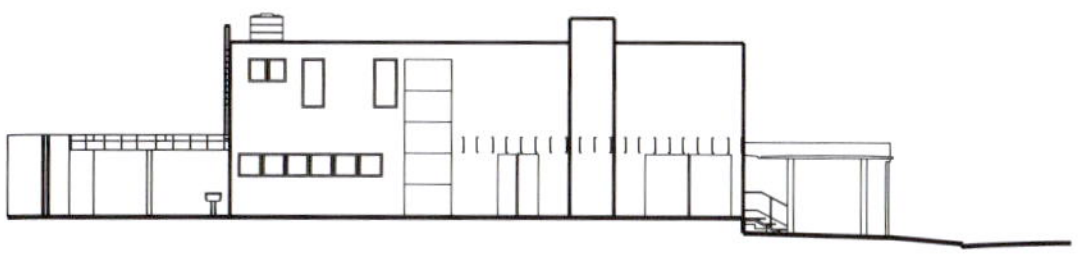

Ilópolis Mill
project: 2005
description: alteration, adaptation and extension of mill to house the Bread Museum and Bakery School
area: 570 m² (680.42 sq yd)
location: Ilópolis, Rio Grande do Sul state

Benedito Calixto Picture Gallery—New set
project: 2005
description: exhibition center, studios, planetarium and internet café
area: 5,000 m² (5,979 sq yd)
location: Santos, São Paulo state

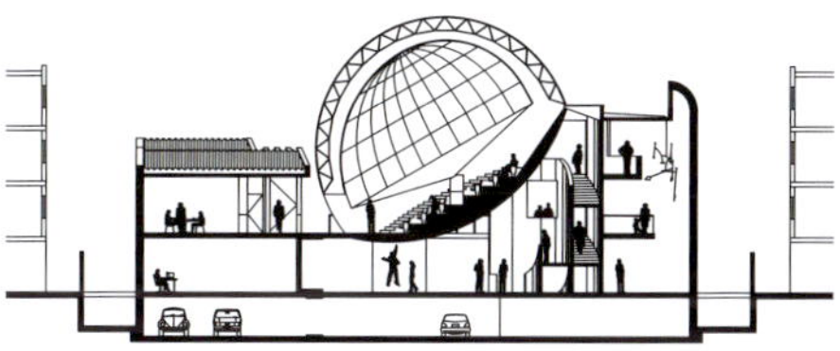

Villa Isabella
project: 2005
area: 318 m² (381.04 sq yd)
location: Henriksberg, Finland
Competition winning design

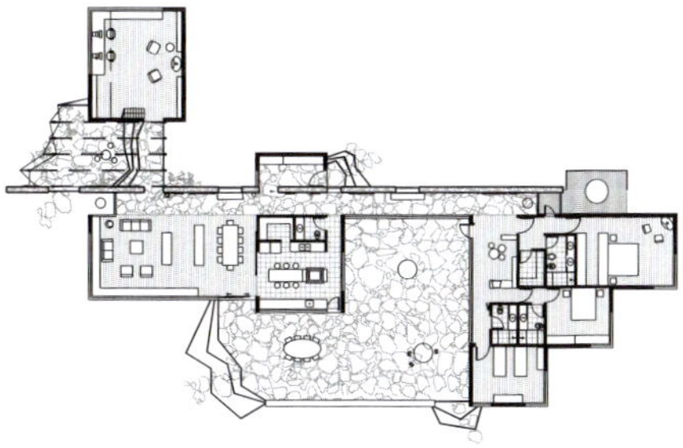

Forte Itapema
project: 2005
description: restoration and extension of the 16th century fort to house the cultural and community center
area: 2,900 m²
location: Guarujá, São Paulo state

Francisco de Paiva Fanucci

Born on April 3rd, 1952, in Cambuí, Minas Gerais state, Brazil.

1971-77 Studies Architecture at the Faculty of Architecture and Urban Studies at the University of São Paulo (FAU-USP).

1974 Together with colleagues from FAU-USP, creates a space for research and design known as Galpão (Warehouse).

1975 Internship with architect Júlio Roberto Katinsky.

1977-78 Works in the practice of architect Abraão Sanovicz.

1978-79 Works in the practice of architect Joaquim Guedes.

1980 Establishes the practice Atelier Vila Madalena with the architects Marcelo C. Ferraz, José Sales Costa Filho, Marcelo Suzuki and Tâmara Roman.

1981 Ends partnership of Vila Madalena Studio, and establishes Brasil Arquitetura Studio with architects Marcelo Carvalho Ferraz and Marcelo Suzuki.

1980-83 Works at the company Eplanco Engenharia e Planejamento, where he creates designs for stores, bank branches, factories, etc.

1981 Participates in the team lead by architect Lina Bo Bardi in the National Public Competition for Urban Restoration Designs for the Vale do Anhangabaú, São Paulo city center.

1982 Designs the Training Center for staff of Casas Pernambucanas (chain store) in São Paulo, with architect Maria Zarria Uehbe Dubena.

1986 Inaugurates the furniture workshop Marcenaria Baraúna with partners from the Brasil Arquitetura Studio, creating and manufacturing wooden furniture.

1991 Participates with the team of architect Lina Bo Bardi in the National Public Competition for the Design of the Brazilian Pavilion at the Seville/ Spain Universal Exhibition.

1993-95 Carries out teaching activities in the discipline of Architectural Design at the Faculty of Architecture and Urban Studies at the Braz Cubas University, Mogi das Cruzes, São Paulo state.

1994 Designs the new head offices of the company Milfra Indústria Eletrônica, in Jaguariúna, São Paulo state, with architect Desirée Pierro.

1999 Takes part in the Seminar *A Floresta e o Pólo Moveleiro no Amazonas* [The forest and the furniture commerce in Amazonas state], Manaus, Amazonas state, invited by the Senai [Serviço Nacional de Aprendizagem Industrial] and by the Professional Association of Forestry Engineers of the State of Amazonas.

2002-04 Teaching activities on Design course at Escola da Cidade, São Paulo capital, a school of architecture of which he is a founder-member.

2003 Lectures at the 2nd Steel Architecture Conference (IAB/Brazilian Institute of Architects, São Carlos, São Paulo state).
Gives inaugural lecture for the Architecture and Urban Studies course at Mackenzie Presbyterian University, in the city of São Paulo.

2004 Gives inaugural lecture at the Faculty of Architecture and Urban Studies at the Braz Cubas University, in Mogi das Cruzes, São Paulo state.

He has organized conferences and participated in debates in schools, universities and museums in Brazil and abroad.

Marcelo Carvalho Ferraz

Born on August 29th, 1955, in Carmo de Minas, Minas Gerais state. Lives in Cambuí, Minas Gerais state, until 1972.

1974-78 Studies Architecture at the Faculty of Architecture and Urban Studies at the University of São Paulo (FAU-USP).

1977 Begins internship with architect Lina Bo Bardi, on the project Sesc Pompéia Cultural Center, in São Paulo.

1978 Obtains degree in Architecture, and starts work as collaborator of architect Lina Bo Bardi. Participates in many projects including the Sesc Pompéia Cultural Center (1977) and the São Paulo Museum of Modern Art (1982). Wins the design competition for the construction of the City Hall of Cambuí, Minas Gerais state, along with architects José Sales Costa Filho, Marcelo Suzuki and Tâmara Roman.

1980 Establishes the practice Atelier Vila Madalena with architects Francisco Fanucci, José Sales Costa Filho, Marcelo Suzuki and Tâmara Roman.

1981 Ends partnership of Atelier Vila Madalena and, together with architects Francisco Fanucci and Marcelo Suzuki, establishes the Brasil Arquitetura Studio.

1986-90 With architects Lina Bo Bardi and Marcelo Suzuki, creates designs for the revitalization and restoration of the Historic Center of Salvador, Bahia state.

1986 Inaugurates furniture workshop Marcenaria Baraúna with partners from the Brasil Arquitetura Studio, creating and manufacturing wooden furniture.

1989 In Évora, Portugal, participates in the World Heritage Cities Conference, representing the city of Salvador, Bahia capital.

1991 Becomes member of the Board of Directors of Quadrante Institute, currently Lina Bo & P. M. Bardi Institute, at the invitation of the couple Lina and Pietro Maria Bardi.

1991-92 With the architects Lina Bo Bardi, André Vainer and Marcelo Suzuki, creates design for the São Paulo City Council Headquarters.

1992 Publishes the book *Arquitetura Rural na Serra da Mantiqueira* [Rural Architecture in the Mantiqueira Mountains], winner of 1992 "Best Art Book" by the IAB/SP – Brazilian Institute of Architects, São Paulo branch..

1992-98 Presents the photographic exhibition *Arquitetura Rural na Serra da Mantiqueira* in São Paulo, Belo Horizonte, Rio de Janeiro, Lisbon, Milan, Barcelona, Delft, London and Mexico City.

1993-2000 Conceives and coordinates the Lina Bo Bardi Project – book, documentary and exhibition on the work of the architect. *Awards received by the book*: "Excellence in Graphic Design", 1993 – Brazilian Association of Printing Technology; "Best Art Book", 1993 – São Paulo Association of Art Critics; "Best Architecture Book", 1994 – 9th Biennial of Architecture of Ecuador. *International tour of the exhibition*: Lisbon, Barcelona, London, Milan, Paris, Vienna, Delft, Bozen, Helsinki, Caracas, Bogotá, Buenos Aires, Montevideo, Santiago, Chicago, Montreal, San Francisco, Mexico City, Macao, Hong Kong, Quito, Berlin, Munich, Copenhagen, Århus and Zurich. *Brazilian tour of the exhibition*: São Paulo, Salvador, Fortaleza, Campinas, Ribeirão Preto, Olinda, Natal, Maceió, Florianópolis, Porto Alegre, Uberlândia, Brasília, Belo Horizonte, Vitória, Londrina, Campo Grande, Rio de Janeiro, São José dos Campos, Caxias do Sul and Goiânia.

1994-2001 Becomes executive director responsible for cultural and publishing programs of the Lina Bo & P. M. Bardi Institute, on Professor Bardi's invitation.

1997 Curator of the exhibition *Design at an Impasse*, presented at the Milan Triennial, in the Monte Carlo Casino, in the Brazilian Embassy in Rome and later, in 2001, in the State of São Paulo Picture Gallery and in the Londrina Art Museum, Paraná state.

Curator of the exhibition *30 Years of MASP*, in the 3rd São Paulo International Biennial of Architecture, presented later, in 2000, at IIT (Crown Hall), Chicago, and at Columbia University, New York.

1998 Receives the "Art Work Award" in the category Architecture and Design of Hotels and Restaurants

1999 Invited to take part in the Curatorial Council of the 4th São Paulo International Biennial of Architecture.
Curator of the exhibition *P. M. Bardi and Architecture* at the 4th São Paulo International Biennial of Architecture.
Together with architect Fernando Vasquez, organizes the exhibition *Mies van der Rohe* at the 4th São Paulo International Biennial of Architecture, which travelled in 2000 to the University of Lisbon. Award for "Best Exhibition" – 4th São Paulo International Biennial of Architecture.
Curator, with architect André Vainer, of the exhibition *Cidadela da Liberdade* [Liberty Citadel], in Sesc Pompéia Cultural Center, São Paulo, presented later, in 2001, at the Aam Gallery, Milan.
Creates the monument in homage to Carlos Marighella, on the occasion of the 30th anniversary of his death, São Paulo.

1999-2001 Designs the presentation of the exhibitions *Território Expandido I, II e III*, at Sesc Pompéia Cultural Center, São Paulo, for the Estadão Multicultural Awards.

2000 Conceives and coordinates the project *Centenário P. M. Bardi*, which comprised the publication of books, exhibitions (at MASP, Lasar Segall Museum, Latin America Memorial and São Paulo State Picture Gallery), and the production of a documentary film about the life and work of Professor Bardi.

2001 Participates in the exhibition *Brazilian Culture* in the Casa das Rosas Cultural Center, with the work *Estudo para o Museu do Inconsciente*.
Curator of the exhibition *Amilcar de Castro*, in the São Paulo State Picture Gallery ("Best Art Exhibition", 2001 – São Paulo Association of Art Critics), presented in 2002 at the Santander Cultural Center of Porto Alegre, Rio Grande do Sul state.

2002 Architectural design for the exhibition *Sem Fronteiras* [No Borders], for the opening of the Santander Cultural Center, Porto Alegre.

2003-04 Invited to coordinate the Monumenta Program, under the Ministry of Culture, for the restoration of historic urban sites throughout the country, for which he conceives the Regional Museums' program.
With architects André Vainer and Marcelo Suzuki, he designs the Museum of the City, for the old Palácio das Indústrias, and the Anhembi Events' Center, in the old Casa das Retortas, São Paulo.

He has published dozens of articles in magazines and newspapers (*A+U, Architécti, Arquitetura e Urbanismo, Projeto, Folha de S.Paulo, O Estado de S. Paulo*, etc.), having organized conferences and participatd in debates in universities and museums in Brazil and abroad. He has also conducted research trips to a wide range of countries in Europe, Africa, North America, Asia and South America, and particularly throughout the various states of Brazil.

Publications and exhibitions

BOOKS

FERRAZ, Marcelo. *Arquitetura rural na serra da Mantiqueira* [Rural architecture in the Mantiqueira Mountains] (English translation and revision C. Stuart Birknishaw) 2nd ed. São Paulo: Instituto Lina Bo e P. M. Bardi, 1996.

FERRAZ, Marcelo; FANUCCI, Francisco, et al. *Theatro Polytheama de Jundiaí* [Polytheama Theater in Jundiaí]. Jundiaí: Prefeitura Municipal de Jundiaí, 1996.

FERREIRA, Avany de Francisco; CORRÊA, Maria Elizabeth Peirão; MELLO, Mirela Geiger de. *Arquitetura escolar paulista: restauro* [School architecture in the state of São Paulo: restoration]. São Paulo: Fundação para o Desenvolvimento da Educação, 1998.

SEGAWA, Hugo; FERRAZ, Marcelo; FANUCCI, Francisco; KON, Nelson. *O Conjunto KKKK* [The KKKK complex]. São Paulo: Takano Editora, 2002.

PERIODICALS

"Paço Municipal de Cambuí" [Cambuí City Hall], *Premiação IAB São Paulo 85*. São Paulo, 1985, p. 53.

"Residência em ilha e campo" [Residence on island and field], *Projeto*. São Paulo,1985, n. 73, p. 82-83.

"Beleza com simplicidade" [Beauty with simplicity], *Marcenaria Moderna*. São Paulo, 1988, n. 27, p. 16-19.

"Marcenaria Baraúna" [Baraúna furniture-making shop], *Design & Interiores*. São Paulo,1989, n. 16, p. 58.

"Paço Municipal de Cambuí" [Cambuí City Hall], *Projeto*. São Paulo, 1990, n. 131, p. 36-37.

BARDI, Lina Bo. "Uma casa no litoral" [A house on the coast], *Arquitetura e Urbanismo*. São Paulo, 1990, n. 32, p. 58-61

BARDI, Pietro Maria. "Estilo que funciona" [Style that works], *IstoÉ Senhor*. São Paulo, 1991, n. 1146.

Design Brasiliano per la Falegnameria, *Ufficiostile*. Italy, 1993, n. 4, p. 37-40.

"Casa em Tamboré" [House in Tamboré], *Architécti*. Portugal, 1993, n. 19/20, p. 42-45.

ORTIZ, Andréa. "A casa moderna dos anos 90" [A modern house of the 1990s], *Arquitetura e Construção*. São Paulo, 1993, v. 9, n. 11, p. 30-39.

SANTOS, Cecilia Rodrigues dos. "Morada paulista" [São Paulo residence], *Arquitetura e Urbanismo*. São Paulo, 1993, n. 48, p. 35-37.

WENZEL, Maria Conceição. "Opção pelo simples" [Choosing simplicity], *Arquitetura e Construção*. São Paulo, 1993, v. 9, n. 2, p. 60-65.

"Diga não à convenção" [Say no to the conventional], *Casa Cláudia*. São Paulo, 1994, n. 10, p. 92-99.

"Reich an Zukunft", *Zeitschrift für Gestaltung*. Germany, 1994, n. 147, p. 44-46.

"Opera interrotta", *Arquitetura e Urbanismo*. São Paulo, 1994, n. 51, p. 38-45.

SANTOS, Cecilia Rodrigues dos. "Quando o concurso comanda o debate" [When the competition drives the discussion], *Arquitetura e Urbanismo*. São Paulo, 1994, n. 54, p. 74-76.

SUZUKI, Marcelo. "Despojamento na ESAN" [Simplicity in ESAN], *Projeto*. São Paulo, 1994, n. 172, p. 55-59.

ANELLI, Renato. "Grave urbanidade" [Serious urbanity] *Projeto*. São Paulo, 1994, n. 172, 56-58.

SEGAWA, Hugo. "Suave rudeza" [Gentle rusticity], *Projeto*. São Paulo, 1994, n. 172, p. 59.

WENZEL, Maria Conceição; CARVALHO, Débora M. de. "O espelho-d'água brilha também à noite" [The reflecting pool also sparkles at night], *Casa Cláudia*. São Paulo, 1994, v. 18, n. 3, p. 56-57.

"Design de mobiliário no Brasil: uma explosão de novos valentos" [Furniture design in Brazil: an explosion of new talents], *Architécti*. Portugal, 1995, n. 28, p. 114-122.

PUGLIESE, Maria Helena. "Arrojada simplicidade" [Daring simplicity], *Casa e Jardim*. São Paulo, 1995, v. 41, n. 480, p. 80-85.

BAVA, Cristina; SCALZO, Marília. "A casa não tem vista, mas o muro deixa tudo azul" [The house has no view, but the wall makes everything blue], *Arquitetura e Construção*. São Paulo, 1996, n. 11, p. 56-65.

"O melhor design" [The best design], *Casa Vogue*. São Paulo, 1997, v. 21, n. 6, p. 11.

"As cores do Brasil" [The colors of Brazil], *Bauwelt*. Germany, 1997, n. 17/18, p. 876.

"Casas do Brasil: residência Kapaz" [Houses of Brazil: Kapaz residence], *Arquitetura e Urbanismo*. São Paulo, 1997, n. 69, p. 54-55.

"Cores brasileiras em Berlim" [Brazilian colors in Berlin], *Arquitetura e Urbanismo*. São Paulo, 1997, n. 72, p. 22-23.

ALCÂNTARA, Denise de. "A restauração do teatro preserva o que é essencial, abrindo espaços para a vida cultural contemporânea" [The restoration of the theater preserves what is essential, opening up spaces for contemporary cultural life], *Projeto*. São Paulo, 1997, n. 210, p. 32-39.

BRANDÃO, Ignácio de Loyola. "Brasileiros vão mudar a cara de Berlim" [Brazilians to change the face of Berlin], *Casa Vogue*. São Paulo, 1997, n. 142, p. 24-25.

BARDA, Marisa. "Brasiliani a Berlino", *Costruire*. Italy, 1997, n. 173, p. 241.

"Regionale e cosmopolita" [Regional and cosmopolitan], *Costruire*. Italy, 1997, n. 173, p. 112-115.

"A arte de ser simples" [The art of being simple], *Casa Cláudia*. São Paulo, 1998, n. 8, p. 52-53.

"Brazil growth is spreading from Rio and São Paulo to a second tier of cities", *Architectural Record*. United States, 1998, n. 9, p. 96-97.

"Trabalho de índio" [Indian work], *IstoÉ Dinheiro*. São Paulo, 1998, n. 44, p. 14.

"Volumes articulados e materiais rústicos definem projeto com inspiração em arquitetura rural mineira" [Interconnected shapes and rustic materials define design inspired by rural architecture in Minas Gerais state], *Projeto*. São Paulo, 1998, n. 219, p. 64-67.

KLINTOWITZ, Jacob. "Hellersdorf: arquitetura brasileira em Berlim" [Hellersdorf: Brazilian architecture in Berlin], *Arc Design*. São Paulo, 1998, n. 5, p. 46-53.

LIMA, Juliana Saboia de Almeida; WENZEL, Maria Conceição. "Histórias do Brasil" [Histories of Brazil], *A&D*. São Paulo, 1998, n. 220, p. 32-41.

MACLNNES, Katherine. "Playing the game" *World Architecture*. England, 1998, n. 63, p. 31.

MARQUES, Sergio. "Casa del muro azul" [House of the blue wall], *Arquine*. México, 1998, n. 3, p. 32-33.

RODRIGUES, Cinthia. "Berlim em cores vivas" [Berlin in living colors], *Época*. São Paulo, 1998, n. 4, p. 88.

SABBAG, Haifa Yazigi. "Espaço Sentinela" [Sentinel Space], *Arquitetura e Urbanismo*. São Paulo, 1998, n. 76, p. 88-90.

"Versão brasileira em Berlim" [Brazilian version in Berlin], *Arquitetura e Urbanismo*. São Paulo, 1998, n. 80, p. 40-46.

"Textures vernaculaires pour une demeure urbaine", *L'Architecture d'aujourd'hui*. France, 1999, n. 320, p. 109-111.

"A influência de Lina Bo Bardi" [The influence of Lina Bo Bardi], *Projeto*. São Paulo, 1999, n. 228, p. 78.

"Em área urbana isolada dos ruídos externos" [In urban area isolated from outside noises], *Finestra*. São Paulo, 1999, n. 16, p. 104-106.

"Hotel-fazenda tem arquitetura simples e linguagem da serra da Mantiqueira" [Hotel-ranch has simple architecture and the language of the Mantiqueira Mountains], *Projeto*. São Paulo, 1999, n. 234, p. 92.

"Os vencedores" [The winners], *Arquitetura e Urbanismo*. São Paulo, 1999, v. 15, n. 84, p. 25.

BRANDÃO, Ignácio de Loyola. "Dos arquitectos brasileños retocan la cara de Hellersdorf, un barrio en el norte de Berlin" [Two Brazilian architects give a facelift to Hellersdorf, a district in the north of Berlin], *Humboldt*. Germany, 1999, v. 127, n. 127, p. 42.

CASTROVIEJO, Alessandro; CALDEIRA, Vasco. "Casas do Brasil: casa Ubiracica" [Houses of Brazil: Ubiracica house], *Arquitetura e Urbanismo*. São Paulo, 1999, v. 15, n. 84, p. 59-61.

CORBIOLI, Nanci. "Liberdade experimental" [Experimental freedom], *Espaço D'*. São Paulo, 1999, n. 8, p. 60-65.

PEDREIRA, Lívia. "Lembranças da Bahia" [Reminders of Bahia], *Arquitetura e Construção*. São Paulo, 1999, n. 9, p. 94-103.

ARAIUM, Cíntia. "Simplicidade planejada" [Planned simplicity], *ViverBem*. São Paulo, 2000, n. 10, p. 52-57.

"Azulejos Kadiwéu" [Kadiwéu tiles], *Revista Ide – Sociedade Brasileira de Psicanálise de SP*. São Paulo, 2000, n. 32, p. 9-15.

CORBIOLI, Nanci. "Obra premiada cria opções de transporte e ajuda a revitalizar região industrial" [Award-winning work creates transportation options and helps revitalize industrial region], *Projeto*. São Paulo, 2000, n. 250, p. 46-51.

NALIO, Alessandra. "A vida é azul" [Life is blue], *Reformar e Construir*. São Paulo, 2000, n. 30, p. 58-63.

"Novos edifícios escolares atenderam maior demanda do ensino privado" [New school buildings serve greater demand for private schooling], *Projeto*. São Paulo, 2001, n. 251, p. 114-115.

"Conjuntos habitacionais revelam valorização do desenho urbano" [Housing projects demonstrate value of urban design], *Projeto*. São Paulo, 2001, n. 251, p. 119.

"Teatro Polytheama: o último ato de Lina Bo Bardi" [Polytheama Theater is last act of Lina Bo Bardi], *Projeto*. São Paulo, 2001, n. 251, p. 102-103.

SABBAG, Haifa Yazigi. "Edifício-rua" [Building-street], *Arquitetura e Urbanismo*. São Paulo, 2001, n. 94, p. 58-61.

"Berlim: o paraíso das sombras" [Berlin: paradise of shadows], *Office*. São Paulo, 2002, v. 13, n. 70, p. 51-52.

"O Conjunto KKKK" [The KKKK Complex], *Architécti*. Portugal, 2002, n. 59, p. 76-83.

CORBIOLI, Nanci. "Recuperados, armazéns transformam-se em centro de informação e cultura" [Restored, warehouses become center for information and culture], *Projeto*. São Paulo, 2002, n. 265, p. 40-46.

"Representações nacionais" [National representations], *Arquitetura e Urbanismo*. São Paulo, 2003, v. 18, n. 115, p. 35.

"Revitalização de edifícios (executado)" [Revitalization of buildings (carried out)], *Projeto*. São Paulo, 2003, n. 276, p. 33.

FIGUEROLA, Valentina. "Rodin em Salvador" [Rodin in Salvador], *Arquitetura e Urbanismo*. São Paulo, 2003, n. 106, p. 34-37.

MELENDEZ, Adilson. "Em dois edifícios, museu combina o passado e o presente, de olho no futuro" [In two buildings, museum combines past and present, with an eye on the future], *Projeto*. São Paulo, 2003, n. 275, p. 40-55.

PAIVA, Cida. "Novo olhar sobre a cidade" [New perspective on the city], *Finestra*. São Paulo, 2003, n. 32, p. 40-51.

SERAPIÃO, Fernando. "Orgânico e racional contrastam em planos horizontais e verticais" [Organic and rational contrast in horizontal and vertical planes], *Projeto*. São Paulo, 2003, n. 282, p. 53-57.

ARAIUM, Cíntia; APSAN, Deborah. "Caipira com orgulho" [Hillbilly and proud of it], *ViverBem*. São Paulo, 2003, n.10, p. 128-138.

"Brasile: nuova architettura/Brasil Arquitetura", *Casabella*. Italy, 2004, n. 723, p. 48-53.

CORBIOLI, Nanci. "Assimétrico, conjunto organiza-se por meio de muros de concreto ciclópico" [Asymmetrical, complex is organized around cyclopean concrete walls], *Projeto*. São Paulo, 2004, n. 287, p. 52-57.

FIORI, Mylena. "Concreto no oásis" [Concrete in the oasis], *Casa e Jardim*. São Paulo, 2004, v. 50, n. 592, p. 64-73.

"Madeira da boa" [Good wood], *Casa e Jardim*. São Paulo, 2004, n. 6, p. 24-25.

EXHIBITIONS

2nd International Biennial of Architecture of São Paulo
Design for Grisbi Nordeste Factory, São Paulo, Brazil, 1993

9th Panamerican Biennial of Architecture of Quito—Brazilian Submission
ESAN Design. Quito, Ecuador, 1994

Baraúna Furniture-Making Shop
Museum of the Brazilian House, São Paulo, Brazil, 1994

3rd International Biennial of Architecture of São Paulo
Designs for Gelbes Viertel, Ubiracica and Tamboré houses, São Paulo, Brazil, 1997

1st Iberoamerican Biennial of Architecture and Civil Engineering
Design for Polytheama Theater of Jundiaí, Madrid, Spain, 1998

11th Biennial of Architecture of Quito
Design for Polytheama Theater of Jundiaí,Quito, Ecuador, 1998

4th International Biennial of Architecture of São Paulo
Designs for KKKK Complex and Riverside Park in Registro and Polytheama Theater in Jundiaí, both located in São Paulo state, São Paulo, Brazil, 1999

Brazilian Architecture in Berlin—The Revitalization of Gelbes Viertel
Goethe Institute, São Paulo, Brazil, 1999

Copyright by Kadiwéu
Ethnologisches Museum Dahlem, Berlin, Germany, 2002

3rd Iberoamerican Biennial of Architecture and Civil Engineering
Design for KKKK Complex, Santiago, Chile, 2002

13th Biennial of Architecture of Quito
Design for KKKK Complex, Quito, Ecuador, 2002

Architectures by São Paulo
Designs for KKKK Complex and Santo André Bus Terminal Delft, Holland, 2002

5th International Biennial of Architecture and Design of São Paulo
Special Hall, São Paulo, Brazil, 2003

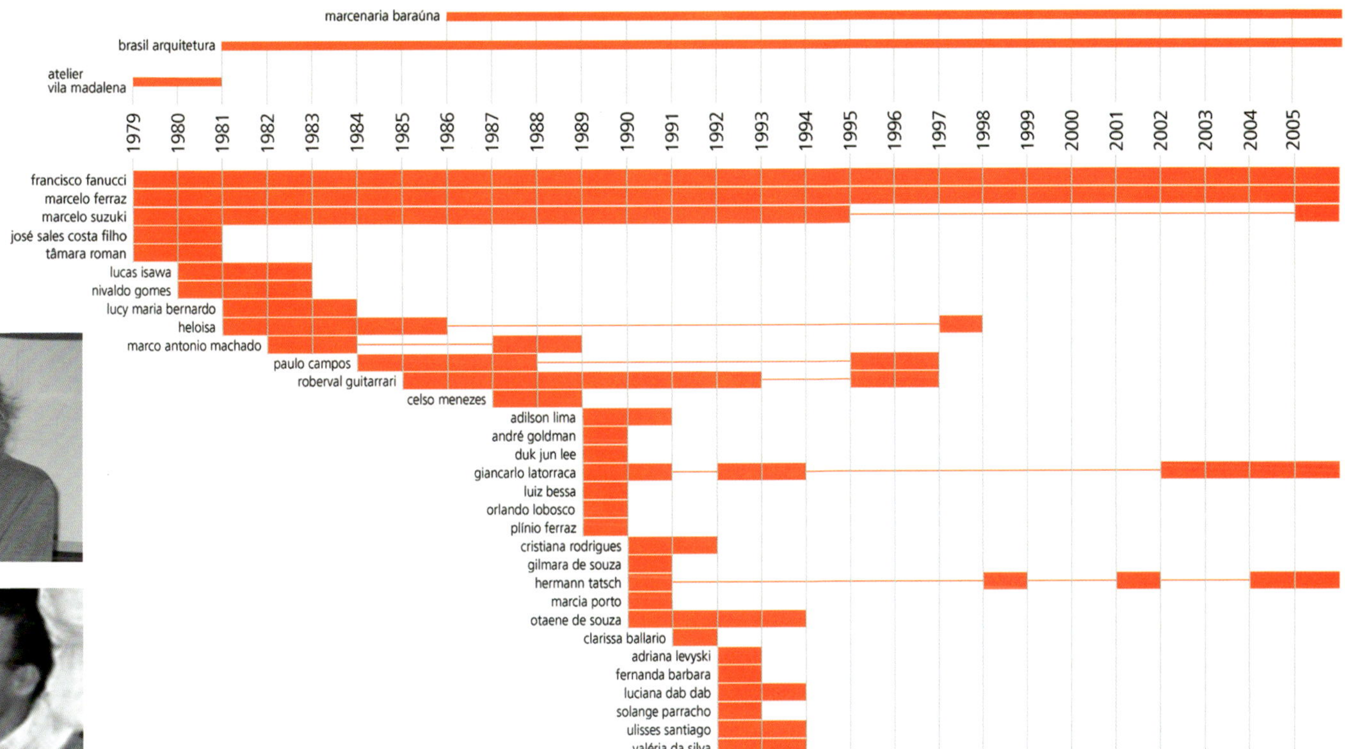

Técnicos colaboradores

Antonio Alfredo Primo
Antônio Roberto M. Nogueira
Aurélio Sandoval
Celso Massola
Claudia Nolasco
Edison Luiz de Almeida
Fabio Oyamada
Francisco A. Corasio Fagundes
Francisco Sanchez
Gabriel Gonsalves
Gilberto Bertoni
Gilberto Pinto Rodrigues
Hercules Castagna
Hisawo Nakamura
José Bojczuk
Manoel Touguinha
Mario Franco
Milton Vilhena Granado
Newton Ribeiro
Oswaldo Campaner
Pedro Moreira
Ramiro Sanches
Raul Pereira
Ricardo Heder
Roberto Rochlitz
Robinson Antonio de Moraes
Thales Azevedo Filho
Wanderlan Paes
William Schepmaker

Grafic design and production
Victor Nosek

Editing and coordination
Denise Pegorim

English version
Mark Lutes

Text editing of english version
Anthony Doyle / Christine M. W. Fonseca

Editorial production assistants
Albert Sugai / Gabriel Grinspum

Proofreading
Carlos Alberto Inada / Clara Ywata

Dutch translation (M. Risselada text)
Getácine Pegorim

Finalization
Fernando Moser (Shadow Design)

Cover photo (Theatro Polytheama)
Nelson Kon

Photos
Arnaldo Papalardo pp. 118, 119, 120, 121, 122, 123, 138, 139
Cícero Ferraz Cruz pp. 19, 23, 77, 78, 79, 125, 126, 127, 158
Francisco Fanucci pp. 20, 54, 84, 101, 102, 103, 165
Frank Ludwig p. 65
Isabel Simon pp. 57, 59
João Liberato pp. 170, 172, 173, 175
Luis Gomes pp. 163, 164, 165, 167 (fotos cedidas pela revista *Arquitetura e Construção*)
Marcelo Ferraz pp. 15, 17, 22, 24, 25, 26, 27, 29, 30, 31, 43, 53, 63, 75, 82, 83, 93, 98, 105, 109, 141, 142, 143, 144, 169, 174
Marco Antonio Galvão pp. 88, 89, 90, 91
Nelson Kon pp. 8, 21, 33, 34, 35, 36, 38, 39, 41, 44/45, 46, 47, 48, 49, 50, 51, 69, 70, 71, 73, 74, 128, 129, 130, 131, 132, 133, 134, 135, 136, 137, 140, 141, 148, 149, 150, 151, 153, 155, 156, 157, 158, 159, 161, 162, 163, 164, 166, 167
Noeci Carvalho p. 82
Pedro Moreira pp. 13, 58, 64
Pilar de Melo Mandelik Pelho pp. 60/61
Rodrigo Izecson pp. 19, 62, 63, 144, 145, 146, 147, 152
Rômulo Fialdini pp. 16, 171, 173

Eletronic designs
Pedro Amando de Barros pp. 20, 75, 80, 85, 87
Roberto Klein pp. 99, 102
Sandro R. Machado p. 88

Perspective
Neco Stickel p. 94/95

Acknowledgements

Adelaide Rodrigues, André Vainer, Ângelo Bucci, Anselmo Turazzi, Antonio Carlos Barossi, Edmar de Almeida, Emanoel Araújo, Francisco Garcia, Guilherme Paoliello, Marisa Moreira Salles, Salomão Grinspum

Dados Internacionais de Catalogação na Publicação (CIP)
(Câmara Brasileira do Livro, SP, Brasil)

Fanucci, Francisco
Francisco Fanucci, Marcelo Ferraz : Brasil Arquitetura Studio / foreword João da Gama Filgueiras Lima, Max Risselada ; essays and project analysis Cecilia Rodrigues dos Santos, Vasco Caldeira ; comments and interview the authors; translation Mark Lutes. — São Paulo : Cosac Naify, 2005.

Original title: Francisco Fanucci, Marcelo Ferraz : Brasil Arquitetura.
ISBN 85-7503-472-3

1. Arquitetura - Brasil 2. Arquitetos – Brasil 3. Brasil Arquitetura (Escritório de arquitetura) 4. Construção 5. Fanucci, Francisco 6. Ferraz, Marcelo 7. Urbanismo I. Ferraz, Marcelo. II. Lima, João da Gama Filgueiras. III. Risselada, Max. IV. Santos, Cecilia Rodrigues dos. V. Caldeira, Vasco. VI. Título. VII. Título: Brasil Arquitetura.

05-5565 CDD-720.981

Índice para catálogo sistemático:
1. Brasil : Arquitetura 720.981

Brasil Arquitetura
Rua Harmonia, 101
CEP 05435 000 Vila Madalena
São Paulo SP Brasil
Tel: [5511] 3815 9511
brasilarq@brasilarq.com.br
www.brasilarq.com.br

Distributed by
COSAC NAIFY
Rua General Jardim, 770, 2º andar
01223-010 São Paulo SP
Brazil
Tel [55 11] 3218 1444
Fax [55 11] 3257 8164
www.cosacnaify.com.br

Font FRUTIGER Paper COUCHÉ FOSCO SUZANO Printed in Brazil by IPSIS GRÁFICA EDITORA